Tell
Me
All
About
It

Tell Me All About It

A Personal Look
at the Advice Business
by "the Man
Who Replaced Ann Landers"

Jeffrey Zaslow

William Morrow and Company, Inc.
New York

Library of Congress Cataloging-in-Publication Data

Zaslow, Jeffrey.
  Tell me all about it: a personal look at the advice
business by"the man who replaced Ann Landers" / Jeffrey Zaslow.
      p. cm.
  ISBN 0-688-08310-2
  1. Zaslow, Jeffrey. 2. American newspapers—Sections, columns,
etc.—Advice. 3. Journalists—United States—Biography. 4. Advice
columnists—United States—Biography. I. Title.
PN4874.Z3A3 1990
070.92—dc20
[B]   89-34788
                                                            CIP

Printed in the United States of America

First Edition

1 2 3 4 5 6 7 8 9 10

BOOK DESIGN BY WILLIAM McCARTHY

To my wife, Sherry,
for her love,
her good advice,
and her great laugh

Acknowledgments

IN THE PAGES that follow, hundreds of people will share their stories, their advice, and their secrets. Without them, this book couldn't exist. I thank them all for allowing me a look inside their lives.

I also must thank my parents, Harry and Naomi Zaslow, for their love, guidance, and good column ideas. My mother led me to the joys of writing, and I'm lucky to share my father's inquisitiveness.

Thanks also to my siblings, Michael, Darrell, Sherri, Randy, and especially Lisa, for their support; my agent, Michael Carlisle, for his contagious enthusiasm; my editor, Lisa Drew, whose enthusiasm picked up where Michael's left off; and my indispensable assistant and friend, Shelley Brown.

At United Media, thanks to David Hendin, Chris Hull, and my pal Denise Flaim. At the *Sun-Times,* thanks to Chuck Price, Sue Ontiveros, Joanie Matthews, Ken Towers, Mary Dedinsky, Virginia Van Vynckt, Joe Pixler, Grace Vavrina, Michael Soll—and Bob Page, for making it all possible. At *The Wall Street Journal,* thanks to Sue Shellenbarger, Dick Martin, and Norm Pearlstine for encouraging me to pursue offbeat stories, one of which led to this book.

Others to thank: Matt Bialer, Bob Shuman, Chris Bearde, Mark Itkin, Todd Musburger, Laura Kavesh, Steven Stern, Beth Kujawski, Mitch Gerber, Jay Boyar, the Regular Joes, and all the readers kind enough to invite me over for dinner.

Finally, thanks to my wife, Sherry, the unofficial adviser to the adviser. Whether she speaks up or simply rolls her eyes, she's a marvelous monitor of my advice. When I'm way off base, she's right on target.

Contents

Ann Landers's Shoes

IN JULY 1981, I spent thirty minutes alone in a Florida hotel room with Ann Landers.

We met, we passed the time, we parted. I was twenty-two. She was sixty-three. This is our story.

A lot of celebrities pass through Orlando, Florida. They come to bring their children on V.I.P. tours of Walt Disney World. They come to play winter golf with northern buddies. Or, if they're like Eppie Lederer (alias Miss Landers), they come for the afternoon, for a hefty payoff, to impart wisdom to a roomful of conventioneers.

On that day in 1981, Eppie was in town to address a gathering of real estate agents. I was in town because I lived there.

As a feature writer for the *Orlando Sentinel,* I was often sent to interview visiting celebrities. I always did too much research. I'd come prepared with a long list of offbeat questions. But the celebrities rarely saw me as a high priority. I was granted just two minutes with Bob Hope, eight minutes with Joan Rivers. I had an hour with Tiny Tim, but only because I offered to drive him from the concert hall to his hotel—and got hopelessly lost. He strummed his ukelele while I tried to read the road map.

So it was that I got the Landers assignment.

There must have been a thousand real estate agents on hand to see her. But first, they had to sit through a few song-and-dance numbers by performers masquerading as real estate salespeople. It was a let's-sell-homes pep rally, with Eppie serving as cheerleader for the finale.

She was a hit. Lots of one-liners, anecdotes, bits of advice. She touched on everything from families to homes to how to sell family homes. She told of how wide-ranging her column had become. When she began it in 1955, she said, it was limited to advice to the lovelorn. "Most columns back then read something like, 'My husband hasn't kissed me in seven years, and then he shot a man who did.' "

Though her talk was peppered with real estate references, her overall message was the same as it is everywhere she speaks. Life, she said, is what happens to you when you're making other plans. And whatever hits the fan is never evenly distributed.

After her speech, I introduced myself. She gave me a look that said uh-huh and I figured, uh-oh, maybe I'll only get three minutes. But she surprised me. She invited me to her hotel room.

A bit star-struck, I was fawning in the way young reporters can be before they learn to be blasé. But I'd done my homework. I knew all about how Eppie had won a contest to get her job. I'd researched the details of her rivalry with her twin sister Popo ("Abigail Van Buren" of "Dear Abby"). And I'd studied how her views on marriage changed after her divorce and her daughter's third wedding.

I was very curious about her—about the insights into America that her job provided. And what impressed me, one-on-one, was that she seemed genuinely curious, too. About me.

The only interest many celebrities show in a reporter is to ask, at the end of an interview, "What's your name, again?" But Eppie was different. She didn't just dismiss me as yet another local kid reporter sent to write about her. She answered questions with questions of her own: Do you have a girlfriend? What do *you* think about premarital sex?

Maybe, I thought, her Jewish-mother tendencies swell when she gets near a Jewish boy. Or maybe she is always playing the role of the concerned Miss Landers. In the end, I decided, part of what made her right for her job was her inquisitiveness. It's a trait she and I have in common. In our meeting, more questions were asked than answered.

We were laughing and getting along wonderfully. I could have sat there all day. And then she said, abruptly but with a smile, "Four more minutes." In other words, my time was running out. Three and a half minutes later, she was standing, showing me the door, thanking me for coming, wishing me success, good-bye, good luck. She'd done this routine before.

No matter. I was thrilled. I sent her a copy of my article when it came out. The piece was quite laudatory, so I could have predicted her glowing response. She wrote back, citing my "marvelous ear" for quotes. She called the interview "superb" and my approach "wonderfully intimate." I knew why she was complimenting me: She appreciated the gushing tone I'd used to compliment her. Still, I saved her letter. After all, she referred to me as a "pal" and wrote:

"You will go far in this business. Your instincts are right and you have the courage and good sense to follow them."

"All the best to you, Jeff," she concluded. "I know we shall meet again."

A couple of years passed. I was invited to interview for a job as a reporter for *The Wall Street Journal.* The job opening was in Chicago, Eppie's hometown.

I knew nothing about business writing, and I'd rarely read *The Wall Street Journal.* But hey, this was the big time. If the Vatican calls and asks if you'd like to be pope, you don't say, "No, I'm just a Jewish kid from Orlando." You say, "Well, yeah, I'll give it a try."

So I accepted the job at the *Journal* and moved to Chicago.

At first, the newspaper had me covering commodities, perhaps the least amusing beat in American journalism. But *Journal* editors eventually realized that they'd hired a ham to cover pork bellies. They took me off commodities and allowed me the freedom to roam the country, tracking down offbeat feature stories.

At the *Journal,* I concentrated on writing stories about people: their struggles, their fears, their quirks, and their triumphs. I wrote about the life-styles of the rich and obnoxious and about people in desperate need. I covered the Miss Agriculture Pageant—the heady competition between the Pork Queen, the Beef Queen, the Wheat Princess, and other ambitious farm girls. I crossed violent picket lines outside West Virginia coal mines to profile a "scab caterer" who risked his life delivering food to scab miners. And I wrote a piece about how department store chains were laying off Santa Clauses because the jolly men weren't hyping Christmas sales. The headline: MANY RETAILERS ARE SHUNNING AND SUBORDINATING CLAUSES.

I'd always been drawn to stories with heart, humor, and hoopla. So in March of 1987, it was natural for me to consider writing about the latest wrinkle in Eppie's life.

Eppie, who was based at the *Chicago Sun-Times* for thirty-one years, had recently negotiated a hardball contract with the paper. The upshot: She won ownership of the Ann Landers name away from the *Sun-Times*'s syndicate. Never anticipating that Eppie would leave the paper, publisher Robert Page had approved the name ownership switch.

It was a shock, then, when she used a contract escape clause and showed up at the rival *Chicago Tribune.* On billboards everywhere, the *Trib* boasted of stealing away the world's most popular columnist. *Sun-Times* editors were left devastated.

The rest of the media, meanwhile, theorized about why Eppie left. Perhaps, after thirty-one years, she felt neglected by her *Sun-Times* bosses and yearned to again be treated like a star. Or maybe, as *Chicago* magazine speculated, "she saw an opportunity to even an old score" with her competitive sister, Popo. By being crowned queen of the *Trib,* where "Dear Abby" had been a staple for decades, Eppie would be pushing her sister from the features page back to the comics page.

Eppie gave little comment beyond a terse statement: "It was time for a change." She admitted she'd be making more money at the *Trib,* but added that she was sure the *Sun-Times* would have matched it.

Sun-Times editors sat around feeling bruised and abandoned, but eventually got off their rumps, stopped sulking, and decided to make the best of a bad situation—lemons into lemonade, as Landers might say. They announced a nationwide competition for a new advice-monger. Modeling it after the 1955 contest that had landed the job for housewife Eppie (over twenty-seven other candidates), the paper printed the largest help-wanted ads in its history. Full-page ads in the *Sun-Times* and *USA Today* announced: "Wanted: Guidance, Guts and Good Advice."

The result: unabated media interest and mountains of entries— from homemakers, moviemakers, sister teams, live-in-lover teams, teachers, convicts, bankers, Jewish mothers, Catholic fathers, you name it! Entries came from every state except, inexplicably, North Dakota, and from as far away as Singapore. Through a tedious winnowing process, the winner would be determined by *Sun-Times* editors, a panel of experts (a psychiatrist, a sex therapist, a religious leader, etc.) and a vote of the newspaper's readers.

The competition—an innovative response to a corporate crisis— was called a masterstroke of public relations. In one swoop, *Sun-Times* editors were garnering media coverage beyond their dreams, while hinting to the world that their competitors at the *Trib* were stuck with a famous, yet dated, advice maven.

The *Sun-Times* help-wanted ads called for applicants with a "contemporary approach" to advice giving, and applauded Eppie for being "still active at sixty-eight." Media pundits saw the faint praise here. Wrote one: "It sounds a little bit like they're describing an old horse going out to pasture to graze, doesn't it?"

"We gave Ann Landers her start," the help-wanted ads concluded. "Now we can do the same for you. Keep your eye on us, Eppie. You're going to have some new competition and we're betting history will repeat itself!"

From the day the contest was announced, I thought of writing a *Wall Street Journal* piece about it. It had all the elements for a wonderful yarn. But the rest of the media was quickly all over the story. My editors said I'd need a fresh angle.

"Why not apply for the job?" a colleague asked.

And so my story became the story of my life.

Ever since my Florida interview with Eppie, I'd been intrigued by the advice column business. So naturally, as soon as I applied for the job, I daydreamed about getting it. The job would offer a great chance to help people, an excuse to meddle in world affairs, and freedom as a writer limited only by my imagination.

I never expected to win. I assumed I was too young (twenty-eight), too irreverent, and too male. Besides, too many other would-be wisdom dispensers (twelve thousand-plus) had also entered.

Still, I worked hard on my application: If I could at least make it to the semifinals, my *Wall Street Journal* article would be that much stronger.

All entrants had to send in resumes, photos, proposed pen names, and plans for the column. I delivered my application to the *Sun-Times* just five minutes before the deadline on March 16. Other last-minute contestants piled in behind me—including a fifty-five-year-old woman who had tapped out her entry with one finger on a manual typewriter while her friend drove her to Chicago from Ohio. "My chances are great," she told me. "I have seven children. I'm always giving advice."

By that same measure, a foster mother handing in her entry figured her chances were even better. "I've had twenty-eight children," she said.

Having told the *Sun-Times* that I was both a contestant and a *Journal* reporter working on a story, I was given a closer look at the selection process. Michael Soll, the newspaper's PR director, ushered me into Landers's abandoned office, a large, two-room suite painted and carpeted in Pepto-Bismol pink. Except for dozens of wall hooks that once bore the advice queen's awards and photos, nothing remained from her reign.

Piled on her chair, desk, and everywhere else were applications of those seeking to ascend to her throne. In a corner, two temporary clerks sat opening entries and counting their paper cuts. Most of the aspirants assumed that hard luck would be perfect preparation for handling other people's troubles. One of the clerks held up a letter: "Here's a woman who has had five children, three husbands, two strokes, and she's been evicted from her home. So that qualifies her to write the column."

Michael Soll stood over a stack of entries already rejected. "They pour their hearts out—how many times they've been abused, raped, divorced," he said. "They think the school of hard knocks is all they need."

I sat down and for the next three hours, scanned hundreds of entries. It seemed as if the paper were sponsoring an angst contest. "There isn't anything horrid my eyes haven't seen," wrote one entrant. Another began: "I am writing this longhand because my typewriter was stolen ten years ago." A third entrant listed "thirty experiences" that made her right for the job. Among them: Her aunt had died returning from her sister's wedding. Her daughter was anorexic. The roof had blown off her house. And a child she had been baby-sitting lost an eye in a snowball fight.

"My husband is ranked number one on A.A.'s most wanted list," a woman wrote. A man explained: "My father committed suicide on my thirteenth birthday. My mother writhed to death in 1981 as a result of medical malpractice. I've seen despair." Another woman listed her lovers: a schizophrenic, a man with a colostomy, a rabbi . . .

Many entrants volunteered salary requirements. Some gave specific numbers ("A $25 raise from my current $350 a week will be fine") and others were less exact: "I'd like to make enough money to fix my double chin and put my mother in a nice nursing home."

People sent singing telegrams, bouquets of balloons, and giant posters of themselves. One entrant sent a resume rolled in an antique typewriter. Another delivered her application in a high-heeled pump. The message: Only she could fill Ann Landers's shoes.

The best entries mixed warmth and compassion with the flippant, pithy tone that made Eppie famous. "I am so good at giving advice that I helped my husband get his girlfriend back," wrote a bookkeeper and "former homecoming queen."

The reject pile had plenty of sarcastic entries. One reminded the judges of how Landers was caught reprinting old letters. "I'm an environmentalist," the entrant wrote. "I can recycle old material, too." He denigrated the job. "All it entails is opening up letters and telling people to see a psychiatrist."

Some entrants were confused. "I'd like to apply for the Dear Abby job," wrote one. Another promised the newspaper's editors: "I'll give your viewers warm, wonderful and accurate advice." (Did she think it would be a televised advice column?)

Applicants ranged from level-headed ("I have an understanding ear") to possibly psychotic ("Give me the job or I'll kill myself"), from barely literate ("I was borned in the South") to overly high-brow ("I got my third doctorate at . . ."). So many were deadly humorless. Dozens of psychotherapists included five- and ten-page resumes, copies of their theses, or videotapes of their speeches. The oldest entrant was eighty-five. The youngest was a four-year-old nominated by her parents for her impressive advice-giving skills.

The clerks told me about celebrity applicants, including a nationally syndicated TV talk host, England's leading advice columnist, Dear Abby's daughter (her entry arrived after the deadline), and a senator's wife. (The senator's office called several times to ask about the "status" of the application—and to lobby for its consideration.)

A healthy majority of the aspirants were women, many of whom gave their ages as fifty-five to sixty-five, but in the tradition of Ann and Abby, provided pictures that showed them a decade—or two, or three—younger. People sent family photo albums, books of their poetry, tax returns, and pinups of themselves in bikinis.

They told their life stories. One woman detailed how she was unjustly fired from her last job and therefore needed this one. A transvestite explained why he was equipped to handle questions from both men and women. A woman not long out of a coma said she felt up to handling the column. And an elevator operator told of all the people he'd met on the way up and on the way down.

"What gives in 1987 that enough people to fill 14 Boeing 747s want to be the next Ann Landers?" asked a United Press International article.

People magazine, which specializes in determining what motivates the masses, responded that the staggering number of entries was no surprise:

> The only surprise, really, is that there weren't more applicants. At any given moment, several million Americans are in mental training to be the next Ann Landers. In dinettes and dentists' offices, Laundromats and lunchrooms, on the phone and on the job, they are dispensing their best advice,

sure that with a prick of common sense and the balm of human kindness, they will avert a crisis, soothe a friend.

And who was the *Sun-Times* looking for? "Someone young and hip, a real trouper of the Sixties who relates to married baby boomers and single yuppies," the *Toronto Globe and Mail* speculated. "The Sun-Times they are a changin'."

Amid all the contest hoopla, Eppie had little to say. At first, she responded to a few questions from the wire services. "People who are applying for the job don't realize I have totally uninterrupted time to do this work," she told UPI. "I don't cook. I don't do any grocery shopping. I don't have any little children. People out there think they can be Ann Landers. There can't be a new Ann Landers. This one is still ticking and has no plans to retire."

After these remarks, she stopped talking.

When I called her new office at the *Trib* for an interview, her assistant told me she wasn't speaking to the media. Sorry.

I didn't give up. I reminded her assistant that I'd met with Eppie years earlier in Florida. I told her about the hundreds of strange and hopeful applications I'd read over at the *Sun-Times.* And I hinted that Eppie might be interested in some of the things I'd learned over in her old office.

Sure enough, fifteen minutes later, my phone rang. It was Eppie. She didn't seem to remember our Florida meeting. But she was cheerful and very curious.

She asked me about all the housewives, cops, bartenders, and grandmothers eager to replace her. She sounded exasperated. "They don't have the foggiest notion of how much hard work there is," she said, "or how vital it is to know top people in medicine, psychology, religion, law. Mrs. So-and-so from Dubuque better think about what she's getting herself into!"

Then Eppie revealed that "for an insane moment" even she considered entering the contest under an assumed name.

It was obvious that Eppie never expected the *Sun-Times* to bounce back so well from her desertion. She thought the media would focus on her arrival at the *Trib,* not on the surprise competition to replace her.

She said she was trying to ignore the contest, but it wasn't easy: She'd been getting letters from confused entrants who thought she was a judge in the competition.

I told Eppie that I had applied for her old job, and she warned me to consider the possibility that I might get it. "Be prepared to work eighteen-hour days," she said, "and you'll need to be stable emotionally to separate yourself from people's problems."

Winning the contest seemed so farfetched then, with twelve thousand competitors. So I just chuckled when she offered potent advice for those of us seeking to replace her. "Be careful what you pray for," she said. "You may get it."

As things turned out, either the other entrants were more careful with their prayers, or I was more reckless with mine. In the days ahead, my life would change forever.

One thing I realized after sifting through stacks of the applications: Mine was far from the norm. For one thing, no one had ever told me I ought to be an advice columnist. That made me a rarity in the competition: Most entrants wrote that their family and friends always tell them they are wise and witty enough to be Ann Landers.

"Everybody reads her column with a hand over the answers to see if they can come up with better advice," Cornell University professor David Grossvogel had told me. "They all think they'd be terrific at it." (I'd interviewed Grossvogel because he conducted a study of thirty-five thousand letters to Landers as research for a book.)

My entry was mostly lighthearted, though I stressed that I'm a compassionate person with a natural concern for people and their problems. As a reporter, I had written about people's fears, struggles, hopes, and despair—and sometimes gotten them help in the process. And my curiosity is limitless: Everyone interests me.

My ideas ranged from on-the-mark to off-the-wall. I proposed a hip pen name with quick reader identification: Stan "the Man" Landers. I promised a lifetime guarantee on all advice. If readers weren't totally satisfied, I vowed, I'd gladly change such advice as "Leave him, the rat," to "Marry him, the swine."

Landers often asks Supreme Court justices or big-name experts to help her answer questions. I, too, would consult know-it-all types. But for commonsense advice, I'd establish "The Regular Joes Advisory Board," consisting of a cabbie, a bartender, a hairdresser, a nurse—all named Joe or Josephine.

My job at the *Journal,* I explained, had been useful preparation. As a *Journal* reporter, I was often asked for advice on good investments. I'd respond with such old lines as: "Want to make a small fortune in the markets? Start with a large fortune."

Such irreverence could help with repetitious, boring letters. To the mother who asks at what age she should let her daughter shave her legs (a perennial question), I'd suggest the reply: "About age fifteen for the legs, but she can shave her mustache any time."

Like all the other entrants, I reviewed my life history. "I've always been an extrovert," I wrote. "In 1960, at age two, I won the annual Baby Parade on Atlantic City's boardwalk. That was the year of the movie 'Hercules Unchained.' In my sword, shield, and diaper, riding a giant float built by my father, I was billed as 'Hercules Untrained.' "

I also told the story of how, in the sixth grade, my pals and I were caught misbehaving. We each had to write "I will not talk with my friends" one hundred times. Instead, I wrote, "I will not chat with my chums." My teacher was miffed, but I was learning to assert myself. Ever since, I have been a contrary wise guy—seemingly a good attribute for an advice columnist.

I explained in my entry letter that I'd always wanted to be a writer. I started writing for local newspapers near my home in suburban Philadelphia at age eight and got a degree in creative writing from Carnegie-Mellon University. I also explained how, over the years, many of my newspaper articles helped people in need.

For example, I'd conducted an in-depth, undercover investigation into the hardships and abuses of Walt Disney World characters (Mickey Mouse, Donald Duck, etc.). Mostly midgets and dwarfs, their problems were little known—low pay, 110-degree temperatures inside costumes, and people who beat them up and kick them between the legs. "The pixie dust wears off pretty fast in this job," Goofy told me. Others described how they must resist responding to all the women who whisper sexual come-ons in their ears. "It's tough," Mickey Mouse told me. "I'm only human."

Anyway, as a result of my piece and the national media attention that followed, the characters joined the Teamsters Union. "A good reporter often helps the people he writes about," I said in my letter to the *Sun-Times*. "It's not so different from being an advice columnist."

On March 23, I received, by Federal Express, a notice from the *Sun-Times* telling me I'd made the first cut, from 12,000 down to 108 semifinalists. The letter also included four test questions.

Others who made the cut included a Vietnamese refugee, a

Chicago cop, a North Carolina bartender, and a former Playboy bunny. They all had something to offer. Linda Sapadin, a Long Island psychologist, described herself as congenitally approachable: "Even walking to the subway, six people will ask me for directions."

Linda Moore, ghostwriter of books with Richard Simmons and Mary Kay Ash, asked the *Sun-Times* where else it could find someone "who had made the best-seller list both as a man and a woman."

Also-rans also made for lively copy in the press. An author from Omaha speculated to the *Omaha World-Herald* that she made a giant mistake by taking the advice of her new agent, a New Yorker. He told her to make her application serious. And come to think of it, she added, "he has yet to make a dime for me!"

Two days after I made the cut, my article ran on the front page of the *Journal*. It began: "Bring me your troubles, America."

America quickly took me up on the invitation.

Journal readers called for financial advice, friends cornered me at parties, and acquaintances I hadn't seen in a decade tracked me down: One even called collect.

As the *Sun-Times* got closer to naming its choice—cutting from 108 contenders to 22 to 7—media attention grew massive. After a mostly anonymous career as a rumpled reporter, I suddenly found myself awkwardly in the spotlight. My job had always been to ask questions, and I was uncomfortable answering them: I stumbled, I blanked out, I talked too fast and mumbled when I did. (My wardrobe, never my strong suit, was anything but telegenic. So I bought two suits, both blue. If you've ever seen me on TV, you've seen one of them.)

Strangers began recognizing me, especially when I wore one of my new suits. At a restaurant, two couples sent over questions written on napkins. On a plane, my seatmate jabbered on about how a man would never get the advice job. And a fruit vendor in Chicago's downtown Loop shouted at me each day as I walked to the subway: "Well, dijagetityet?"

Friends warned me to seriously consider what I would be getting myself into. I read Nathanael West's *Miss Lonelyhearts,* a powerful and depressing book about a young male adviser, and did quite a bit of soul-searching. Some people called the job one of the most influential in America, on a par with Nancy Reagan's. Others said I would be leaving journalism for a circus. (My reply: "Come on, journalism *is* a circus!")

At times, however, I did feel as if I was in the center ring. While preparing an article on the finalists, *People* magazine sent a Pulitzer Prize winner to photograph me in a Landerslike bouffant wig. Despite his Pulitzer, I declined.

I heard from an endless procession of newspaper and radio reporters—most asking the same questions. (You're so young, they all said, how would you have the audacity to give advice? My reply: "I'm twenty-eight, but I have the wisdom of a twenty-nine-year-old.") For Mother's Day, two radio DJs from opposite ends of the country called with the same trouble-making question: "What's the worst advice your mother ever gave you?"

In the midst of all this attention and pressure, I lost twelve pounds. I attribute six of those missing pounds to anxiety over the job and five to the hubbub over planning my July Fourth wedding. One pound remains unaccounted for.

Sherry, my fiancée, was supportive, though nervous. *The Wall Street Journal* had agreed to transfer me to Detroit, where she was a TV anchorwoman, after our wedding. But if I got the advice job, we reasoned, we'd end up stuck in a commuter marriage. Sherry sighed a lot at our situation—big, long sighs late at night on the telephone. But she stood by me.

Strangers also were supportive. People phoned my home. An elderly woman called to compliment me on my appearance on *Donahue.* But I hadn't been on that show. "You most certainly were!" she said, and I thought better than to argue.

I got letters from people I'd written about years ago. A psychic I once interviewed informed me that he had predicted I'd be a famous advice-giver (a prediction I don't remember). And an elderly Chicago man whom I had profiled when he illegally fixed people's parking tickets wrote that he'd go back into business to fix my tickets, free of charge.

The limousine driver for ABC-TV's *Nightline* show was the first person ever to ask for my autograph. The request made me uncomfortable and, not knowing what to write, I signed: "Rob, thanks for the ride."

Would-be agents and book publishers called to sign me up. If I got the job, they said, I could write my life story. And if I didn't, they promised me ghostwriting assignments. Worst-case scenario: I'd lose the competition and end up penning *Vanna Speaks Again.*

I tried to remain humble and unassuming, but my colleagues at the *Journal* saw stars in my eyes and teased me mercilessly. They warned of advice malpractice suits. One asked if he could "be Jeff Zaslow" for just one radio interview: "Who would know?"

My editors at the *Journal* at first considered asking me to drop out of the contest. Though they're a fun-loving bunch, they were worried about the paper's image. Another concern: distractions in the Chicago bureau caused by visiting TV camera crews and the unending phone calls from reporters, agents, advice seekers, an obscene caller, and someone I once met briefly during college. This college acquaintance had troubles and my phone number. I had a sympathetic ear. What the heck, I needed the practice.

Once I made it into the finals—along with two other men and four women—my editors realized, hey, our guy might actually win this thing. They let me continue in the contest. If I lost, they figured, I'd write a close-but-no-cigar story for the paper. And if I won, well, maybe I wouldn't take it.

By then, however, I knew I'd grab the job if it was offered. The challenges of the column and the chance to be innovative outweighed the potential negatives: Would I tire of the question and answer format? Was the idea of a modern advice column too lowbrow? Was I somehow selling out?

My mind was spinning with ideas for the column. I pictured myself as an advice columnist working the streets, making house calls, talking to people about their hopes, their loves, their lost dreams.

One of the reasons I went into journalism was to try to make a difference: to provide readers with a forum for their thoughts, their joys, their heartaches—while giving them some direction for their lives. An innovative, entertaining advice column would be the perfect vehicle—one of the greatest challenges in journalism.

Through a succession of TV appearances, I got to know the other finalists. The whole process was a cross between an athletic competition, a TV game show, and the SAT exam. Under the bright lights, with the world watching, we had to be wittier, smarter, more sensitive, and quicker than our competitors. All of us were nervous TV amateurs, and we knew *Sun-Times* editors were watching—judging us and our advice.

The six other finalists all seemed bright, creative, and driven, and all had some degree of writing experience. There was author Linda Moore from Evansville, Indiana; Gary Provost, from Lancaster, Massachusetts, who'd written thirteen books; New Yorker Linda Stasi, editor of *Beauty Digest* and author of *Looking Good Is the Best Revenge;* and Carol Wells, a California sex therapist. Two of the finalists asked to remain anonymous for reasons of job security.

They were described to the media only as a male editor for a Chicago publisher and a Massachusetts lawyer (whom I'd soon learn was Diane Crowley).

These other finalists weren't my only competition. Oprah Winfrey had us on her show and kept topping our advice with hers. She was pretty good, too. Several times, when a person in the audience asked for advice, Oprah gave a quick, sharp answer, and moved on to the next question—almost forgetting to give those of us onstage a shot. (I guess that's why they call it *The Oprah Winfrey Show.*)

Several of the shows we appeared on had studio audiences, and I was constantly amazed by people's willingness to discuss personal problems live on national TV. For instance, on Oprah's show, a woman admitted she was having an affair with her best friend's husband. Should she tell her friend? I gave the obvious answer: "You probably just did!"

Oprah planned to have her audience vote on a winner at the end of the show, but decided that would be humiliating for the losers. If she had taken a vote, I'm sure Oprah herself would have won, and might now be penning "Dear Oprah." (Appearing on Oprah's show is more hectic than glamorous, by the way: During commercial breaks, those of us onstage kept asking for glasses of water. Eventually, a producer brought us a glass of water, which we all shared.)

Nightline was the most brutal experience. The show had flown finalists to various cities (I was dispatched to Detroit) because Ted Koppel likes people popping up from different spots on his map of the United States. Ted, of course, usually deals with heavier issues than the advice business, and heavier guests, too: contra leaders, sham evangelists, deposed rulers. Maybe that's why he came on rather strong with me and the other would-be advice queens. "Why, in heaven's name, would you want to leave *The Wall Street Journal*?" he asked me. And what qualified me to give advice? I told him: "I'm a wise guy, but not the wisest guy in the world. . . . What I do have is a big heart and a quick mind." I explained that, as a reporter, I'd know where to go for answers. As a writer, I hoped to communicate with readers in ways that would move them, make them laugh, and help them think.

Halfway through Ted's most probing questions, the entire Detroit camera crew pointed at their ears. Were they telling me to speak up? Is Koppel hard of hearing? No, my earpiece had fallen out and was dangling from my head. That explained why Ted's voice was getting fainter! I nervously poked the earpiece back in my ear and heard Ted's suddenly loud, soothing voice: "That's all right.

Don't worry." In living rooms across America, millions of people were surely snickering.

Everyone I met in those weeks had an opinion about my TV appearances. I happened to interview film critic Gene Siskel for a *Journal* article and he volunteered a stinging, thumbs-down critique of my *Nightline* performance. I longed to be rescued by Roger Ebert.

Other finalists also felt the pressure. The *Sun-Times* had asked for tax returns, data on every job we'd held, and a list of all the homes we'd lived in. The paper stopped short of asking about every bed we'd ever slept in, but did hire private investigators to check into our personal lives. "I started to think I should wear makeup to put out the trash," said finalist Linda Stasi.

"We have seven people as pure as the driven snow," *Sun-Times* editor Matt Storin told *The Washington Post*, "but the competition has gotten so much attention, we want to know that [they're pure] beyond any doubt. Our paper's name is attached to this."

(I didn't, however, quite understand the need for all the questions about our driving records: Why would an advice columnist need to be a good driver? Or had the *Sun-Times* slipped us an employment form meant for its truck drivers?)

Meanwhile, through all the media madness and private detective work, I still had to answer the *Sun-Times*'s test questions. I worked late into the night, advising a 213-pound woman whose husband was threatening to leave her unless she lost 80 pounds; a homosexual whose lover was dying of AIDS; and a husband who had a hunch that his wife was having an affair with his brother.

Another sample letter was from an eighty-year-old woman complaining about teenage boys on the bus who spout off obscenities. "Am I just an old fussbudget," she asked, "or do today's teens really have filthy minds?" I took her question to a host of "experts," including Gray Panther Maggie Kuhn, who advised: "Don't generalize about teens any more than you would want them to generalize about old people." I also called comedian George Burns, who, by that point in his career, was more familiar with limousines than public transportation. He suggested: "If you don't want to hear language like that, stay off of buses."

Another test question asked for my definition of the word *chutzpah.*

My answer:

Edward Koch. John DeLorean. Joan Rivers. Frank Sinatra. Malcolm Forbes. John McEnroe. The Pope.

These are just seven of 906 people with chutzpah, my favorite computer tells me. I punched the word "chutzpah" into Mead Data's Nexis machine, which found every time the word was used in 87 publications since 1983.

The Yiddish word is more an insult than a compliment, but it can be either. It means moxie, nerve, supreme self-confidence. The classic illustration: A man who kills his parents and pleads for leniency because he's an orphan. My 906 examples bring chutzpah into the 1980s. Consider the big-league pitcher who asked for a $100,000 raise after a 5–12 season; or the inmate who kills another prisoner, a lifer, and argues that he did so to save the government money.

I also called Elliot Jaffa, who teaches "Chutzpah 101," a class for adults, in Washington, D.C. He had the chutzpah to call me back collect. "Chutzpah is the epitome of risk-taking," he said. He should know. He bills doctors for his time when he waits too long in their waiting rooms.

I, too, have chutzpah. I love to crash weddings. Once, during a particularly jubilant bunny hop, I ended up second in line—right behind the bride. Halfway through the dance, she turned around and did a "Who is this guy?" double-take. I smiled back at her, held fast to her hips, and just kept hopping.

Weeks went by. Finalists' answers were printed in the *Sun-Times* each day, and readers were asked to vote on their favorites. At first the *Sun-Times* promised a late-April announcement. Now here it was, late May, and no word. "It felt like when I was pregnant and all I got were 'You're still home?' calls," Linda Stasi said.

Finally, the call came. Could I be at publisher Bob Page's apartment the next morning? I was given no details and was told to keep the whole matter secret. I hung up and felt my heart racing. I was incredibly excited and more than a bit scared. I left my desk at the *Journal* and went for a long, surreal walk through Chicago's Loop, somewhat oblivious to red lights and yellow cabs. The next morning, Page had coffee and doughnuts ready. I couldn't eat.

Page is the sort of guy who likes to do everything with a flourish, from the way he dresses to how he runs a newspaper. He had decided that he'd get maximum punch from his contest by selecting two winners, a man and a woman, and having us write our own separate columns, five days a week. Page wouldn't identify the woman, but he said she'd be writing a more traditional column, to appeal to the many readers who like advice in a question and answer format. I was expected to depart from convention. Page promised me free rein.

A few days later, I met the mystery woman for lunch. My first impressions of Diane Crowley: attractive, smart, personable, and driven, with a quick sense of humor. But why was that last name so familiar?

Soon, features editors Susan Axelrod and Scott Powers clued me in. I was familiar with how Eppie got the job, right? The woman who had created the Ann Landers name and written the column for thirteen years had died suddenly in 1955. A contest was held to replace her. Housewife Eppie won. The real name of the original Landers? Ruth Crowley.

Diane, now forty-seven, was her daughter.

When her mom died, Diane was fifteen. She eventually moved out of Chicago, had a full and varied career as a feature writer, actress, and teacher, then, in her late thirties, put herself through law school. It was while practicing as an attorney in Longmeadow, Massachusetts, that Diane saw a notice about the Landers replacement search in her local paper. Friends and family encouraged her to enter. Having grown up watching her mother dispense advice, she had an obvious affinity for the job.

In many ways, I liked the idea of having Diane as a partner. She wanted to write a Q and A column, as her mother had. She'd appeal to the many readers who'd prefer that familiar brand of advice. And that would allow me freedom to experiment with my column.

While the *Sun-Times* held off inquiring reporters by saying that the final decision could come at any moment, Diane and I were flown to New York for two days of training with Lilyan Wilder, a well-known and intimidating TV coach. (Her clients include network anchormen, talk-hosts like Oprah Winfrey, and politicians like George Bush.) Her crash course in on-air poise was intended to help us weather the media barrage in the days ahead. Lilyan taught us how to turn negative questions into positive answers by always giving "the minipeech"—hammering home our qualifications, our personalities, our messages. We practiced before a TV camera in her office studio. Lilyan liked Diane's TV persona, but couldn't stop telling me to sit up straight, quit mumbling, remember the mini-speech—and where'd I get that tie? She rolled her eyes a lot, but at the end of the sessions, said I'd improved somewhat. It wasn't such a ringing endorsement, especially since in a matter of hours, I'd be on my own in front of dozens of cameras and reporters.

On June 3, Diane and I flew back to Chicago to sign our contracts with the *Sun-Times*. The *Sun-Times* was adamant about avoiding an Eppielike desertion. So the paper made sure that it had total control of our columns—especially the columns' names.

Diane's would be called "Dear Diane." My column would be a takeoff on the name "Zazz," which has been the Zaslow nickname for generations. Page agreed, that night, to permit me to call the column "All That Zazz"—if the *Sun-Times* would own the rights to it. My brothers and sister, luckily, could continue to be called "Zazz" (without "All That") by friends.

Near midnight on June 3, I got together with Matt Storin, the *Sun-Times*'s editor, to sign the contract and drink a champagne toast.

He didn't hand me the keys to Ann Landers's former office. That would come some days later. But he did let me know that this was a moment of transition. From then on, my responsibility would be to help fill a space in the newspaper that Landers had occupied for thirty-one years.

Of course, I'd be getting a lot of assistance—from readers who in the months and years ahead would share with me their stories, their troubles, their lives.

Confessions of a Sob-Brother

ON THURSDAY, JUNE 4, 1987, I began working for the *Chicago Sun-Times.*

It was an odd way to start a new job. No one showed me to my new desk, pointed the way to the office coffee machine, or asked me to visit the personnel office to fill out forms.

Instead, Diane and I were ushered into a crowded auditorium where more than sixty reporters, TV cameramen, and photographers from across the country were waiting. The whole scene—flashing cameras, shouted questions, a forest of microphones—was surreal to me. It was the first press conference I'd ever attended where I didn't have to return to my newspaper office afterward to write a story. Here, I was the story—and it felt awkward.

All this media attention would soon translate into an inability to ride the Chicago subway without being stared at—or asked for advice. And people in the media, whom I considered friends and colleagues, were suddenly regarding me differently, warily. They asked pointed, personal, and brusque questions about my age, background, qualifications, and ideologies. Their stories weren't always accurate or well-intentioned. It was a view of the media I'd never had before.

In many ways, this was the most frightening time of my life. After being liked and respected in my career thus far, I suddenly discovered that not everyone was sold on me or my abilities. "You're twenty-eight and single. What can you know about life?" a reporter asked. Another demanded: "If you're such a regular guy, why are you moving into Ann Landers's fancy office instead of sitting in the newsroom with all the other regular guys?" And: "Aren't you embarrassed to be taking this job?"

In hindsight, I realize that I wasn't always giving an honest picture of myself. I gave a lot of pat answers that might have seemed flip. How much would I be earning? "Five dollars for each piece of bad advice," I said, "and ten bucks for each piece of good advice.

So naturally, I hope to give mostly good advice." Journalists, wrongly assuming I was making Ann Landers-like millions, didn't always like the smug nature of such comments.

Hours after the press conference, Diane and I took off for New York to start a nine-city media tour. *Sun-Times* PR director Michael Soll orchestrated the promotional blitz. He worked the phones, scheduled photo sessions, got us to our TV and radio interviews, told me which of my one-liners wouldn't be appropriate on *The Today Show,* and kept promising us bathroom time—"but not now."

In the first few days, press coverage ranged from good-natured to unconvinced. Dozens of newspapers ran our story under such headlines as IT'LL TAKE TWO PEOPLE TO FILL ANN LANDERS' MASSIVE SHOES. Or: ANN'S SHOES TOO BIG FOR ONE PAIR OF FEET. Some papers lent a supermarket-tabloid tone to their headlines. LANDERS' SUCCESSOR HAS TWO HEADS, announced the *Stockton* (California) *Record.* Naturally, Diane and I preferred the friendlier headlines, such as TWO HEADS BETTER THAN ONE.

The Wall Street Journal ran an illustration of the headline that it had printed ten weeks earlier over my original article about the contest: DEAR JEFFREY: TAKE OUR ADVICE, STICK TO REPORTING. The *Journal*'s headline this time around: OUR REPORTER (AS USUAL) DECIDES NOT TO TAKE HIS EDITORS' ADVICE. In its story, the *Journal* jokingly announced that it would hold a contest to replace me.

News of our selection even spread overseas. President Reagan was in Venice for an economic summit and his spokesman, Marlin Fitzwater, opened a press conference by asking, "Who is the new Ann Landers?" After reporters gave him our names, he joked about rejected applications from the White House press corps.

Through the newspapers, I got a new understanding of how I appear to other people. "He's jittery, up and down, in and out, coat on, coat off, coat on again," wrote the *Philadelphia Inquirer,* which also determined that I "look vaguely like Harpo Marx" and that my suit coat was too big for me. The *Phoenix Gazette* suggested I look like the Eddie Haskell character on *Leave It to Beaver.* No papers noticed a resemblance to Robert Redford. (A few stories, however, mentioned my only previous claim to fame: Zazley Jeffrow, the *Easy Street Journal* reporter in the *Brenda Starr* comic strip, was based on me. My friend Mary Schmich coauthors the comic.)

Pundits weren't so quick to accept "a kid" in Landers's old chair. The *San Jose Mercury News* observed that I'd never been married and, after my stint in financial journalism, probably "wouldn't know a mother-in-law from a pork belly." The *San Francisco Examiner* took issue with the selection of two contest winners, "a committee": "And such a typical committee, too, so reflective of modern times. Evenly divided between the genders and totally white."

On the media tour, I found that very few people had the story straight. Some TV interviewers assumed that Landers had retired—or even died. Others announced that we'd replaced "Dear Abby."

In a couple of cities, TV reporters took me in and out of shopping malls. Shoppers weren't sure who I was or why TV cameras were following me around—but they asked me for advice, anyway. What the heck: Anything for the cameras.

I had several unexpected shocks on the tour. On a radio talk show in Orlando, a woman called and asked whether it's impolite to accept a date with one guy while on a date with another. "If you do it," I replied, "you'd better be very discreet." Turns out, I dated this woman once when I lived in Florida. She proceeded to announce to the radio audience that she met her future husband while on that date with me. When I went to the bathroom, he asked her out and they lived happily ever after.

On his Chicago radio show, acerbic talk-host Morton Downey, Jr., casually asked me what advice I might give to a pregnant girl in her early teens. He listened patiently as I gave a detailed, basically pro-choice response. Then he gave me the big news: He's vehemently opposed to abortion, and the girl in question was his daughter. It was as if he'd said, "Gotcha!"

In interviews, I had to decide what of my personal life should be open for discussion. The media wanted to know what made me different from the mostly conservative advice brigade that came before me. Do I smoke pot? Did I sleep with my fiancée when we visited my parents' house? Which of my sexual experiences might help me answer the sex questions? At first, I tended to be open about some of these personal questions. But I soon learned to be more withdrawn, more careful.

I had trouble sleeping at night. Consider the irony of this tour. Diane and I were on the promotional circuit before we'd even answered our first letters. We'd logged tens of thousands of bonus miles before turning in even one paragraph to the cause! I suppose it's a sign of the times—that fame in America can arrive before any real work is done. But I kept wishing I'd been given the chance to settle into the job first. I felt like an author doing a book tour before writing the book. All I could say was how wonderful I was going to be. "Just stay on the road and you'll never have to start working," advised a *Boston Globe* reporter.

Back in Chicago, the *Tribune* and *Sun-Times* were engaged in what the media were calling Advice Wars. On every newspaper rack in the city, you could find either my face, Diane's, Ann's, or Abby's. An extensive *Tribune* ad campaign announced: "ACCEPT NO SUBSTITUTES! READ THE REAL ANN LANDERS, ONLY IN THE CHICAGO TRIBUNE." The ads were everywhere, even on news vendors' change aprons.

Meanwhile, malcontents at the *Trib* were leaking to the media details of the paper's in-house Advice Wars—a sibling rivalry for the record books. Abby, already sore from being knocked back to the comics page, was angry that the *Trib* was promoting Ann's column on the front of its features section every day. So the *Trib* began alternating its promos—Ann, then Abby, then Ann. "There's been a lot of grief in the design and layout," a *Trib* staffer told the *Chicago Reader.* "I had to do 16 damn things to accommodate the two columns."

And Ann wasn't pleased with any of her new *Trib* photos. "I don't know how many hours it took to shoot the right picture until she was happy," a colleague told the *Reader.* The selected photo, it turned out, ran in the paper a third of an inch larger than Abby's photo. And part of Abby's head was chopped off. "There was all this background music," a *Trib* insider told the *Reader.* "She wants this, she's unhappy about that."

Though I viewed myself as just a regular guy—a reporter eager to write a newspaper column—some in the media viewed me as if I were a product designed in a Procter & Gamble marketing meeting. A PBS-TV public affairs program interviewed a Northwestern University professor who said the *Sun-Times* was marketing Diane and me like tuna fish—and doing a good job of it. *Chicago* magazine noticed that the *Sun-Times* gave plenty of space to our baby photos, our life stories—even details of how I proposed to Sherry (at a Chinese restaurant, with a doctored fortune cookie that said, "Say Yes"!). "The Sun-Times tried to hype the two into personalities as quickly as possible," the magazine wrote. The paper "showed a selection of photos from their family albums: Zaslow as a perky one-year-old and Crowley with her hair in pigtails. The subtext: These people are your friends."

Meanwhile, the *Sun-Times* was sending batches of letters to us on the road. We wrote our first columns—the ones that would have to prove to the world that we were right for our new jobs—on personal computers as we flew between cities.

By this time, it was late June, and to complicate matters, my wedding was still set for July Fourth. I kept calling Sherry from hotel rooms on the West Coast and she filled me in on the wedding plans. Maybe it was a good thing I was out of her hair in those days before we married. I got to experience some heavy prewedding tensions with space—the Rocky Mountains—between us.

Finally back from the tour, I packed a stack of letters in a suitcase, and after a forty-eight-hour break for the wedding, went on a working honeymoon. I had to. The column was already under way. It needed to be filled.

We honeymooned in St. Thomas. Sherry sat by the pool and got a great tan. I holed up in the hotel room, pasty-skinned, tapping out columns on my personal computer. I even wrote a column about all the marriage advice that I'd gotten from guests at our wedding. Sherry was justifiably fearful that I might use her in my column the way Henny Youngman abused his wife in his act. "You can write about the wedding, just don't mention me," she said, straight-faced, on our first day as husband and wife.

One thrill on the honeymoon (besides the obvious ones, of course) was reading news of our wedding in the *San Juan Star.* The paper printed an AP story under the headline NEW "ANN LANDERS" WEDS TELECAST NEWSWOMAN. (Implying that two women had tied the knot, it may have confused the natives, but it thrilled us.)

By the time I returned from the honeymoon, United Feature Syndicate had signed on to handle the column (fifty papers have since picked it up), and the pressure was on. The buildup had been so huge that even if I'd been Hemingway, I would have had trouble living up to the hype.

As *Chicago* magazine wrote: "What got lost in all the hoopla were some fundamental questions: Do readers in the 1980s any longer care about advice columns? Are they a tradition worth continuing or the newspaper equivalent of the last brontosaurus?"

Tough questions. And my success or failure would provide the answers. In the fourteen-hour days that followed, I had to put into practice all the ideas I'd promised in my winning application.

To signal a change in regimes, the *Sun-Times* painted over the pink walls in Ann Landers's old office. It took more than a few coats of white paint to do the job. By the same measure, it took more than a few "All That Zazz" columns before many *Sun-Times* readers adjusted to a new brand of advice giving.

Some readers, accustomed to the predictability of Ann Landers,

didn't know what to make of my column. Landers had been part of
their daily routine for thirty-one years. She printed a question. She
gave an answer. Question. Answer. Question. Answer.

Suddenly, I was messing with that old formula. And in my
eagerness to prove myself innovative, maybe I came out of the box
too strong. One day I'd give unsolicited advice to Elvis Presley in
heaven, the next day I'd play *Jeopardy!* with readers (I'd give an
answer and ask readers to send in matching questions). I put out a
call to Joes, Joannes, and Josephines to join my Regular Joes Advisory Board. And, vowing to be an advice columnist who makes house
calls, I invited readers to invite me over for dinner.

Many readers liked the change of pace, and wrote in to encourage me and suggest offbeat column ideas. But the reprimands, the
you're-full-of-it letters, and the unprintable hate mail began pouring in the very first week. "Dear Zazz: Who are you, where the hell
did you come from, and why don't you go back there?" wrote one
reader. Another letter began, "Dear Zasshole." Then I heard from
all the Elvis fans who were offended by my tongue-in-cheek advice
to the King. "If you live a hundred years and write a million columns," one woman wrote, "you will never be fit to touch the tip
of Elvis's shoes."

Several of the negative letters came from friends or relatives of
people who had entered the Landers competition. "You're crazy and
I hate you," wrote one. "They should have given the job to my Aunt
Betty." (I also suspected that a number of the unsigned unfriendly
letters came from losing entrants. One began: "They sure made a
mistake when they picked you. I'd have done the column right!")

Though the column remained serious and straightforward three
or four days a week, I tried to stretch the definition of advice giving
on the other days. I gave unsolicited advice to corporations, movie
stars, and *National Enquirer* readers. I took up the cause of Chicago's
piano players, who complained to me of broken, out-of-tune pianos
in the city's famed blues bars. And I advised couples never to play
the home version of *The New Newlywed Game.* (That board game
seems designed to ruin marriages. Look at the questions: "Ladies,
which one of your husband's friends has the lap you'd most like to
sit on?" "Gentlemen, who has more looney-tunes, your family or
hers?")

I vowed I'd never get my laughs from the people who wrote in
to me with serious problems. Still, figuring out when and how
humor fit in an advice column was a hit-and-miss learning process.

A columnist at the rival *Chicago Tribune* gave me little time before going public with his observations: "An irreverent advice columnist is a lot like a funny preacher. It sounds good until you go to church. Then the congregation might not feel so comfortable with the jokes."

I tempered my irreverence, and kept retooling—trying to redefine the Landers formula, while not alienating her longtime, mostly female readers. Soon enough, many readers were writing to say they liked my columns—both the lighter ones, and the sensitive essays. "You took some getting used to," a woman wrote. "But now I wouldn't want it any other way. So keep coming up with surprises!"

Many people now welcome the idea of having a male doling out advice. The advice business had been a sorority for so long that a lot of readers—male and female—say they're desperate for a huskier voice.

Every day, male readers begin their letters: "Zazz, I'm writing to you because I need a man's advice." By the same token, many women write to me hoping that, as a man, I can give them insights into their husbands, fathers, sons, boyfriends, or illicit lovers. One woman wrote: "I'm baffled by 99 percent of the men I meet. Maybe it takes a man to understand a man. So Zazz, I hope you can help."

Some readers write to say that Diane and I complement each other by being so different, and by lending a male/female perspective to issues. In the *Sun-Times,* Diane's Q and A column runs on the left side of the page; my column runs on the right. At the bottom of the page each day, in large print, is the "Daily Double" question with Diane's answer on the left, mine on the right. Readers have a choice: They can write to my post office box, Diane's, or ask that their question be a Daily Double.

Lighter questions make the best Daily Doubles, and Diane and I don't see each other's answers until the paper comes out.

"This question may seem petty, but it raises the hair on my head," a woman wrote during our first week on the job. "When my husband and I pick up his mother to go out to dinner and a Sunday drive, is it proper to let 'the little woman' sit in the front seat of the car with her son, or should she sit in the back?"

Diane responded: "If his mom seldom gets a chance to see him, why not let her sit next to the apple of her eye? If she lives across the hall (or if you're driving cross-country), all three can take turns in the front seat and at the wheel. All seats of the car will get you where you're going at just about the same time."

I told the young wife: "Your rightful place is in the front seat, with the 'little woman' in back. If your husband doesn't agree, suggest that you drive and he sit in back with his mother. Then drop them both off for Sunday dinner and drive home alone. They'll find their way."

My volume of mail rose steadily, from a few hundred letters in the first month to four thousand in the sixth. The only way to make it in the advice game is to prove yourself, one column at a time. After people trust you and decide they like your advice, they bring you the stories of their lives in fascinating detail.

Very quickly, I realized that few other jobs allow such access to real life in America. From the start, the scores of problems, opinions, and heartaches that traveled across my desk covered quite a range—poignant, funny, depressing, strange, perceptive, paranoid, uninformed, and, often, unintelligible. My post office box became a window into people's innermost feelings—and the secret absurdities that rule their lives.

Diane and I also installed a special phone line, allowing readers to call us, twenty-four hours a day, and have their questions or comments taped. Since then, the tiny red light on the office answering machine has welcomed us to work each morning. Overnight, the world always leaves the same message: "HELP!"

In those early days, I was too curious to wait for transcripts of the tapes to be typed up. So every few hours, I'd rewind and listen. A typical day:

"Shocked," age seventeen, calls to announce a discovery: Her boyfriend, who claims to be nineteen, is actually twenty-nine. "Maybe I should leave him, huh?" she says.

"Disgusted" complains that every time she argues with her fiancé, he takes back the engagement ring. "This time he took back the watch he gave me, too," she says. "I'm tired of him taking things back and giving them to me again like he's doing me a big favor. What should I do?"

"New to the Neighborhood" tells of moving into a new home with his new wife and learning that a woman he dated eight years ago lives next door. "She claims I'm the father of her eight-year-old son," he says. "It's not true. Should I tell my wife about this before my old girlfriend does?"

The tape plays on. Spurned loves spin their tales—and their animosity. A man complains about his stepmother-in-law—"a real shrew." A half-dozen teens give life to the term "puppy love": "I can't decide between Tim and Robert," says one fifteen-year-old. "Tim's cool. Rob's cool, too. I really love them both. Who should I pick?" She pauses, thinking, then adds, "Sign me, 'Confused.' "

Every advice columnist ought to have an answering machine. The bewilderment, excitement, and confusion in people's voices give a glimpse of their emotions in ways a letter never could. The only problem with my answering machine, however, is that it doesn't have answers, only questions. I have to come up with the answers myself.

Eventually, I told "Shocked" that her boyfriend, the twenty-nine-year-old teenage impersonator, sounds like trouble: "Do the smart thing. Say good-bye." I told "Disgusted" that her fiancé, the Indian giver, sounds immature. "He's obviously not ready for marriage. You might want to reconsider your engagement. In the meantime, get your own watch."

As for "New to the Neighborhood," I responded: "If you're not the boy's father, then be honest with your wife. Together you'll come up with a solution. It could be tough, though, if your old girlfriend tells her son to start calling you Daddy. At that point you'll have to either spend a lot of time playing ball in the yard next door, or move to an apartment complex that doesn't allow children to live there."

Spotting fake questions is never too hard. The fact is, a surprisingly small number of letters are put-ons. Sure, we get a few less-than-believable calls on the hot line. One of my favorites: "I'm a Siamese twin. I want to go to the movies, but my brother always wants to stay home. How can we settle this?"

Still, I've found that the vast majority of those who write or call are quite serious. Most people these days are too busy to waste their time writing fiction. The truth is usually compelling enough. And if I'm even slightly suspicious, I keep the letter out of the column.

That's not to say that a lot of letters aren't surprising, or even shocking. It has taken me a while to adjust to the steady procession of strange tales from readers. In my mind I'll say, "You must be kidding!" But I've learned not to rush to judgment.

When I first started the job, I heard from a woman whose friend visits her fur coat in cold storage during the summer. The letter writer asked: "What is she doing, stroking the fur? Asking if the fur is having a nice summer? I think she's nuts, Zazz. What do you think?"

I replied: "Fur coats don't get lonely in the summer, especially when they are locked up with other furs." A furrier I interviewed was reassuring. "Why would you visit your fur?" he asked. "To see if there's any news? If you have friends, you stop by and say hello. But you never have to say hello to your fur."

I concluded: "Maybe fur storage houses aren't bad places to pass the dog days of summer. They're cool, with low humidity. And if you get bored shooting the breeze with your lynx coat or mink stole, I could line up some psychiatrists who would love to join your conversation."

Well, as soon as the column was printed, I heard from several other women who also enjoy visiting their furs. One wrote: "Haven't you ever put on your favorite sweater in the middle of summer, just because it feels good? Anything that makes a person feel good is not crazy. It may be self-indulgent, but is that bad?"

A letter about breast-feeding led to more surprising mail. A young mother wrote me about her neighbor, who breast-feeds friends' children after she finishes feeding her own: "If one of her friends is going away or needs a few hours off, she steps in and feeds their kids. She's even enthusiastic about it! She thinks it's a great way to help out and get to know her friends' kids. As for myself, I don't feel like sharing my breasts with the neighborhood. If someone asks for my breast-feeding services, what should I say?"

I was pretty firm: "Tell inquiring mothers that your breasts get more than enough business from your lovely daughter. Besides, breast-feeding is a personal matter you'd rather share with your child alone."

Again, much of the follow-up mail suggested that breast-feeding can, indeed, make sense as a community activity. "Forty years ago that was standard practice, at least in the hills of Tennessee," one woman wrote. "Most of us didn't have refrigerators and had never heard of breast pumps. It was convenient and neighborly to breast-feed a friend's child. These loving gestures gave the child an extended family."

The people who write to an advice column, I discovered, can be separated into two major categories: those commenting on (or complaining about) yesterday's column, and those looking to have their problem solved in tomorrow's. Readers who write in with comments come from all social groups, from everywhere on the economic scale. Those writing in with serious problems, however, are almost always people who can't afford a therapist, don't know one social agency from another, and in essence, have nowhere else to turn. They are lonely, unhappy, or disenfranchised, and even though I'm a stranger, they share with me their innermost anguish.

My appointment to the job was a signal to some of these readers that I must have superhuman wisdom and half the secrets of the universe. I came into the job viewing myself as merely a chronicler of people's lives. Yes, I'd try my best to track down answers. But my basic skills were limited to those of a good listener, reporter, and writer. To avoid feeling like a fraud, I often found myself apologizing to readers and pointing out the limitations of an advice columnist.

I was especially surprised by the number of desperate readers who get me on the phone to ask advice—and even stop by my office.

For a long while, a man in a mental hospital called me weekly. I didn't always get on the phone with him. That wouldn't have been a smart idea for either of us: He needed help I couldn't provide. But when I did speak to him, our conversations would remain in my mind. "I don't want my name to disappear from the face of the earth," he'd tell me. "I'm a somebody like everyone else."

People who deliver their letters in person invariably ask my secretary if I'm in and available. They'll ask for just a few minutes of my time, but often, I'd need hours, days, years, to help them. Still, I find it hard to turn them away. One young man came in, closed my office door, and confided, "I'm addicted to prostitutes." After spending four thousand dollars on prostitution over a two-year period, he said he still considered himself a virgin because he'd never had sex without paying for it. He talked about how ugly he thought he was, how ashamed he felt, how desperately he needed help. The five minutes became thirty. I tried to listen compassionately—and to point him toward therapy. But as I asked him questions and heard his confessions, I wondered if part of my interest in him was voyeuristic. Indeed, advice columns are popular, in large measure, because they reveal the dark sides of human nature, and confirm that other people's woes are the same, or worse, than our own.

To better understand my job and responsibilities, I studied the history of the advice column business. When and why did people start writing to "expert" strangers in newspapers? What lessons might I learn from my advice-giving predecessors?

I found some answers in dusty old clippings, others on microfilm. Beginning in 1942, there was Diane's mother, Ruth Crowley, who created the Ann Landers column and introduced the snappy, down-to-earth tone that would later become Eppie Lederer's trademark. This was a departure from the more spiritual lovelorn column, "Dorothy Dix Talks," which began in the 1920s and attracted a loyal female following.

Still, to appreciate the genesis of the advice column in America, I had to trace advice giving back to the turn of the century in the Jewish villages of Eastern Europe. In that era, people knew where to go for advice. Whatever the problem—rude neighbors, overbearing in-laws, anti-Semitic persecution—wise rabbis had an answer. Many rabbis even gave the ultimate advice: Leave your troubles behind—go to America.

Idealistically, 2.6 million Jews did just that. They arrived here full of hope, but with nowhere to turn for advice. The old system of problem solving didn't translate to America. Yes, the rabbis also emigrated here. They came on the same ships and lived among their congregants in the slums of New York and elsewhere. But in America, the rabbis knew no more than anyone else. They didn't know how to ride the subway or use the toilet. They didn't know what a banana was.

Sensing the immigrants' helplessness, the *Jewish Daily Forward*, a Yiddish newspaper, in 1906 created an advice column called "A Bintel Brief" ("A Bundle of Letters").

The paper soon was inundated with mail. At first, readers wrote mostly of how bewildered they were by the American life-style. But as they adapted, matters of romance and family strife took priority. One typical letter: A woman complained that her mother-in-law "didn't like how my furniture was arranged so she moved it around while I was gone one afternoon."

The column supported the best New World values while weaning readers of Old Country superstitions. Consider this letter:

"Worthy Editor: I recently met a wonderful girl. She has a flaw, however: a dimple in her chin. I'm told that people who have such a dimple quickly lose their spouses. I love her very much, but I'm afraid to marry her, lest I die because of the dimple."

The *Forward*'s answer: "The tragedy is not that the girl has a dimple, but that some people have a screw loose in their heads."

As readers grew more assimilated, letters came from matchmakers decrying the death of their trade, and from homemakers worried about their addiction to TV. Readers lamented their children's disdain for Yiddish, and their grandchildren's inability to speak a word of it.

Today, Yiddish is spoken mostly by old people. The *Forward*, which once had a daily circulation of two hundred thousand, now is a weekly with a circulation under twenty-five thousand. The language is dying with our parents and grandparents.

Though the advice column ended a decade ago, I was eager to learn what made it so popular in its heyday. I talked to several retired *Forward* editors, who spoke of how the column became an integral part of people's lives. After World War II, for instance, thousands of desperate readers used the column to search for relatives who might have survived the Holocaust.

These editors told me to focus my column on issues that consume people's thoughts and weigh heaviest in their hearts. Readers should view the column as a place they can communicate with one another, learn about one another, even find one another. So from the start, I often modeled my column after the *Forward*'s. A mother used my column to try to contact her runaway daughter. A girl given up for adoption at birth asked me to print a letter to the birth mother she'd never seen. The friend of a boy who murdered his stepfather used my column to convey a message of sorrow to the victim's family.

All of these people sensed that an advice column, as a communication tool, might make a difference in their lives. Through my job, I have the ability to entertain, inform, amuse, and give a little guidance. But I'd say the column is most powerful when readers use it to talk to one other.

Your Neighbors' Secrets

TAKE A TRIP across America, by way of an advice column, and the people you come upon are in one sense quite familiar: the husband who vegetates in front of the TV set, ignoring his wife; the woman who can't accept being dumped by her boyfriend; the teenager who is being pressured to smoke pot.

Ordinary lives, you might say; predictable problems. And yet, when these people's stories are told by way of an unsigned letter to an advice columnist, there is a raw honesty that surfaces. Each problem often takes on a new dimension, an unexpected spin.

That husband who sits on the couch, switching channels and avoiding his wife: Why? His daughter wrote me to explain:

> My father is about to retire and all he wants to do is watch TV and write letters. When it comes to doing anything around the house, he's not interested—much to my mother's frustration.
>
> Television seems to be simply a diversion for him, but the letter-writing is a preoccupation. All his letters are to the same person: a woman in Europe whom he met during World War II. My mother says these are love letters.
>
> Obviously, my father no longer is interested in my mother, so she has a very lonely, depressing existence.

What about that woman whose boyfriend broke off their relationship without explanation? She wrote me an unsigned letter that read like a confession:

> I tried winning him back with kindness, but at the same time I wanted to punish him for leaving me.
>
> One day, I found myself eyeing the biggest knife in the kitchen. I slipped it under my coat and went to his house. He answered the door and I pulled out the knife. I might

have sliced his throat, but we struggled and he got it away from me.

That night, I called to apologize, but he wanted nothing to do with me. A month later, I discovered I was pregnant with his baby.

And then there was the teenager who felt intense pressure to smoke pot. In his case, suggesting that he "just say no" would seem simplistic, almost useless. He wrote:

I get along pretty well with my parents. However, my mom and dad smoke marijuana a few times a week. None of my friends smoke pot, and I've never had a problem with peer pressure. But since I turned 16 a few weeks ago, my parents have been trying very hard to convince me to get high with them. I don't want to do it, and I'm starting to panic.

Reading people's letters—especially those that run for five or ten pages—is a bit like getting deep inside their heads. What arrives in my office inside a sealed envelope is often a jumble of thoughts, fears, musings, questions—many of which are starting points for tangents that lead to more tangents.

After her father died in an airplane crash, a young woman wrote me to say how miserable she felt, how lost and alone. She said that she'd been having trouble sleeping and was overeating. "I've gained 10 pounds," she wrote. Then suddenly, her letter took on a different tone. It got almost cheery, as she asked for my advice on dieting. What's a surefire way to lose ten pounds quickly? How about an easy exercise program? Her father wasn't even mentioned in the last two pages of her letter.

Suicide letters, which arrive weekly and usually have no return address, have a tendency to ramble from subject to subject. One man devoted the first half of his letter to a dissection of his sad life, and his plans to end it. Then he changed the subject, offering an articulate and optimistic overview of the Chicago Cubs' chances for the pennant. By the end of the letter, it seemed that his impending suicide was incidental to the baseball season. Was the letter legitimate? I'm almost positive it was. Here was a person—distraught and without much hope—who still had a passion he believed in. Because he never signed his letter, I don't know what became of him: The Cubs finished last in their division that year.

When I get a suicide letter that has a return address, I quickly try to get the writer in touch with a suicide counselor. I've called people at home and written them encouraging letters. But mostly, I realize, there's not much I can do.

And yet, often, I get more credit than I deserve. An eighteen-year-old wrote of how her boyfriend's suicide had left her contemplating suicide herself. "It's been three months and I haven't been able to get a decent night's sleep. In my dreams, I constantly see him killing himself. He even talks to me. . . .

"My family thinks this is 'a phase' and my friends tell me to try to forget him. I don't want to die, but that's what I seem to be driven toward."

I responded that losing loved ones to suicide is often much more painful than losing them to illness or an accident. There are always unanswerable questions after a suicide. Survivors often dwell on things they did that they shouldn't have done, things they said that they wish they hadn't. I gave this young girl the phone number of the Youth Suicide National Center, which would put her in touch with a survivor's support group in her area.

In essence, all I really did for this girl was give her a phone number. It's not as if she'd been dialing at random and I gave her the secret code. She could have gotten that number from many sources.

But she called me a few months later to say I'd saved her life. Had I not responded with those supportive words and that phone number, she said, she would now be dead.

Incidents like this one don't give me an inflated view of my own advice-giving skills. When it comes to passing out information, I am no more adept than a good social worker. And there are other writers who might be just as eloquent at putting together words of encouragement. Still, when someone says I saved her life, I don't dismiss it. For people in desperate need of human contact, even a pen pal relationship with a newspaper columnist can have great importance. At times, it's a mighty responsibility. I can never take it lightly.

Readers have novel ways to get my attention: Many scrawl the word "Personal" in the bottom corner of their envelopes. One woman taped a Band-Aid to her envelope and wrote, "Help! I'm hurting!"

Scores of readers send pictures of themselves and their loved ones. If I know what they look like, they reason, I might understand them better and give better advice. On several occasions, widows have sent me photos of their late husbands clipped to long letters describing their marvelous marriages and their current loneliness. I try to respond to all of them. I return the photos and offer a comment that makes this point: "It sounds as if your husband was a wonderful man. You were lucky to have had him in your life."

So many letters contain information that is extraneous to me, but vital to the letter writer. I frequently hear from people who think it pertinent to include their astrological signs in their descriptions of their problems. Though I'd give the same advice to a Leo that I would to a Taurus, it's not for me to belittle anyone's beliefs. I've got to respect readers if I want them to respect my advice.

I've learned to overlook atrocious grammar and spelling. I try not to dismiss letter writers just because they're uneducated or can't express themselves well. As long as I get the gist of a letter, I'll consider it.

A lot of letters are brimming with clichés and mixed metaphors. "My boyfriend definitely has a screw loose upstairs," a woman wrote. "If he wants my love, he'd better clean up his act. There's a very thin line between love and hate and he has brought push to shove." Her message was clear, even if her delivery was a bit stilted.

I try to give everyone a hearing, no matter how strange their approach might be. A man in his sixties wrote to tell me that he had devised a way to "eliminate AIDS without drugs or operations." His long letter was a study in riddles. He didn't spell out his plan, but he sure seemed to have confidence in it. In fact, he said, he owed his own good health to his "philosophy"—and to prove his point, he included a photo of himself wearing nothing but boxer shorts. Yes, he did look healthy and fit for a man his age.

So, okay, I bit. I wrote him back and asked him to flesh out his philosophy. He replied with two letters totaling twelve blustery pages. He still didn't reveal his philosophy, but he did make this offer: "If you foot the expenses and provide me with a roomful of so-called AIDS victims in a meeting hall close to my house, I will show you how to eliminate not just AIDS, but diseases in general. Ultimately, we'll empty a lot of hospitals."

Maybe the guy is on to something. Maybe he's a crackpot. Then again, maybe he's got some kind of shady pyramid scheme going. Whatever the story, I put his letters aside and didn't mention them in the column. In his last correspondence, the man suggested I was a coward for not meeting his challenge.

He's not the only reader who is disappointed in me. Sometimes, readers are so incensed by something I write that I can feel their anger rising from their letters. I often go back and reread, and even reconsider, whatever column had set them off.

An angry California woman wrote: "A girl asked you if it is proper to date her stepbrother. You said yes. But according to the Bible, it most certainly is not. If your roots were in God, you'd know that! For the same reason, homosexuality is wrong. God's laws come first, not man's. If I was that girl's mother, I'd want to slap you in the face!"

I didn't remember ever advising anyone to date her stepbrother. Shelley, my assistant, couldn't find such a letter in our files. Hmmm. Well, a week later, the mystery was solved. The woman wrote back: "The other day, I slammed the hammer on you. I've just discovered that I wrote to the wrong guy. I really apologize." It turned out that another columnist in her local paper gave the advice she found so offensive. It was nice of the woman to write back. But since so many of my beliefs—regarding premarital sex, homosexuality, etc.—are obviously at odds with hers, I assume it's just a matter of time before she writes to complain about an answer that really is mine.

I can't always be as empathetic as a letter writer might like. I've never been abandoned by my spouse. I've never suffered a catastrophic illness. I've never felt as if no one loved me. I've never hated myself.

So how do I give advice to people whose hurts I can only imagine? Partly through research. I'll call doctors, psychologists, lawyers, social workers—anyone who might have some insight. And there is no shortage of experts. Their publishers send me their new books. Their PR firms mail me their resumes. Their spouses stop me in the supermarket and hand me their cards.

I frequently go to clergymen: They've been in the advice business longer than I have. I then weigh their answers with mine. (I once called four rabbis and got seven opinions.)

Of course, there are many questions that no expert can answer definitively. And neither can I. So I say so in my response to a letter writer, and often, that can be of help.

A man called our hot line to say he had suffered a stroke several months earlier that left him crippled, in pain, and confined to a wheelchair for the rest of his life. "Everyone wants to live forever," he said. "Not me. My wish is to die.

"I don't want to commit suicide, but I'd like to figure out a way to die more quickly, so my family doesn't have to suffer with me. They all suggest ways for me to cope, but I can't.

"My family is very devoted to me, so obviously I can't give my name or address." He ended his message by calling himself "Looking for a Way Out."

My response:

None of us can pretend to know your pain, hurt and depression. Words of encouragement—whether from me or your family—can sound hollow and forced. But it is human nature to strive to overcome the worst adversities. Your loved ones are pulling for you, as they'd expect you to pull for them if circumstances were reversed.

You say you'd like to die so your family won't have to suffer with you. But your death, especially if it is in some way "quickened," would likely be even more painful for your loved ones. They may get great pleasure in caring for you. You can bet they'd rather have you in their lives in a seated position than see you laid out at your funeral.

People who've survived terrible injuries or illnesses often say they contemplated suicide—at first. But many have learned to live productive, joyous lives. It has only been a few months since your stroke. In time, you may find the adjustment easier.

Some readers wrote to say they approved of the answer I gave "Looking." They felt it was realistic, yet provided some hope. Other readers responded that "Looking" has every right to consider quickening his death. One woman addressed her letter directly to "Looking": "Your family loves you, but they should show their love by supporting whatever you choose to do with your life. You don't have to be any stronger than you're able to be. Don't feel obliged to live by someone else's definition of strength. God will love you no matter what you decide."

Another reader's response:

I have degenerative arthritis. There is no real treatment. Doctors can give me pain-killers—that's all. There is no cure, and not much hope. I can't work, I sleep and eat poorly, and

I can't have a normal sex life. All I can do is hope for a relatively quick and painless death.

As for the people who want me to hang on: I go through more pain in a day than they will know in their lives. My advice to Looking: Don't spare other people's feelings at the cost of your own.

On many days, I page through my mail and wonder, "Where are the easy questions?"

But I've come to realize, if these questions were so easy to answer, people wouldn't need to write to me. Just as they struggle for solutions, I struggle, too. What I come up with is often a thoughtful opinion rather than the absolute right answer.

A woman wrote to say that her parents had recently gotten divorced. A month later, her father was diagnosed as having cancer. "He has now been told he has six months to live," the daughter wrote. "It's an awful and complicated situation for my mother, because the family is ganging up on her. They say she should go back to my father. But what about her independence and her feelings?"

I responded:

I get the impression that your mother initiated the divorce, and at this toughest moment in your father's life, he wants and needs her.

It's understandable that your mom is being asked to return to your dad for the sake of family unity. "Do him a favor," people must be saying. "It'll all be over in six months anyway."

Well, I can't recommend that your mother remarry your father, or even return to him. God willing, your father could live for a decade. You hear stories of miraculous recoveries all the time. Then what happens to your mother's independence? It's too much of a sacrifice.

If your mom is willing, she ought to visit him from time to time and offer support. She can let him know she is praying for him without reuniting with him. She should also be supportive to you and the rest of the family. You all will need her in the months ahead—probably as much as your father does.

I wish strength to everyone in the family.

More tough questions:

A young woman wrote that, as a girl, she was sexually molested by a relative: "Recently, my boyfriend asked me if I was a virgin. I didn't answer him, and I didn't tell him about the incest. Am I considered a virgin?"

My response: "By the definition of the word, no. But if you'd be uncomfortable telling your boyfriend about the rape and would rather tell him you're a virgin, that's an honest answer in my book. At least for now. As the relationship gets more serious, you may consider sharing your secret with him. If he cares for you, he'll be understanding."

A woman wrote that her ex-boyfriend used to get drunk and beat her: "Now he plans to marry a good friend of mine. Should I tell her about my experiences? If he starts to beat her, I'd feel very guilty."

My answer:

Let your friend know how much you care about her and want the best for her. First, try to speak positively about your ex-boyfriend. Give her reasons why he'd make a good husband—if there are any. You don't want her suspecting sour grapes or some ulterior motive.

Then tell her of the beatings. She might be familiar with his violent side. Or, in the time since your "ex" dated you, he might have gotten help for what could be alcoholism. Regardless, as someone who cares, speak up.

A sixteen-year-old wrote to say she'd been raped a few years earlier by her father's brother: "Now my uncle is in the hospital, dying, and he wants to see me. Should I go or should I just let him die without paying my last respects?"

I arrived at my response after consulting several therapists:

I hope your family knows of the rape, and that you've sought counseling to deal with it.

If you were to visit your uncle, examine your reasons for going. How will seeing him again make you feel? Will you feel guilty if you don't go? And is there someone—a counselor, relative or friend—who can help you talk through your feelings?

Should you decide that you'd feel uncomfortable visiting

your uncle, that's understandable, and your family should respect your decision.

Several rape victims wrote to offer support to this girl. Wrote one:

It's hard for a rape victim to face her attacker. It's even harder for her to forgive him. But until she does, she will never really be able to put the incident behind her.

I was raped twice as a child, and for years, I let my anger, guilt, fear and desire for revenge run my life and make me miserable. Only when I learned to forgive was I finally at peace. I pray every day that the person who raped me has gotten help and will never hurt anyone else.

This young girl's uncle is dying and probably wants to get her forgiveness before he faces his maker. She has a right to scream and tell him how much he hurt her, but she should also forgive him—not so much for his sake as for her own.

Among the worst tragedies, I find, are the ones where fingers are pointed, blame is identified, and hatred gets in the way of healing. A woman wrote:

My closest girlfriend and my husband's brother fell for each other at our wedding two years ago. They soon moved in together, but the relationship was troubled from the start. She'd go out and leave him to take care of her kids from a previous marriage. Then she said she wanted space. They were on and off for months.

Then one day, he went to pick her up for a date and found her with her ex-husband. My brother-in-law was devastated, but everyone told him he was lucky to be rid of her. Despite their problems, she and I remained good friends.

Well, one day last August, he called her, played "My Way" by Elvis Presley over the phone, and said goodbye. He killed himself the next morning.

Everyone blamed her for the suicide. She wasn't allowed to go to the funeral and no one ever wants to see her again. Except me. She was my best friend.

My husband and in-laws are very angry that I stay in touch with her. She and I have to sneak around to see each other.

My family says my husband is silly to blame my friend, and that I'm letting him run my life. Am I a traitor to my husband and his family?

I responded:

People who commit suicide are severely troubled, and it's unfair to pin all the blame on anyone else.

Your husband's family is hurt and angry in ways you may never understand. Even if it isn't fair of them to blame your friend, you should respect their feelings.

It may be too soon for you to be palling around with your friend. Out of loyalty to your husband, explain this to her. Tell her you don't blame her and you care for her, but at this time, it would be best if you put your friendship on hold.

In time, your husband's family may realize your friend shouldn't be blamed. But for now, and for the sake of the marriage, withdraw from the friendship.

Readers came down hard on both sides of this woman's dilemma. "She can respect her husband's feelings by not inviting the friend to her home," one reader wrote. "But she should be allowed to choose her own friends, otherwise she'll be bitter and resentful."

Other readers felt otherwise. "I know that the girlfriend didn't pull the trigger," a woman wrote, "but it seems she contributed to the suicide. It's understandable that she'd be barred from seeing the family. I feel the wife is simply heartless. Her husband's brother is dead, and she's still running around with this irresponsible girlfriend. Where is her loyalty? Her husband ought to take a long look at the woman he married."

An advice column is a place where readers go to be reassured. Other people's problems help put our own in perspective. And when other people describe their emotions, we can see that we're not alone in even our most disturbing thoughts.

That's why I sometimes print questions that take issue with the whole world at once. Don't all of us get angry at everything once in a while? Two such questions:

Dear Zazz: Sometimes, I look at my loved ones and see only the things I hate about them. I look at my friends and suspect they don't have my best interests at heart. I look at myself and wonder how I got involved with all these people.

People I meet casually seem to have more to offer than the people in my life now.

At times, I just want to run away. Maybe I'd make a new life with new friends, and maybe I'd just stay a loner. I wonder if I'd somehow be happier.

I don't have these feelings all the time. Usually, my friends and family bring me joy and I'm thrilled they're in my life. But I worry when these dark emotions surface. Is this normal?
—R.G., Chattanooga, Tenn.

I responded:

There are days when all of us like our acquaintances more than our friends, days when we can name a dozen people who understand us better than our spouses do, days when the neighbors' kids seem human and lovable, while our kids are monsters from the deep.

These feelings are usually natural, brought on by the pressures of commitment, family responsibility and proximity to the same circle of people.

When we care deeply, we often can't help but enhance negative emotions as well. We've invested so much of ourselves in these people that we're disappointed by what we get in return. Strangers seem more appealing, only because we don't know their faults.

Your feelings are most likely healthy, but if you continue to feel distraught, a counselor can help you sort through these emotions.

A similar letter:

Dear Zazz: Newspapers are filled with tales of rape, violence, murder, child abuse, and car accidents. People die of horrible diseases. I feel like a victim who hasn't been hit yet.

I'm afraid for my children and depressed about our society. How can I stop living with this fear and frustration?
—S.M.

I replied:

The happiest people subscribe to what might be termed "the charmed life theory." They tell themselves that they'll avoid the major traumas, the worst diseases, the random crimes. They're careful, but positive. They force themselves to live "the charmed life" because they know the alternatives.

Yes, there are evils in our society. Yes, we all die in the end. But if we focus on the negative, we'll be afraid to get out of bed. I think we have no choice but to try to live that charmed life. And if crime or disease does hit us, well, what option do we have besides doing our best to survive?

Teach your children to be wary and aware, but stress the beautiful things in life. Encourage them to face the world with hope and a smile; the good usually outweighs the bad.

Religions have thrived because for centuries people have struggled with these same questions. Perhaps you might find comfort and more answers through your church or synagogue.

Of course, not all questions are so heavy and humorless. Many lend themselves to a lighter touch. And even if they don't, sometimes I just can't resist.

A good advice-column must have a quickness about it—at least on some days of the week. Selected questions should be bite-sized and intriguing. Answers should be sharp, precise, unexpected. Sarcasm really has to work, or it should be avoided. Quirkiness is fine as long as at least one reader per household will "get it." (Then he or she can explain it to everyone else.) Entertaining answers are great, but they are best if they're useful, too. And finally, jokes about animals are very risky: Even if the animals have a sense of humor (and that's hard to tell one way or the other), their owners invariably do not. So a smart advice-columnist skips all but the most irresistible cat, dog, and canary jokes.

Given the guidelines above, how would you answer the twelve questions below? (Remember, all were sent to me by earnest readers in search of legitimate answers.)

Question: "I dropped out of high school without graduating. Now the 10-year reunion is coming up and I'd like to go. Should I?—Unsure"

Answer: "Go to the reunion and have a good time. Most of your former classmates will be too busy worrying about their own appearances or histories to remember (or care) that you didn't graduate. And if some snob brings it up, reply: 'You're right, I didn't graduate. By the way, what happened to your face?' "

Q: "I'm an Elvis impersonator and I work private parties, charity groups and small clubs. I love doing my Elvis act, but it's not full-time work. My problem: I find it hard to keep a regular job. Things don't work out. I end up quitting. I can't concentrate. Any advice?—Forever Elvis"

A: "Have you considered getting an Elvis-related day job? Maybe you could be a tour guide at Graceland mansion, an Elvis souvenir wholesaler, or a DJ on one of the nation's four all-Elvis radio stations. Is there a book inside you? One good title not yet used: *Elvis, Priscilla, the Colonel, the Lord & Me.* Elvis is still alive, at least as a cottage industry. Find work in the empire he left behind."

Q: "How do I tell my boyfriend that I'd feel uncomfortable wearing a bikini at the beach?—Shy"

A: "Tell him in English, if that's his native tongue. There's no need for long explanations or apologies. If he cares for you, he'll accept your simple statement: You'd be uncomfortable in a bikini."

Q: "My girlfriend's table manners are disgusting. I'm embarrassed to be seen eating with her. How do I let her know this without hurting her feelings?—Fed Up"

A: "Tell her gently, using words like 'honey,' 'darling' and 'sweetheart,' while limiting use of the words 'gross,' 'disgusting,' and 'animal-like.' While her feelings might be hurt, her table manners will likely become more civilized. That will make her more popular at every dinner table she frequents. When her habits improve, take her to dinner to celebrate."

Q: "I often see references to 'older men and younger women.' How much older than a woman does a man have to be before he's an 'older man'? Five years? Ten years? Twenty?—Woman Who Needs to Know"

A: "You certainly should think about the age difference if a man has toupees that are older than you are. And be especially careful if his last 'younger woman' was old enough to be your mother—or grandmother."

Q: "I couldn't finish my meal in a fancy restaurant—I'd eaten about half of it—so I asked for a doggy bag. Walking back to the kitchen, my waitress tripped and dropped my plate. Needless to say,

I never got my doggy bag. Should I have asked for another meal to replace the food she dropped?—Hungry Now"

A: "A smart restaurant manager would offer a replacement doggy bag. A kind customer would decline it, with thanks. If no overtures are made, you may ask for a make-good on the dropped food. And next time, if you suspect your waitress is clumsy, have the doggy container brought to your table so you can pack up your meal yourself. Just don't trip on the way out."

Q: "My wife's best friend comes over all the time when my wife isn't home. She and I really want to get involved with each other, but don't know how to go about it. We don't want to ruin our friendship. What do you suggest?—Mixed Emotions"

A: "What do I suggest? I suggest that your wife spend more time at home. Maybe that way, she'll catch you and her best friend making goo-goo eyes at each other. What follows after that can't be predicted. But one thing is certain: Your friendship with your wife's best friend isn't the relationship that needs the most work."

Q: "I've been dating a girl who seems sincere and honest. I've even thought of marrying her. Recently, however, she told me that she has spotted UFOs several times in her life. Each time she saw the UFO while out walking alone. This really makes me wonder about her. Is this a sign that she's off the deep end?—Worried"

A: "Give her the benefit of the doubt. Maybe she mistakes bright stars for flying saucers. Or maybe she really has seen UFOs. Of course, if she starts telling you that Elvis lives in her closet, or that she knows a 9-year-old who gave birth to quintuplets, be prepared for the worst. Once the supermarket newspapers get on to her, she might end up leaving you for Bigfoot."

Q: "I have a twin brother who is always getting into trouble. I'm better behaved, but when it comes to punishment, my father treats us like we're the same person. I'm tired of being punished for my brother's actions. What can I do?—Half of Double Trouble"

A: "If your twin is wearing a blue shirt, wear red. If he has long hair, wear yours short. Make it easy for your father to figure out who is making trouble and who is innocent and angelic. And tell your dad that you need a separate identity even in matters besides misbehavior.

"If your brother remains a troublemaker as you both grow older, always wear different clothing and hair—especially in police line-ups."

Q: "My husband and I are going to his brother's third wedding in 10 years. Are we obligated to give the same amount as a gift?—Enough Is Enough"

A: "I assume that each of your brother-in-law's weddings has been less lavish than the one before. Gifts can be downsized as well. However, if you can afford to be a sport and want to avoid trouble, keep your gifts uniform. The latest bride will appreciate your welcoming her into the family with the same enthusiasm you showed her predecessors. I might, however, have different advice for the fourth or fifth wedding. Feel free to write back then."

Q: "Can you base a relationship on money alone?—Wondering"

A: "Your relationship with your automatic teller machine can be based on money alone. But between family, friends and especially lovers, a relationship based on money lasts only as long as the money holds out.

"If you're the one with the money and feel used, cash in. If you're seeing someone because of money, think about what that person sees in you. You could be being used, too."

Q: "My fiance insists on allowing his big, black Labrador retriever to sleep on his bed. When there are three of us in the bed, let me tell you, it's a crowd! How can I get him to make alternate sleeping arrangements for his dog? He won't budge on the issue.—Man's Best Friend, or Am I?"

A: "You can get a bigger bed, a smaller dog, or a more considerate fiance. Assuming you keep your fiance, consider giving him an ultimatum: 'It's the dog or me, at least at bedtime.' In a marriage, all parties (in your case, man, woman and dog) must compromise. Your fiance's refusal to do this bodes poorly for everyone in your relationship except the dog."

House Calls

SITTING BEHIND A desk all day, opening mail and answering questions, is awfully confining. From the start, I had this nagging urge to meet the people behind the letters, to see the families they describe come to life.

So one day, I figured, why not?

At the end of my column I wrote:

> Attention Readers: I want to come over for dinner. I'd like to visit your house one night and hang out with the kids, grandmom, whoever's around. Let's talk about the family's concerns and beefs (with each other and the world) and I'll try to give some good advice.
>
> Write me a letter explaining why you'd like me to visit. Also, don't forget to let me know what's for dinner.

Well, I quickly learned that an advice columnist who makes house calls must be ready for any kind of family strife, any problem, any meal. When I put my little note in the column, I never expected the range of questions, issues, and menus that might be thrown my way.

Hundreds of readers responded to my request for a free meal, including typical suburbanites, homosexual couples, a college dorm, and children who hadn't yet asked their parents if they could have me over. Their letters offered a captivating view of American home-life.

"I have daydreams of being kidnapped by a group of men who like 200-pound women," wrote one female reader, who promised "the best breaded pork chops you've ever eaten."

"I can't tell you what's for dinner, but it won't include red meat," wrote another. "One of my roommates is a vegetarian. That's one of my beefs!"

One family wrote that they have "mostly Cosby-type problems," which I figured could be solved in a half hour. But others' woes were more complicated—alcoholism, dead marriages, "acute housewife boredom."

One woman invited me "only if you don't mind mortar dust, glass, brick, and seeing the remains of what used to be a living room." Five days earlier, she explained, a drunken driver had smashed into her house, stopping six feet from where she was sitting.

A suburban Chicago woman hoped that my coming to dinner and writing about the experience might help her husband find a job. He had just been laid off after twenty-six years.

The most unexpected letter came from a woman who lived in a van and said she read my column each day in the library. She wrote: "When you visit people's homes, tell them to be thankful they have a home to have problems in."

I was charmed by the understated eloquence of many invitations: One woman wrote: "I'm 29, black and live in a small apartment with my 6-year-old son. I take care of him and he takes care of me. We get by. Sometimes we eat breakfast for dinner, sometimes dinner for breakfast. We'd enjoy company."

Many readers gave pithy rundowns on family members I'd meet at dinner. A teenage girl wrote that I might be giving advice "over the red and white bucket," since her mother doesn't cook. The girl described her younger brother in three words ("very sports oriented") and herself in four ("not very sports oriented").

Some readers invited me so I'd help around the house. One woman wanted to know if I'm a licensed driver, since her kids needed to be taken to Math Olympiad practice, and music and tumbling lessons. Another mother reminded me to bring cash to buy Girl Scout cookies from her daughter. She also warned that her son, whose IQ is 142, plays chess for money.

Then there were the combat zones. One homemaker wrote of "hapless diners" at her house who'd been hit by flying food. Her husband eats in five minutes ("Marine chow line" syndrome, she explained), so I wouldn't have to worry about a long, boring dinner.

Another reader said her husband "invented the word obnoxious" and warned that her children might test their karate chops on me. She promised "to put Super Glue on the tennis balls so they won't be bouncing off the walls during dinner." Still, she suggested, "bring your catcher's mask."

Many readers were kind enough to invite "Mrs. Zazz," my wife;

I guess they didn't want me leaving her in the car. Others tried, unsuccessfully, to make me feel special. One man wrote: "The kids are dying to meet you, Zazz, even though they don't know who/what you are."

So many of the dinner invitations (and menus) were enticing. The many columns that would originate at these readers' dinner tables turned out to be among the funniest and most touching I'd write.

In the first batch of invitations, I was drawn to one in particular. Written by a woman named Caroline Depcik, the invitation was so challenging that I had to visit her home first.

LOVING HANDS

Caroline began her letter bluntly: "Unless you're a coward, what could be more fun and interesting than visiting a family of seven deaf people who live normal lives?"

So I drove out to Lyons, Illinois, and was welcomed by the Depciks with big smiles and cold beer. Robert and Rita Depcik have five children—Michael, Valerie, Paul, Caroline, and Kay—ranging in age from eighteen to twenty-five. The parents and children have all been deaf since birth.

I quickly learned that in their world, I was the handicapped one. As they conversed effortlessly with their hands, my ears were useless. Luckily, the Depciks also invited a few deaf friends who hear to some degree or read lips. They translated for me. (The quotes that follow are translated from sign language.)

The Depciks are attractive, well-adjusted, and love a good laugh. Responding to sign language commands, their dog did tricks for me. Michael gave a few hand motions and the dog rolled over. Another sign language command and the dog played dead.

Except for touches like flashing-light alarm clocks, their suburban home looked like any other. It was the dinner-table conversation that was so different.

Michael, eighteen, had just returned from Australia. Though Australians speak English, "their sign language was like French to me," he said. He felt self-conscious, signing with an American accent.

Caroline told me of how a man approached her in a loud, crowded bar. She motioned to him that she couldn't hear. He thought the loud music was the problem. He kept shouting, then gave up, confused.

Scott Morrison, a family friend, explained how he went deaf: "I was eleven years old and watching *The Twilight Zone* on TV. The sound kept getting lower. The next morning, I couldn't hear. My hearing went into the Twilight Zone."

Scott's wife, Deeadra, is deaf, but their son, Daylon, two, is not. Deeadra told of how she and Daylon were on a playground, signing to one another. "Parents looked at us like we were freaks," she said. "Daylon wasn't embarrassed. But I know he'll go through a stage where he'll be ashamed of me."

I wanted the Depciks and their friends to help me write a column giving advice to hearing people. So many of us don't know how to respond to the deaf. Well, as soon as I asked for complaints about hearing people, a half-dozen hands started signing at once. Scott said he hates people who gawk: "In a restaurant, I ask to sit facing the wall, so I won't see people staring when I sign."

Some people are ignorant about the deaf. "They ask if we read braille, or if we can pray, or how we communicate when we make love," said Iris Martinez, a family friend. "I say, 'Date a deaf person and find out!'"

The old phrase "deaf and dumb" still stings. "There's a lack of confidence in us," Valerie said.

Another complaint was that local TV news is not captioned for the deaf. Mayor Harold Washington of Chicago had died just a few weeks earlier, and the Depciks described their frustration at not being able to follow the special reports on TV.

They had plenty of advice for the hearing: Don't bother screaming; even a bullhorn won't help. If your children are deaf, learn how to sign. (They gave me a poem written by a deaf child for his family. It begins: "What I want most is to hear your loving hand . . .")

"We don't want sympathy," said Iris, adding that she has been sent free drinks by people who see her signing in restaurants. "All we ask is patience, understanding, and if you can't communicate by speaking, write it down. People can hear with their eyes. They can talk with their hands."

While the Depcik women watched *Dynasty* (with captions) on TV, I had another beer and some laughs with the men. Soon enough, it was late. I thanked Rita for a great meal and we said our good-byes.

Once in my car, I listened to the radio self-consciously. Then I turned it off and drove home in silence.

A SECOND CHANCE AT LIFE

Some readers send me detailed menus with their dinner invitations. Others send detailed lists of their problems.

Maria Zajczenko-Varela sent both.

She described everyone in her family, from her three-year-old "Rambo-like" son to her eleven-year-old daughter ("typical 'dumb blond'; dances, plays piano, aspiring model"). Her topics for my visit: "in-laws, divorce, suicide, backstabbing friends . . ."

Maria's letter was so clever that I mentioned it in a column I wrote about interesting invitations I'd gotten.

A few days later, Maria sent me this note:

> My daughter, Lisa, was so excited to read your column when I told her you'd be mentioning us. However, after she read it, she said, "Mom, how could you say that about me? Now my friends will laugh at me even more!"
>
> You see, Lisa has a speech problem. We've been working to clean it up, but sometimes kids make fun of her pronunciation, and it hurts.
>
> Our family teases her about being a "dumb blond" and she doesn't mind. But printing it in the paper is another matter. Could you please print a "Confidential to Lisa Z-V," stating that her family loves her no matter what? Thank you.

I felt awful, and guilty of an insensitivity so common among media people. We put names in the paper or faces on TV without always considering who might be hurt.

I called Lisa and apologized. I spoke to Maria, too. She was glad I called, and said the dinner invitation was still open. So two weeks later, I headed out to their Chicago home.

What I found was a house full of love—and an unexpected story of a family rallying against adversity. Because their friends and relatives already knew their story, the Varelas agreed to let me tell it in a column. Perhaps, they said, they might inspire other families.

When I got to their home, Tony, three, got me a beer from the refrigerator, then settled onto the couch for his twentieth viewing of *The Wizard of Oz* on videotape. (He recited the dialogue before the characters did. Bright kid.)

Lisa and her sister, Francesca, fourteen, gave me a tour of the family photos and school projects. I was impressed by the girls' politeness and maturity. (Lisa's speech problem was hardly noticeable. And to set the record straight, I found her to be a smart blonde.) The girls are half sisters, products of Maria's two previous marriages.

Soft-spoken, friendly, and very spiritual, Eric Varela is Maria's third husband, Tony's natural father, and the girls' adoptive dad.

We talked about Maria's teaching job, the girls' schoolwork, Tony's fascination with Oz, Eric's former job as a credit manager and his current unemployment. Then Eric told me "what happened."

A few months earlier, Eric was depressed and deeply in debt. He had a $100,000 insurance policy, and wrongly assumed his family could collect after his suicide. It was Lisa who discovered him in the garage, unconscious in his car. She saved his life.

"I felt I wasn't up to standard as a husband and father," Eric said. Through counseling and "my wife's persistent love and concern," he'd learned to be positive again. "God gave me a second life. If I tried to kill myself again, it would be a slap in His face."

The family told me they were learning to discuss problems openly. "The other night, Francesca blew her top at me," Eric said. "She told me, 'Stand up and face your problems.' She's right."

Despite the heaviness of "what happened," the Varelas impressed me as a family celebrating life. "We leave the Christmas cards out all year," Francesca said. "We like to reminisce about Christmas. It's a special time for us."

Maria said she was thankful that she married Eric. She talked of his kindness and his love for the kids. She said she learned to forget that her two ex-husbands never see her daughters. And she told me she's buoyed by a Mae West line: "Never cry over the man who left you. The next one may fall for your smile."

"This line applies to life in general," Maria said. "You can't cry over the past. I always try to imagine something better down the road."

By the TV, Tony was singing "If I Were King of the Forest" when Eric confided: "Our dream is to pay off our debts and go to Austria for a family vacation. Whatever we do, we do as a family."

I was glad I picked the Varelas' home for a house call. Like every family, they have their troubles. But I decided that they also have enough love and strength to carry them through.

GREEN JELL-O

Ted Manning wrote me to say he was a resident assistant on a dormitory floor for honor students at Northern Illinois University. He figured that for nostalgia's sake, I'd appreciate "the fine cuisine" at a college dorm, and he promised that no matter which day I visited, "there will be Jell-O."

The availability of Jell-O sealed my decision to make a house call at NIU, and I headed up to the De Kalb, Illinois campus, where about forty NIU honor students were waiting for me.

The food, I found, was pretty bad, but there was indeed Jell-O. Flavor of the day: green.

Having made house calls in all sorts of alien environments, I figured a student dorm would be familiar terrain. After all, I was just eight years out of college. I never expected so pronounced a generation gap.

We were talking about student activism, and almost in unison, the students told me that "cool" kids don't join the John Lennon Society.

I'd never heard of this group before, and so the honor students filled me in.

With their long hair and tie-dyed shirts, the Lennonites were known as the campus oddballs. They roamed the campus, talking of social change and student involvement in social issues. But few of their peers ever listened. "A lot of students look at the John Lennon Society as a bunch of freaks," one student told me.

For millions of once-young people, the generation known as baby boomers, John Lennon was a mythical hero. But these NIU honor students said they found him—and the passions stirred by his name—to be rather passé.

One thing I discovered quickly while eating dinner at NIU was that these students (ages seventeen to twenty) have strong opinions about baby boomers (ages twenty-four to forty-two). "I'm tired of reading about them," said Ted. "Every time you turn around, the media are reporting, 'Baby boomers turned forty yesterday,' or 'Baby boomers are getting married,' or 'Now they're getting divorced.' or 'They're all going shopping.' "

For many students, the term "baby boomer" applies to their parents. For others, boomers are their older siblings. They certainly don't identify with us. But they do have sharp advice for us: Enough already!

The NIU students told me they appreciated an article that appeared a while back in various alternative newspapers. "Some of us are not part of your baby boom," postboomer Julie Phillips wrote. "We don't really care what you were doing the day Kennedy was shot. We don't want to know how you watched the war on TV, or how you wished you'd been at Woodstock. We are sick of hearing about you, tired of reading about you, and bored senseless by your self-absorbed prattle. In short, we are Boomed Out!"

I tried to tell these students that I clearly remember when John Kennedy was shot, even though I was a mere kindergartener. "We don't care!" two students yelled out in unison. They didn't seem to have the same reverence for the big events of their early years. "Yeah, we have memories of Watergate," one student said. "Bozo wasn't on."

They didn't seem to regret that their generation lacks a spokesman, a Lennon or a Bob Dylan. "We have Tiffany," someone said, and everyone laughed.

We've all read about how today's students don't want to save the world. They'd prefer an M.B.A. and a piece of the action. These honor students didn't deny this. "There doesn't seem to be anything left to protest," one said.

In fact, aside from the pet causes of the tiny Lennon Society, the few sparks of campus activism at NIU that semester focused on safe issues, such as cuts in the state's education budget. "People don't want to get in trouble anymore," a female student said.

Not all of them were proud of this. Students in the 1960s "had the guts to say what they thought was wrong," one student said. "We don't." And they said they sometimes question their disdain for the Lennon Society. "We laugh at them, but we're not doing anything and they are," a student said.

Still, they defined baby boomers as self-centered and idealistic and themselves as self-centered in a realistic way. Their view of the protest era: "The majority of students today think it was a waste of time," a student said. "In the '60s, they smoked pot, grew their hair long, and didn't really accomplish anything."

The students also said that they doubt all 1960s students were activists. "There must have been a lot of people who were never involved—people like we are now," one said.

Others believe that baby boomers spend too much time looking backward—reliving or rewriting the good old days. And the media, populated mostly by boomers, indulge them. "We can't just dwell on the past," one student warned.

Meanwhile, a student named Russ Talley said he had a clear view of the future. And like it or not, he said, he's tied to the baby boom. "We'll be paying your social security," he told me.

Only the green Jell-O seemed familiar.

GOLDEN GIRLS MINUS FORTY

Usually when I visit someone's home, I just bring my reporter's notebook and a bottle of wine. But on one unforgettable house call, I brought along something else.

I picked it up in the street, on my left shoe, moments before entering the house. The family dog sniffed it out. What an embarrassing moment: There I was, meeting people for the first time, and I'd tracked a healthy dog dropping into their home.

Worse still, a three-man TV camera crew for a show called *PM Magazine* happened to be following close behind me at that inopportune moment. They were shooting "a day in the life of a modern advice columnist." They got everything on tape: the moment I entered the house, my discovery of the dog dropping on my shoe, the this-can't-be-happening expression on my face. I pleaded with the cameraman to turn off his lights and camera, but he was laughing too hard. Luckily, the TV show's producer cut out those scenes before sending the tape off for national syndication.

As you might expect, I spent the night in my stocking feet, apologizing. Luckily, my hosts were forgiving.

Alison Brown had invited me with a letter that explained: "We're not a real family, but we're three roommates who consider each other family. . . . One 'must' topic of dinner conversation: Why are single men so desperate and boring? We hear you're happily married and we'd enjoy an optimistic viewpoint."

Alison, Edie Paterson, and Kris Kalapos, all twenty-four, lived together in a spacious apartment on Chicago's North Side. They described themselves as "the Golden Girls minus forty years."

They'd been together since they were college roomates six years earlier. Kris is a management consultant. Alison is a fabric sales rep. Edie schedules commercials for a traffic-reporting network.

After the TV crew left, the three women made a three-course meal. Each prepared her single-woman's "specialty." Alison's course was popcorn. Next came Edie's chips and dip. Kris, the most domestic, made a salad.

The household dynamics were such that Kris was in charge. As she explained: "They throw the bills on my bed and I figure out who pays what."

"Then we complain about it," Edie added.

Despite some predictable peeves, this was a tight, supportive threesome. "When I get married, it would be great if my husband could move in here," said Alison, only half jokingly.

These are three very attractive women, so they didn't ask me the typical "How do I get a date?" questions. They were more interested in learning how to get men to back off.

The phone rang several times during dinner. In each case, it was a man who "never exactly took the hint."

"When the phone rings, we all scream, 'I'm not here!'" explained Alison. The answering machine, obviously, is a necessity.

They told horror stories of boring dates. "Some men take you to trendy restaurants and all they do is talk about how great they are," Alison said. "I'm not impressed."

"I went out with a pilot," said Kris. "All he wanted to talk about was how his parents' divorce affected him."

"A lot of men like to talk," Alison added, "but they don't listen."

"What?" I asked.

These women recognized that they may be too critical. "The three of us can analyze a guy all night, and pick him apart right down to his socks," said Edie, the only one with a serious boyfriend. "If we lived alone, we wouldn't be able to do that."

They had no sense of when or if the right men might come along. "I do a lot of dating and weeding," said Kris. "It takes so much energy. I wonder if there's a light at the end of the tunnel. It's a very blind future."

Living for the moment, though, can be a lot of fun. They said they enjoyed making "home movies" on videotape. They had even danced along with the stereo and made music videos.

"If a guy asks me out for a weekend, I'll often postpone it until a weeknight because I'd rather be with the girls," Alison said.

Girls? "I don't consider myself a woman yet," said Kris. "I'm a girl." (Soon enough, of course, they'll feel like women. Maybe they're smart not to rush it. They've heard the testimony of those of us over twenty-four: Life somehow speeds up as we age.)

My advice to these women centered on giving men a break. It's not just men who don't listen, who are self-centered and boring: It's people.

Alison, Kris, and Edie agreed: They ought to be less judgmental and more open-minded. Good men are out there. It's a matter of time.

Maybe the men they meet seem so underwhelming because the roommates enjoy each other too much. Time could change that, too. As Alison said: "Maybe at some point, I'll have enough of the single-working-woman-roommate phase." She paused. "But not yet."

After dinner, I found my shoes on the front porch. I cleaned them off as best I could, thanked everyone for dinner, and watched my step as I headed home.

PETER SANCHEZ, JR., GROWS UP

When Peter Sanchez, Jr., was in his early twenties, he was impulsive, immature, and irresponsible. Just ask him. He'll tell you.

In fact, when I went to his apartment for a house call, he related this "typical" adventure:

One day, Peter and his friend, Mario, decided it must be better in the Bahamas than in Chicago. So, impulsively, they blew most of their savings on airfare. Hours later, they hit the beach. "We landed at nine A.M.," Peter recalled, "and with the money we had left, we started buying things—T-shirts, headbands, straw hats. By nine P.M., we were broke."

They'd already checked into a hotel. Eventually, they'd have to pay that bill. In the meantime, they were hungry. How would they eat?

Peter had an idea. He made a collect call to Peter Sanchez, Sr., and asked him to wire money. But his father, perturbed by Peter junior's antics, refused. Instead, he offered advice: "You're hungry? Okay, here's what you do. Go into the hallway of your hotel and look for room service carts. Some people will be finished with their dinners. See what you can scrounge up."

And with that, Peter senior hung up.

Peter junior wasn't angry. He knew his father had ways of teaching a lesson. Besides, the advice made sense. So he and Mario hit several carts before a bellhop confronted them.

Peter senior waited a few days. Maybe his son deserved to land in whatever Bahamian prison locks up room service thieves. But he couldn't let that happen. So as he'd done many times before, he came to his son's rescue. He wired five hundred dollars.

"Everyone should spoil their kids," he told me that evening over dinner. "You show them love and affection. You try to guide them. That's all you can do."

But enough is enough. When Peter junior sped through the five hundred dollars and called for more, his father was finished playing Santa. He said good luck and good-bye.

That incident wasn't so long ago. Neither was Peter junior's overnight jail stay for fighting, his heavy drinking, his womanizing, his failed marriage. "I was bad," Peter said. "Irresponsible and un- trustworthy."

And yet, when I met him, he was twenty-six and said he felt like a changed man. Perhaps that's why he invited me over: to chronicle his maturation. He wrote:

> **Dear Zazz:** I live with my girlfriend Robin, her daughter, and her brother. I'm a construction worker. Robin is a wait- ress. We are hardworking Mexican Americans. We're also party animals, though we've cut back. (I guess we're getting older and more responsible.) You seem like a cool dude, Zazzman, so if you're too busy to come over and offer advice, no sweat. We'll understand.

Well, I went to the Sanchezes' and was met by a warm crowd of relatives and friends. Robin served terrific enchiladas as I heard stories about the Sanchez clan. For instance, Peter senior's mother, ninety-three, was once an old Indian fighter. "My father was an old Indian," explained Peter senior.

Peter senior, an avid sky diver, refused to marry his second wife, Sally, until she took the plunge. They've since given Peter junior a half brother, age three.

Peter junior was a rebellious kid who never got along with his mother and moved in with his dad at age thirteen. Sally, his step- mother, told me he was as wild as a kid could be. Just five years older than Peter junior, "I had to be his friend, rather than his mother," she said. "Nothing else would have worked."

"My dad and Sally provided the family unit," Peter junior said. "Everyone else gave up on me. I was bullheaded. It took me a long time to learn what they tried to teach me."

Peter junior was proud of himself. "It would've been easy," he said, "to fall into the traps of this neighborhood—crime, drugs. But I want better things for myself and my family."

He told me he planned to marry Robin when their divorces were final. She was pregnant, and they said they hoped to have more children.

They were trying to speak Spanish in the house, though both grew up speaking English. "I don't want to be distant from my culture," Peter junior said.

Peter senior was still offering advice: "I tell my son to love himself. If he takes care of number one, he'll be able to love and take care of numbers two and three."

Peter senior stood by his philosophy of lovingly spoiling kids. His son turned out well, he said. Peter junior agreed: "Each day is a challenge. But I love Robin. I love my family. We're going to make it."

Male Call

AS A LONE male in the advice sorority, I've found that men and women often have very different agendas when they write to me.

Men want empathy. A lot of them want me to say, "Buddy, I'm with you all the way," even if they're cheating on their wives, lying to their mothers, and annoying every woman they meet with cheap come-on lines.

They expect me to reinforce their most sexist contentions, redress all the wrongs committed by the female population, and respect their assertions that "a man's gotta do what a man's gotta do."

When women write, they often hope I'll share with them the secrets of being a man. They want to know what makes men tick and how to "fix" them when things go wrong. Since men don't come with a user's manual, women write to me as if I'm the men's service department.

Women also use me as a fact checker. One middle-aged woman's husband told her that he'd need to sleep with a younger woman to cure his impotence. Her question: "Can a young woman really help an impotent man in ways an older woman can't?" She signed herself "Not Convinced," and with good reason.

My job is to give reasonable advice to both sexes. But in many ways, I feel more responsible to men. It's a matter of kinship, I guess.

Men often write to me to be reassured in matters that they assume Ann, Abby, or Diane wouldn't understand. "Always remember that you're a man," wrote a male reader when I first started the job. "Don't ever let us down."

Since then, men routinely have written to say I've let them down, but I do try to be supportive. Consider this letter:

> **Dear Zazz:** OK, so men will never know the pain of childbirth. But can women ever know the physical torment brought on by a hit below the belt?

My wife takes great delight in playfully tapping me in the groin area and gets a good chuckle out of my reaction. I'm at the point where I often "take a bow" as we pass in the house. She doesn't realize how painful even light contact can be. She says, "How can that hurt? I hardly touched you."

For the benefit of all men so abused, please back me up. This is no joke.

—Hurting

I replied: "Football players wear protective cups. Husbands shouldn't have to. Next time you go to your doctor, take your wife. Ask him to firmly give her the lowdown on how sensitive men are down there. If she doesn't cut it out, she's sadistic. I feel for you, man—in ways a woman never could."

As sex roles become increasingly reversed and unclear, I feel for a lot of men. "My wife makes more money than I do," a man wrote. "She wants me to stay home and clean the house, cook dinner—in essence, just be her househusband. Despite all the money she makes, I don't think she has the right to ask this."

My response:

If another guy were married to your wife, he'd quit his job, clean the house, do the laundry, cook dinner, and, just before she got home from work, he'd head for Hawaii with all the money from the joint bank account. You needn't take such drastic measures. But be firm: You don't want to be a househusband, and your wife had better respect that. If she can't, she's threatening the marriage.

Then there was the twenty-nine-year-old bachelor who began his letter by saying that he respects women. "I was taught that ogling women is rude and that pornography cheapens sex," he wrote. "I work with six women, some single, some married. I like them all, but their behavior puzzles me. They often bring in Playgirl magazine and drool over the naked men. They show the photos to me and laugh when I blush. I'd never insult them by forcing them to look at photos of nude women."

I replied:

Slowly, but surely, a lot of men are becoming sensitized to women's feelings. They've learned to keep locker-room talk and blatant ogling out of mixed company.

But because exploitation of the male sex object is a more recent development (and less pervasive in our society), not all women are aware of how their public man-watching might make men fidget.

Your co-workers are inconsiderate. Tell them that you're uncomfortable when they force you to react to Playgirl photos. Just as men must learn to consider how their comments and behavior play to the opposite sex, women need to do the same.

I don't always side with men unequivocally, of course. Where they want me to see black and white, I can't help but see shades of gray. And then, invariably, readers of both sexes respond with a rainbow of opinions.

A man wrote to say he was having a drink with a female colleague. She suddenly kicked off her shoes, and placed her feet on the seat next to his. As a playful, innocent gesture, he stroked her feet with a cocktail straw. She then scolded him for what he considered "a sexual come-on." The man wrote: "I thought she overreacted. What's your opinion?" He signed himself, "Sorry I Did It."

"Perhaps you did take some liberties," I replied, "but if you've already apologized, there's no need to dwell on the matter. Just be careful in future dealings with this colleague. Also, here's a way to look at whether this was a sexual come-on or just playfulness on your part. If a male co-worker had kicked off his shoes, would you have stroked his feet?"

I thought I'd given an even-handed response, and was surprised when readers, many of whom were women, came to the man's defense. "A lady shouldn't take her shoes off and plop them on a seat in a public place," a woman wrote. "If her feet were hurting her or she was tired, she should have gone straight home. 'Sorry' should be careful around this woman. She probably is a tease and would be the first to yell sexual harassment." Another woman said Sorry's colleague had issued the sexual come-on by putting her feet on the chair: "Would a male co-worker have kicked off his shoes in such an environment?"

The issues men bring me are often male variations on a female theme. For instance, women have long complained that men leave the toilet seat up. So a male reader wrote:

Dear Zazz: I'm glad the Sun-Times hired a male advice columnist. Perhaps now we'll get a reasonably unbiased perspective on a topic many men feel strongly about—fuzzy toilet-seat covers.

Don't play naive, Zazz, you know what I'm talking about. It's those toilet-seat covers that have so much pink or blue fuzz on them that every time a man stands to urinate and lifts one of them up, it flops back down. This can make for embarrassing moments in the bathroom.

In this man's case, the fuzzy seat covers pointed to a female conspiracy led by his fiancée's mother. He wrote:

> Rhonda's mother gave her the seat covers as a gift, and Rhonda feels obligated to use them. My complaints were met with scoffs of "You'll just have to make do." Well, one dark night, the toilet-seat cover flopped down at the wrong time. I made a mess and Rhonda was livid. She said if I couldn't deal with her seat covers, I'd have to use the gas station down the block. That was the last straw. I said it was either me or the seat covers. She's still deciding.

I heard from other men on the subject. One said he threatened to shave his wife's seat covers. Another said he would flush them down the toilet, if not for the potential plumbing problems.

My solution:

> Fuzzy covers can be pulled off toilet seats easily. When you need to use the bathroom, take a few seconds to remove the seat cover. When you're finished, replace it. Rhonda won't know what went on behind closed doors. Her mother can visit and proudly see her gift prominently on display. And you won't have the problem of a toilet seat slapping shut at the wrong time.
>
> If you do end up marrying Rhonda, you always can install a urinal in your first house. That's one way to make sure her seat cover doesn't put a lid on your love life.

I thought my answer was a compromise. Some men felt otherwise. Wrote one:

> You could have taken a stand against this kind of petty feminine bull, but you chose to wimp out. Fuzzy seat covers are clearly obnoxious. I, too, have been a victim of falling seat

covers. It's embarrassing. But, in essence, you told the man he was being too sensitive.

If a woman complained about something her man was doing, you would advise her that the man should accommodate her sensitivities. Women who insist on being so inconsiderate should be told to get their heads out of you-know-where and show respect for the man's wishes.

The man signed his letter "Not A Wimp," which made it obvious what he thought of me.

Actually, when I don't support a man 100 percent, I'm often called a wimp—and worse.

A man wrote a long letter complaining that women are only interested in dating hunks. "There's no man shortage," he concluded. "Women are just totally obsessed with cute, gorgeous hunks. I'm average-looking at best and, as a result, I've had enough rejection to last a few lifetimes. At age 34, I've joined the 'Given Up Club.'" He signed himself "No CGH."

I told him I was sorry to hear he'd joined the Given Up Club, but he seemed to have the right criteria for membership: a pessimistic attitude, a chip on his shoulder, and low self-esteem. I told him:

> Don't blame all women. Many grow out of the CGH stage after their teen years. And those women who still demand cute, gorgeous hunks have a definite function in our society: Without them, where would cute hunks find dates?
>
> Sorry, my friend, but I don't buy your arguments or your anti-female tirade. Quit complaining about women as if they all were cut from the same mold. Quit moaning about the hopelessness of your life. And quit the Given Up Club. Rejection often is a painful part of being single. Lots of people— men and women—go through it. But there are special women out there who would appeal to you—and vice versa. Keep your spirits up, your eyes open, and your negative attitude in check.

The women who wrote in response to No CGH suggested that he take a look at himself. Does he bathe regularly? Is he still wearing polyester leisure suits? Is he looking only at younger women? I even heard from a female stripper who said she had danced at many bachelor parties. "Most of the guys I've danced for are far from cute, gorgeous hunks," she wrote. "Some are downright ugly. Well, women somewhere are marrying these guys!"

Most of the men who wrote about No CGH, however, were disgusted with my answer. "You either are unwilling to lose favor with female readers or are sadly naive," a man wrote. "The letter was not an anti-female tirade. The man merely was expressing reality."

Another man wrote:

Dear Zazz: Why did your paper go to the trouble and expense of hiring a male advice columnist? After a few months of publicity and female attention, he's just a woman with male hormones.

Any man (like you) who manages to have his grinning image beaming daily from a newspaper is likely to have dozens of women offering him sexual favors at no cost or at a drastic discount. This puts him in an elite group of males who don't have to beg, lie, borrow and steal to obtain sex.

You, sir, now are one of the elite. Your fame and presumed fortune make you unfit to advise the average mope who constantly must endure brutal rejection and tedious sexual negotiations with women who want only a quick ego boost.

In case you've forgotten:

—Sex is a seller's market and women own the store.

—If a man isn't rich, handsome, famous or a believable liar, he won't get a woman.

I must assume, Zazz, that you are reading this letter after yet another night of sexual abandon provided by some nubile young creature. I therefore have no sympathy. I only suggest that your newspaper stop this phony "male" viewpoint angle. I resent smug female advice coming from a male mind.

—W.A.L.

Well, minutes after reading W.A.L.'s letter, I phoned him. He was surprised to hear from me, but we had a nice chat. It turned out that the guy was "happily married." Explain that!

I told him I'm married, too, and that my mug shot in the paper had resulted in zero come-ons by available women. He didn't sound convinced. And in the days that followed, I got many letters supporting his theories. Blinders Wide Open wrote:

> I'm a man who bathes regularly. I brush my teeth and wear only the finest suits. I'm not cute, but I'm intelligent with a great sense of humor. I'm kind to animals and small children and once, I sent $10 to the National Organization for Women. But I can't get a date with a woman.
>
> I'm aware that there are not-so-cute men who do very well with women. However, to follow their examples, I'd have to be a drug-dealer, an alcoholic or a criminal. It seems women today are more interested in some bizarre sense of "excitement" than they are in decent men with substance.
>
> My advice to the men with "low self-esteem" (as you've described those of us who see the reality of women today) is to become social deviants. If you can't be cute, be cruel. Women will love you for it.

Mail here at Advice Central runs in predictable cycles. If I print letters from men who complain about women, women soon demand equal time. Then back and forth it goes.

A woman writes: "Since I'm not a young sexy bimbo, no man is interested in me."

A man responds: "Ha! Women won't even talk to a guy unless he's rich or powerful!"

"Ha!" a woman counters. "I'd go out with almost anybody, but since I'm 43 and overweight, I can't get a second date."

Well, after one particular round of female rebuttals to male rebuttals of female rebuttals, I heard from Fredric Hayward, director of Men's Rights, a male support group in Sacramento, California. A female advice-columnist might have been unlikely to give Hayward space in her column. But I decided, what the heck, I'd give the man a forum. He had some intriguing arguments, and I knew he'd elicit an emotional response from readers.

Hayward's message: A woman who claims she is overlooked by men is a hypocrite. "So many women dump the dirty work on men," he said. "They expect men to do the risking, courting and financing—offering nothing as motivation but their simple presence."

The fact that men seek younger women and women prefer older men is seen by society as an example of female inequality: Older men supposedly have their pick of women, while older women are often stuck alone. Hayward wrote:

It is fashionable to blame men for this inequality. But female fingers pull the triggers that set this pattern in motion.

Long before women are rejected for being "too old," men are rejected for being "too young." At age 16, it is not the boys who think, "Why go out with my peers? I'd rather find a 14-year-old girl with fewer wrinkles and firmer breasts." No, it is the 16-year-old girls who decide, "Why go out with my peers? They ride bikes and collect allowances. I'd rather find an 18-year-old with a car and an income."

Hayward contends that this begins a process where men are "success objects," valued for their power and money. And as men age, they accumulate more money and power, making them more "attractive."

"This process also makes women into sex objects," Hayward said. "They're admired for their bodies. And since age generally erodes the body, age generally makes women 'less attractive.'"

Hayward believes the "man shortage" exists because many women refuse to abandon their expectations that a man is eligible only if he is older, wiser, and richer.

He pointed out that an older woman is a common male fantasy: "The most memorable character in 'The Graduate' was Mrs. Robinson. But most women aren't interested in teaching an inexperienced man. They don't want to waste time on a man unless he already has it together."

Men, meanwhile, enjoy teaching inexperienced women. "There is danger in this male fantasy for both parties," Hayward said, "but there is also something healthy in wanting to foster someone's development."

For the older woman/younger man scenario to work, Hayward said, we must change how we raise our children:

We urge boys not to consider someone attractive just because she has a pretty face. We must also teach girls not to consider someone attractive just because he's a football hero or BMW owner.

A woman can attract younger men the same way that men attract younger women: Share with them the benefits

that come with age—the knowledge and wealth you've ac-
cumulated.

The female experience lulls a woman into feeling, "I'm
giving him my time. The least he could do is pay my expenses." The woman who continues to think her mere presence is a gift to men is the woman who must worry most
about what age will do to her beauty.

Predictably, many women were unimpressed by Hayward's
theories. Wrote one: "Hayward fails to acknowledge that women
earn far less than men. If a woman takes the financial responsibility
for a date, it usually costs her 50 percent more of her income than
it would her date's income. If women were paid equally, picking up
checks would soon reach parity."

Another woman, who signed herself "Eve," complained: "Since
Adam, men like Mr. Hayward have been busy blaming women for
the pain and ignorance men have inflicted on themselves. The most
arrogant sexual cripples are the ones who continue to blame women,
and keep professing their own innocence."

Naturally, I heard from many men who appreciated Hayward's
remarks. A Chicago dentist offered one of the most eloquent explanations (others might call it a rationalization) for why it's okay for
men to seek women with big breasts:

> **Dear Zazz:** We need only peruse personal ads to see what
> males and females consider important in the opposite sex. In
> their ads, women generally seek "a professional" (or some
> other security-related euphemism). The desired man's physi-
> cal attributes are secondary—or aren't mentioned at all.
>
> Meanwhile, men's personal ads are replete with refer-
> ences to the physical beauty, slimness and hair color they
> seek in a mate. Few ever contain references to the need for
> education or financial status.
>
> I say a female's attraction to a man because he's finan-
> cially secure is no better (or worse) than a man's attraction
> to a woman who has large breasts.
>
> It might be my male perspective showing through, but I
> find that many women view their attraction to rich, powerful
> men as "understandable" or "a minor flaw." However, these
> women view men's attraction to "young beauty queens" as
> the lowest type of vile behavior.

When I look within myself, I find that my attraction to female beauty comes not from some dark corner of my soul, but from organic drives that seem natural and honest.

I'll concede that there may be a natural part of the female soul that views the security implication of wealthy men in the same way, but which I will never understand.

The dentist who wrote the letter above seemed to have a bit of Alan Alda in him, a bit of Hugh Hefner, and a bit of Margaret Mead. The engineer who wrote the letter below had more than his share of the King of Siam in him. He wrote:

Dear Zazz: I'm convinced that monogamy is a failure. If men were allowed by law to have two wives, our society might be better off—and women might be happier.

Consider this familiar scenario. A virile businessman's eyes light on the sexy chick in his office. He divorces his plain old wife and shares his bed with this new, young exciting partner.

The pathetic old wife, who probably helped make the man a success, is cast aside. Maybe she ends up with financial support. But in the long run, she's the loser in the deal. She would make out far better if she remained the man's wife, along with the new sexpot.

Let's face it: Since the dawn of time, men have been built to handle several women sexually.

Print my letter, Zazz. I think it will be a blockbuster for you.
—W.H.

I replied:

Dear W.H.: Let's think this through. Perhaps the "pathetic old wife" can continue to cook and clean for her virile husband and his new love. Maybe she'll even deliver breakfast in bed to the stud and the babe from the office.

What an interesting threesome they'll make. Imagine the dinner table conversation! Wife No. 1 can tell Wife No. 2 about the Studman's exciting early years. And Wife No. 2 can provide commentary, for comparison's sake, on more recent sexual escapades.

When Mr. Virile has to work late at the office (selecting Wife No. 3, no doubt), the two wives can stay home together watching "The King and I" on the VCR.

Sound feasible?

It sounds loony to me. Any first wife with any self-respect would tell her husband to take a quick hike off a tall cliff—and to hold the bimbo's hand when he does it.

Men may be physically capable of more than one sex partner (as are women, don't forget), but polygamy seems to work only in isolated cases—and usually in societies where women are second-class citizens.

A MONEY-BACK GUARANTEE

There is one area where I always take it upon myself to rally for men's rights. Many men feel they're under attack by all the how-to books for women, the advice columns penned by females, and the women's magazines that offer lists, tips, secrets, and facts (and fiction) to give women the edge in dealing with men. Men need someone looking out for them, so I try to monitor the various media.

One instance where I felt obliged to sound a warning was after the book *How to Marry the Man of Your Choice* became a best seller in 1987.

For a husband hunter, the $14.95 book is a sensational deal. If in two years a woman hasn't yet married Mr. Dream Guy, she gets a full $14.95 refund. It's no risk.

Except to men.

The book, written by attorney Margaret Kent, teaches women to be conniving, bitchy, and critical. "Yes, it's manipulation," Kent cheerily admitted to me in an interview.

Kent was in the midst of a never-ending tour promoting her brainwashing technique. Women couldn't get enough of her. Men paid no attention. "Men really don't bother to read the book," she told me.

Well, I bothered to read it, and after I did, I felt compelled to make an attention-getting offer to male readers. If a man read my column about the Kent technique and still got snagged by one of her followers, I'd give him twenty-five cents—a full refund on the price of the newspaper.

Though I used the column to give the lowdown on the hazards of Kent's approach, I tried to be fair. She does offer a few good tips:

how to dress, how to "interview" prospects, and what occupations women should get into if they want to meet men—IRS agent, men's shoe saleswoman, security guard, etc. (As a guard, "you can stop whomever you want and ask him questions," writes Kent.)

I was afraid, however, that some women would take the book's directions too literally. Kent says that by criticizing a man, a woman builds herself up. "Never let him think he's too good for you. ... The key to a successful relationship is to know his inferiorities." Kent suggests saying: "You're so smart, I'm surprised you're not richer."

Men—especially doctors and lawyers—try to overwhelm women with the importance of their jobs, Kent says. So she suggests put-downs: "When do you expect the Nobel Prize for your work?"

Praise a man in front of his friends, family, and coworkers, Kent advises. "However, if your praise will inflate his ego, remove the praise privately. A comment such as 'Your boss really believed everything I said about you' will suffice."

Sensing that men like well-bred wives, Kent teaches women to mask their "lower social class" by using "higher-level words" such as "dentures" (instead of "false teeth").

I provided male readers with telltale signs of a Kent disciple:

• She'll sound self-serving. Tell her she's pretty; she'll answer, "Yes, everyone says that." (Kent advises: "Let him know you're a treasure!")
• She'll stop reading horoscopes because men don't believe in them.
• She'll first make love on the twelfth date.
• When a man is dead-tired (and most susceptible, says Kent), she'll pitch her wifelike qualities.
• She'll have a messy closet to help her man "displace" his anger. "Your man won't complain [about the mess] except when he's in a bad mood," Kent writes. "The messy closet is a safety valve that helps him blow off steam."

I told men to be especially wary if their girlfriends change from "the Fan"—supportive and fawning—to "the Bitch." Kent says niceness "doesn't get a man to love us, need us, marry us"—but demanding, complaining women have men at their mercy. Kent figures a man feels special if he's chosen by a woman who hates everything and everybody.

Kent also tells women to "feather the future nest." If a Kent follower has a dog, she'll ask her man to wash him. Kent explains: "The first time, he's doing you a favor. The second time, he's doing Rover a favor. The third time, it's 'his dog.' Let him invest those emotions."

On Kent's advice, a husband hunter shouldn't sound materialistic. What does she want for Christmas? She should answer "You," rather than "A ring."

Kent told me that before she married her husband in 1984, he'd say, "Honey, you're manipulating me and I love every minute of it!"

Maybe so, I wrote. But any reader unhappily bamboozled into marriage by a Kent disciple was invited to send me the sad details. He could use the quarter I'd send back to pay for the newspaper— and to call his mother.

My column might have been a help: No men took me up on the refund offer. Many, however, wrote to thank me for the warning. "Margaret Kent must think men are weak, dim-witted, masochistic creatures who desire the company of mean and conniving women," one man wrote. "I'd like to believe that in the majority of cases, she is dead wrong."

Several men commented on Kent's suggestion that a woman should ask her man to wash her dog so he grows to think of it as "his dog." A reader named Tom Farrell wrote:

Here's an idea. Let's say you meet a woman who has read this husband-hunting book. First, you let her henpeck you for a week or 10 days (no longer or it's not worth the effort). Let her think you're hookable. Let her tell you, as Kent advises, that you're not as good as you think you are. Then walk and wash her dog a few times. And when she tells you that the dog is really yours, you dump the bitch and keep the dog.

You see, Zazz, I love dogs. Dogs are man's best friends!

KEEPING TABS

Naturally, when I try to be supportive of male readers, I risk getting myself into trouble with female readers. Some women make it their mission to monitor my advice—and give me hell when they're not pleased. It's as if they send my columns to the lab for analysis, find traces of sexism or chauvinism, and feel obliged to write up their reports. Sometimes, they even organize letter-writing campaigns among their friends and neighbors, just to hammer home their points.

I got a letter from a man who doesn't like shaving every day. He wrote:

> **Dear Zazz:** I need a man's advice. I shave all week long, so it's nice to give my face a rest on the weekends. Of course, if I have to go out on a Saturday night, I'll shave.
>
> Well, my wife hates it when my 5 o'clock shadow turns into two days' growth. She says she can't stand kissing me when I'm full of stubble. She thinks I look rotten, too. If I loved her, she claims, I'd shave every day.
>
> Also, because we have more time to make love on weekends, she says those are the most important days for shaving. I say it's more crucial to be clean-shaven for work.

Hoping I'd be empathetic, he signed his letter "Counting on You."

I suggested a compromise: "If you shave Friday morning for work, your beard shouldn't be too heavy for Friday night kissing. Saturday night, your wife can live with your stubble or live without your lovemaking. But promise her you'll shave Sunday night before bed (instead of Monday morning)—which should help you two close your weekends with, well, a bang."

Bad answer. Dozens of women wrote in to complain. One woman suggested: "Zazz, take a wire dog brush and scratch it all over your face for five minutes. Pretend it's a quickie. That should feel a little like someone who shaved Friday morning and kisses you Saturday night."

Another woman wondered why I didn't give the question to my partner, Diane. "Unless you're in the habit of necking with women who have hormonal problems, what could you possibly know about the repercussions of five o'clock shadow? I suggest you get some sandpaper and rub it across your lips and chin."

Even my wife told me that my answer rubbed her the wrong way. And the negative feedback kept coming. One woman wrote that she long ago gave her husband an ultimatum: "Either you start shaving your face or I stop shaving my legs." Another woman wrote: "Ninety percent of lovemaking occurs above the neck." (I was a newlywed when I answered that question. I didn't know.)

So I goofed. In a follow-up column, I admitted that "with the help of a piece of sandpaper, I've reconsidered." My revised advice for husbands: "Try to accommodate your wives by shaving when requested." And for wives: "If you know lovemaking isn't in the cards, give your men a break and let them skip a shave or two."

Sometimes I think I'm coming down rather hard on a sexist or inconsiderate male letter-writer. And then immediately, women write back to say, in the words of one female reader, "Not hard enough, Bozo!"

A man from Spokane, Washington, wrote to say he was in desperate need of a man's advice. He and his wife had visited California. One day at the beach, his wife got very upset because he kept eyeing all the pretty women walking by. His wife complained that she couldn't even hold a conversation with him because his head kept turning.

Well, at the motel that night, she got back at him. She hid his contact lenses. "The next day," he wrote, "I couldn't see well enough to drive the rental car. We argued all day."

His wife eventually returned the lenses, but the man was still angry with her. "Zazz, I love my wife and have been faithful for our four years of marriage. I say married guys are entitled to look around. Do you agree?" He signed himself "Innocent." I responded:

> I assume your wife's ploy backfired. A man at the beach without his contact lenses won't stop looking around. He'll just look harder, squinting to make out shapes.
>
> You're right. A married man is entitled to look. But how flagrant was your roving eye? Next time bring sunglasses (not a bad idea at the beach anyway) and learn to move your eyes without moving your head.
>
> Be sensitive to your wife's insecurities. Reassure her. Tell her how much you love her, how attractive she is to you, and how bored you'd get if you spent too much time at the beach. And be sincere when you deliver these lines. Take off your sunglasses.

I quickly discovered that a lot of women found Innocent to be anything but. And they weren't too pleased with me, either. A woman from Alta Loma, California, wrote:

> Boy, am I mad at you, Zazz. Innocent sat gawking at the beach, drool running down his chin, while his wife sounded

like the adults in a Charlie Brown movie. And you let him off easy!

Anyone who pays so little attention to a person speaking to him is rude. Instead of suggesting dark glasses, you should have advised him to grow up. This man said he was innocent—but of what? His wife wasn't accusing him of infidelity, just insolence. Hiding his contacts wasn't the answer. A child would have been sent to his room. An employee might have been fired. Zazz, you're gonna get letters!

Yes, I got letters. "You aren't faithful if you have lust in your heart," wrote a religious woman. "Men are always looking for someone to tell them it's OK to look. So that's what you did, Zazz. If Innocent can't straighten himself out, he ought to stay at the beach and drown. He's already drowning in sin."

"I, too, am married to a faithful 'innocent' man whose head is always turning to look at women," another woman wrote. "His tongue hangs from his mouth." This woman said she understood why Innocent's wife hid his contact lenses. "It's common courtesy to be discreet. Some men say, 'Start worrying when I stop looking.' That's an excuse. They're just inconsiderate. Period!"

A woman who signed herself "Looking Only at My Husband" wrote: "Your answer to Innocent was typical of a male. I say, if you need to look, you shouldn't be married. Looking at other women is asking for trouble. It's temptation. When you spend a day window-shopping, you go home dreaming. If Innocent gets sunglasses, be prepared to hear from him next year. He'll write that the woman looked back at him, and they exchanged phone numbers."

One angry woman argued that Innocent's wife wasn't insecure. The problem was that Innocent was insensitive—"and I'm sick of women being blamed for men's insensitivities!"

Some women monitor not just my advice, but my choice of words. After I wrote a column about my wedding, a woman sent a postcard stating: "You used the phrase 'man and wife' instead of the less-sexist 'husband and wife.' Why? And don't do it again." She signed her postcard "Not a Friend."

I responded: "Dear No Friend of Mine: I slipped. Had I been more careful and thoughtful, I wouldn't have made that mistake." The letter writer had a point. Wouldn't it be odd if a married couple were referred to as woman and husband?

Another good catch by a reader: I printed a letter from a sixteen-year-old girl who was preparing for a fistfight. Naturally, I discouraged the idea of fighting. I thought my answer was innocuous enough until a woman responded: "I take exception to your highly sexist remark that fighting is 'unbecoming to 16-year-old girls.' What about boys? And is it 'becoming' at any age? I know you know better, Zazz, judging from your generally unbiased advice."

I've also been reprimanded for using the word *housewife*. An officer of a feminist group wrote:

> The correct title for a non-wage-earning chief caretaker of the home and children is "homemaker." The term "housewife" is a 19th century relic that is thankfully becoming obsolete because: 1) There is no such word as househusband. Men have wisely decided it's a ridiculous moniker. That makes housewife blatantly sexist; 2) The word housewife identifies gender and marital status. This is discrimination against non-wage-earning women. Businesses don't hire workwives and officehusbands; 3) Some homemakers are divorced, widowed or single. Rather than call someone a housesingle, homemaker makes no mention of gender or marital status.
>
> Like broad, bimbo, and office girl, housewife is demeaning and conveys a negative stereotype about women.

I replied: "You raise some good points. I don't know if you'll ever get 'housewife' out of the dictionary, but you may help it fade from popular usage. By the way, 'houseboy' and 'houseman' remain in the dictionary. So it is not only women victimized by negative stereotypes."

The backlash to this feminist's letter came mostly from women. One wrote:

> I am not the least bit offended when I'm called a housewife. I use the word "homemaker" also, but only because feminists conceived and perpetuated the notion that there's something wrong with a married woman who has the job of being a wife.
>
> Being a housewife is very rewarding. My husband provides for the family and I manage what he provides. I say the word "housewife" is perfectly suited for the 20th century. And I don't think the majority of Americans want language changes dictated by a fanatic fringe element of society.

I guess that because I'm a man, my column is a lightning rod for tales of double standards and inequities between the sexes.

One woman complained to me after her boss invited his fourteen male employees to watch the Super Bowl at his house: "He never mentioned his little party to the 11 women who work for him."

Another woman, age sixty, wrote: "As fate would have it, and because I'm a woman, I am left taking care of my mother (who has Alzheimer's disease), my 88-year-old father, and my twin brother. Talk about 'learned helplessness!' Mothers, please teach your husbands and sons to be self-sufficient."

A dozen women in Mensa, the high-IQ society, wrote to me after a man complained about his superintelligent girlfriend. "I'm no moron," the man had written, "but I always feel inadequate when my girlfriend comes back from a Mensa meeting. She brags about all her witty Mensa friends. I'm a professional, and I earn more than she does, but I worry that if I marry her, I'll be destined to feel inferior forever."

This struck a nerve with the Mensa women, who complained about "the intellectual double standard." As one explained: "An intelligent man is considered a good catch. An intelligent woman is an intimidating freak who turns men off."

Many Mensa women who married less intelligent men wrote me of their regrets. One woman divorced her college professor husband and married a man with a tenth-grade education. At first fascinated by her second husband's street smarts, she said she'd become "bored to death" with him: "He's threatened by my intelligence. And his sense of reasoning and comprehension are so limited, I now feel dumber. At times, I feel my brain has turned to slush."

A former Mensan, married to a "domineering and sadistic" man with a 100 IQ, wrote: "You may well ask, if I'm so smart, why am I still married to this man? I've been in therapy for two years and still don't know why. My self-esteem is falling fast. I'm getting dumber and have dropped out of Mensa at my husband's insistence."

(These letters led me to look into a research project at the University of Washington. For thirty years, the study tracked 175 married couples with varying degrees of intelligence. The study's early findings suggest that when less intelligent women marry smart men, they get smarter; when smart women marry less intelligent men, they get dumber; and a man's intelligence hardly changes, regardless of his wife's brainpower.)

Women notice inequities between the sexes in all facets of life—and even death. A Pennsylvania woman wrote me the letter that follows after attending a string of funerals:

> **Dear Zazz:** I'm disturbed by a noticeable difference in the way the deceased are dressed at viewings. The men are always in business suits, while the women wear frilly nightgowns with lots of lace.
>
> It amazes me that feminist groups are not aware of this. Should men be dressed in lounging robes or the women in business suits? I believe the same standards should apply to both sexes.
>
> By the way, I've directed my children to close the lid on me when I go. I think the practice of viewing is barbaric.
> —Stewing over Viewings

I replied:

> **Dear Stewing:** The family of the deceased picks the clothing. And funeral directors tell me that families like their loved ones in clothing they "normally wear." (Men, of course, normally wear T-shirts and bathrobes, but they never seem to be buried this way.)
>
> A nightgown seems like appropriate garb for eternal rest. So some families choose to dress their late mothers or sisters that way. But put a man in his pajamas and he looks sort of silly. Hence men always are sent off in suits and sport coats.
>
> Sure, there's an inequity at work here. But our society is full of such sexism. And you can't mandate a dress code for the hereafter.
>
> Actually, when it comes to viewings, I agree with you. A funeral is one occasion where the guest of honor, whether male or female, needn't be seen to be appreciated.

New-Age Angst

MANY OF THE letters I receive could have been addressed to any advice columnist in the last half century. A philandering husband—like an overbearing mother-in-law or a dreaded sweat stain—is a perennial staple of the advice business. Sure, I try to give a new twist to the predictable, to rethink and restate what has become universal and obvious. But I've learned to face facts: There are only so many ways to deal with the who-keeps-the-engagement-ring-after-the-awful-breakup controversy. Likewise, dandruff today is like dandruff long ago. Only the faces and hairstyles have changed.

And yet, as our society makes its way into the 1990s, a new breed of questions has emerged. Many age-old problems now have a technological spin on them. And I often find myself overwhelmed by a host of modern dilemmas that would have been unfathomable five or ten years ago.

For instance, the creation of tinted contact lenses made this etiquette question inevitable: "I just got tinted contacts that make my brown eyes blue. As a result, I've been getting a lot of compliments on my 'beautiful blue eyes.' Should I tell people about the contacts, or graciously accept the compliment?"

New dilemma, familiar ring. I replied:

> If people say you have a pretty face, you wouldn't respond, "I just had a nose job." If they compliment your hair, you wouldn't say, "I'm blond from a bottle." If they talk about your pretty smile, you wouldn't say, "My teeth were full of plaque, but the dentist cleaned them." Similarly, when anyone mentions your beautiful blue eyes, just say, "Thanks."

Advances in phone technology have led to numerous etiquette questions, including this one:

"I have call-waiting service on my telephone. When I'm talking to one person and another person calls, is there any particular etiquette you recommend? Is it OK to abandon the first person to talk to the second?"

I didn't want to make an outright condemnation of call-waiting. But as more of us install call-waiting, more of us will be waiting on hold. My answer hinted at the farcical side of this new phone development:

> If you decide to talk to the second caller, apologize profusely to the first. Use phrases like "emergency," "long distance," and "very ill." If you want the first person to feel important, ignore the clicking that signals an incoming call. Of course, if both of you have call-waiting and get calls at the same time, you can hang up on each other simultaneously with no hard feelings.

Telephone answering machine etiquette questions can be more clear-cut. The gadgets have created all sorts of new ways to be rude. Consider this question from "Disrespectfully Dumped":

"I went out with a guy for four months—we were very close—and he broke it off by leaving a message on my answering machine. I haven't acknowledged his message or called him back. Should I? Or should I just forget him?"

My answer: "Erase his message from your tape machine and him from your life. Don't call him. If he thought you were worth only a tape-recorded kiss-off, let him know that he's not worth even that. If he doesn't hear from you, he might assume you didn't care enough to call him back. That's what he deserves to think."

Meanwhile, toll-call party lines have altered the way people meet, date, and even make love. A twenty-three-year-old woman wrote to say she'd met a man on a party line. "We've spoken frequently," she said. "Last night, we practically made love by phone. We've never met in person, and now he's trying to set up a date. I'm nervous. What do you suggest?"

I replied:

> You're a grown woman and if you'd like to meet this man, do so. For safety's sake, pick a very public place: a brightly lit restaurant, a shopping mall or—hey, why not?—a police station lobby. If you're embarrassed to have engaged in over-the-phone lovemaking before setting eyes on each

other, maybe you've learned something. Go slow. That can be fun, too.

In terms of its ability to tear apart an American family, the toll-call party line may be the most dangerous telephone innovation of all time. I've gotten dozens of letters from scared kids who rack up phone bills of hundreds of dollars. They want me to give them some kind of magical solution before the bill arrives and their parents find out.

Parents write, too. Often, they're beside themselves. One of the most shocking letters came from a woman whose daughter ran up a six-hundred-dollar phone bill dialing a party line at twenty cents a minute. "I take the phone to work so my daughter can't use it," the mother wrote. "But she borrows phones from friends, plugs them in at our house, and calls the party line. I'd like to cut off her dialing finger!"

This issue goes beyond how to punish children who selfishly and irresponsibly spend their parents' money. The misuse of the phone is a symptom of family disharmony that is far more troubling. The girl who borrows friends' phones isn't simply addicted to the party line. For whatever unhealthy reasons, she's intent on driving her parents crazy over her behavior.

Luckily, some gadget-addicts are more harmless. They irritate loved ones unintentionally—and their loved ones ought to learn to take it in stride. "My wife is addicted to photocopying," a man wrote. "She's a secretary, so she has access to a machine. She makes copies of everything—magazine articles, recipes, letters from her family, our kids' school papers, even junk mail. It really gets on my nerves. How do I get her to quit?"

"What's it to you?" I asked in my reply. "It's not such a bad addiction, though your wife could get into trouble at work. Remind her of the cost to her employer, and the possible waste of her time. Maybe she'll slow down her reproductive habits. And if not, let's hope this is the worst complaint you ever have about her."

Technology addictions run the gamut. Women complain to me about their "computer nerd" boyfriends and husbands. Wrote one wife: "He'd rather plug into his computer than into me." Motorists send letters taking issue with cellular-phone users who can't stay off their carphones. "They're dangerous one-armed drivers in speeding phone booths negotiating big business deals," one motorist wrote. "Big deal!"

Technology also creates new problems between neighbors. "My

next-door neighbor has a giant satellite TV dish in his backyard,"
a New Jersey man wrote. "We live in a rustic suburb, and his giant
dish ruins the scenery. There's no sense talking to him about it. He's
obsessed with his big-screen TV. What can I do?"

Probably not much, I discovered. Court records showed that in
1988, a self-proclaimed "TV addict" in Redding, Connecticut cut
down his neighbor's eighty-three-year-old oak tree to get better
reception on his satellite TV dish. The neighbor sued, and a judge
sentenced the TV addict to an easy two years' probation. The judge
also denied the neighbor's request that the dish be taken away
during the probationary period. "He's going to be able to enjoy the
fruits of his crime," the neighbor was quoted as saying. (Indeed, the
dish owner admitted he was getting terrific TV reception since he
cut down the tree. "Now I can get the Disney channel," he boasted.)

Modern gadgetry can make for embarrassing moments that
would have been avoided years ago. I heard from a young mother
after she hosted a party at her house. During the course of the
evening, she had invited a friend to take a look at her sleeping baby.
In the baby's room was one of those new, voice-activated intercoms
that allows parents to monitor their kids from anywhere in the
house.

Well, while looking at the baby, the young mother complained
to her friend about her mother-in-law. "My mother-in-law was in
another room in the house, and I think she heard what I said," the
woman told me. "Later, she said I'd better be careful about what I
say on that intercom."

All of these technology-related problems might be new, but
human nature remains constant. One word describes the question
that follows: Predictable.

> **Dear Zazz:** Though we've been cable TV subscribers for
> six months, we've never received a bill. Until recently, we
> couldn't afford to pay it, anyway. Now things are getting
> better and we could pay up. Should we call the cable com-
> pany or let it slide?

> My reply:

> Your letter is a commentary on our times. You install
> cable TV that you can't afford, but you're saved because,
> despite having the technology to wire your house and send

you programs from around the globe, the cable company can't get its act together well enough to send you a bill.

The right thing to do is to contact the company. You knew that before you asked your question. Maybe cable companies need to supplement their weather, sports, and financial channels with an ethics channel.

THE MOM/DAD DILEMMA

Offbeat medical advances have created a new breed of modern questions, too. Before doctors could turn men into women, questions like the ones that follow wouldn't be possible.

I heard from a man who was married and fathered two children, then had an operation to become a woman. Shortly after the surgery, his ex-wife died of cancer. Then, as a woman, he married a man and they adopted two more children. His problem: Of the four children in his house (ages three to thirteen), two know him as Dad and two as Mom. "It is really confusing for the little girls to hear me called Dad because they see me as the woman I now am," he wrote. "Still, I can't bear to ask the older ones to start calling me Mom, particularly so soon after their mother died." He signed his letter "Struggling."

My response:

> Wow, I'm struggling with this one, too.
>
> I suppose that since you're now a woman, it is more natural for your adopted kids to call you "Mom." Your older children are now entering their teen years and will have to come to grips, emotionally and intellectually, with your sex-change. They ought to call you whatever they're most comfortable with.
>
> No matter what, it's probably a good idea for you and the kids to visit a counselor so you can sort out where, as a family, you're all going from here.

Another question on the same topic came a few months later. But this one was easier to answer.

> **Dear Zazz:** I'm an active almumnus of a large men's college that will soon celebrate its 100th anniversary. In honor

of the occasion, I've agreed to compile and edit an alumni directory.

I contacted thousands of alumni and heard every life story imaginable, from heart-warming to depressing. But there were two responses I didn't expect.

Two of the male alumni have undergone sex-change surgery and are now women. One is a nurse who fathered children before changing his sex. The other is married as a woman to another alumnus. And both want to be listed in the directory as women. One of the transsexuals says she's coming to the celebration because it's a perfect opportunity to face up to important people from her past.

Some school administrators say I shouldn't print these transsexuals' biographies in the directory. What do you suggest?
—Confused Alumni Editor

My response:

Dear Editor: As long as these transsexuals met the necessary graduation requirements of your all-male college, it doesn't matter that they no longer have all the necessary parts of the male anatomy. They belong in the directory.

The word "née" is used to identify a woman's name before she got married. Since both of your transsexual alumni were or are married, you might identify them this way: Susie Jones, née Sam Jones, and Betty Smith, née Bob Smith.

If one of your goals is to get people to read your directory, printing these ladies' bios should do the trick.

School officials or other alumni may be embarrassed by these listings—but that's too bad. They ought to be men about it and just accept these women for who they are—and were.

FREE MONEY, BUT YOU LOSE YOUR HONEY

Before women were willing to ask men out on dates, before airline companies started apologizing for their screwups by giving away free flights, and before women were so pervasive in the work force, the dilemma that follows could never have happened.

But modern times make for modern arguments between lovers, would-be lovers, and forever ex-lovers. This one is a doozy:

Dear Zazz: I began dating a wonderful woman, and a month later, she won a sales contest through work. The prize was a free seven-day ski vacation for two to Colorado. Though we had been dating only a short while, my new girlfriend asked me to go along.

The vacation was terrific. First-class. I thanked her by buying her a sweatshirt and a cowboy hat.

When we got on the plane to return to Chicago, we learned the airline had overbooked the flight. To give up our seats, we each were offered a free roundtrip ticket to anywhere in the United States, plus a check for $500. What a deal! We bolted off the plane.

While we waited for the next flight to Chicago, we got our free tickets and money—and that's when the trouble began. My girlfriend felt that because she had made the trip possible, she should get both of our $500 checks.

We've been arguing about this since we got back. Her family believes she is entitled to my $500 check. My family thinks that because I gave up the seat, the ticket and the check belong to me, no matter who paid for the trip.

This issue has put a horrible strain on our relationship. She feels I took advantage of her hospitality. I feel she and her family are being greedy.

At the moment, I am in possession of the $500. Should I write her a check and forget about it—and her?
—Tired of Fighting

My reply:

Dear Tired: If you both want to make a go of your relationship and still care for each other, don't give up yet.

Tell your girlfriend that you've put the $500 aside—so you can spend it together. Maybe in a few months, you can go on another vacation together. Or else you can spend the $500 on a half-dozen romantic dinners in Chicago. And you may want to surprise her sometime with gifts that are more pricey than a sweatshirt and hat.

Of course, if she turns out to be greedy in other respects,

or breaks up with you, you'll still have a little something to help you through your sorrow: the unspent $500.

The day this question ran in my column, everyone seemed to have an opinion. I got a flood of calls and letters. Those in Tired's camp called his girlfriend a greedy vulture. Others labeled Tired an audacious heel. A sampling:

• "No woman deserves such an egotistical, ungrateful excuse-for-a-boyfriend. She should take back the $500 and then dump him. If he's still making a fuss, she should give him back the sweatshirt and cowboy hat he gave her and call it even."
• "The ticket was issued in Tired's name, entitling him to the benefits that came with it. The decision to give up his seat was his to make, not hers. Therefore, the money is his, too. If he had won $500 at a casino craps table on the vacation, would his girlfriend have demanded that tidy sum, too? I think she's a self-centered monster."
• "If it cost Tired's girlfriend $500 to find out that he is a greedy cad, then it was worth the investment."
• "We've taken a poll around the office and we all agree: If Tired had one ounce of self-respect, he'd have offered his girlfriend the money and plane ticket as thanks for the lovely free vacation. Tired should find a doormat to support him in the manner which he and his family think is suitable."
• "Here's a hypothetical question: What if the plane had been in an accident on the ground, and Tired dislocated his shoulder? Let's say he had to spend a few weeks in the hospital, and the airline settled with him for a large sum of money. Would his girlfriend feel she was entitled to all that money because it had been her free trip that got him in the hospital?"

So, whatever happened to the once-happy couple?
Well, they ended up taking their argument to the airwaves. After my column ran, a top Chicago disc jockey invited both onto his show to talk it out. Listeners got to vote and, like my readers, were equally divided.
The couple resisted the urge to hold a catfight, and eventually reached a truce. Tired walked away from the relationship richer than when he entered it—he kept the money. Meanwhile, his one-time lover said she was happy with her part of the settlement: She never had to see him again.

THE FAX MAN

There are many ways to get a date as we enter the 1990s. And Paul Hohendorf hit on what may be the perfect technique for our time.

He faxes for foxes.

Paul is vice president of the Roostertail, a major Detroit catering facility. I happened to meet his boss, Tom Schoenith, at a party. Tom said something like: "So, you're the lovelorn guy? Well, maybe you have some advice for a man who works for me." He then told me about how Paul was trying to be a high-tech Casanova. I knew I had to share the story in the column.

Paul uses his office facsimile machine many times a day to communicate with businesspeople. Often, he'll fax a woman a document, then call her back to make small talk. He knows how to flirt, what lines to use, and, most important, how to fax photos.

Photos of himself.

If a woman interests him, he'll fax himself anywhere in the country.

"I'll send a photo and my vital statistics," he told me. "I'm thirty-two, single, love to eat, love to spend money, and believe anything goes when it comes to having a good time."

His photo speaks for itself. The earring. The wild hair. That look of self-confidence. If you squint, he looks exactly like Rod Stewart. "I tell women to post the picture in their office: 'For a good time, call Paul.' Or: 'Win a dream trip with Paul'!"

When I first spoke to Paul, he had faxed blowups of himself into thirty-five offices. Most of the women were pleased to see his smiling face amid the boring documents that usually come their way. Some even faxed back photos of themselves.

Bonnie faxed Paul an eight-by-ten head shot of herself. "She was beautiful," he said. Impulsively, he invited her for a weekend in New York. She accepted. On the day I spoke to Paul, they were preparing for the trip and hadn't yet met in person. "I assume the picture she sent was really of her," Paul said. And if not? No matter. They'd go to New York anyway. Paul said he knows how to have a good time with anyone, anywhere.

Paul's boss, Tom, is also impulsive and fun-loving, and he told me that Paul's technique was just fine with him. He didn't mind that Paul's photo introductions tied up the fax. "It's the modern pickup technique," Tom said. "I admire him. He's a hustler."

Tom forgave Paul for sending photos to a few women who he

never realized were married. "There were only a few complaints at a couple of companies," Tom said.

Tom also excused Paul for accidentally sending his mug shot to the private fax of Tom Monaghan, founder of Domino's pizza and owner of the Detroit Tigers. "Paul was just trying to reach some young lady down the hall," Tom said in Paul's defense.

We all should have such an understanding boss.

Paul, meanwhile, said that faxing is the hobby of the future. Every day, there are more fax outlets. In 1989, there were about 1.6 million fax units in America—a majority of which, it seemed, were attended to by women.

Paul said he recognizes that faxing alone won't guarantee a winning social life. "A fax machine breaks the ice," he said. After that, the romancing takes on more human dimensions.

Well, I thought his approach was fairly harmless. Yes, there are costs involved. Every time Paul faxes his photo, his company pays any long-distance phone charges. Also, the company receiving the photos pays about ten cents for the thermal-coated paper. But if Paul's boss was willing to pay on his end, I decided it was worth readers' dimes just to get a look at Paul.

That's why, on behalf of curious readers everywhere, I made an unprecedented offer. With the permission of Paul's boss, I printed the phone number for Paul's fax. The last line of the column: "Ladies, start your faxes."

The *Sun-Times* edition carrying my column about Paul hit the streets a few hours before dawn on a Monday. At 3:30 A.M. central time, Paul received his first faxed photo from a woman. By 10:00 A.M., faxes were arriving every minute. This continued, unabated, for two days.

"Make my day—send a photo!"

"We are a manless office and we need your picture for our wall!"

"Let's see what you've got, big guy."

Lori and Susie sent a photo of themselves gazing through prison bars and wrote: "Set us free. Date us! Date us!"

Another woman sent a photo of the Chicago skyline and wrote, "Send me your photo or I'll jump."

Then there was the woman from Inland Steel Company who asked Paul to send a message back by code so her boss wouldn't find out she was using the fax.

It was an incredible response.

Women sent resumes, sketches of themselves, detailed body

measurements. Paul received photos of women in cheerleading uniforms, bikinis, halter tops, and leather miniskirts.

By midweek, more than eighteen hundred Windy City women had faxed messages and photos to Paul. (His phone number was printed only in the *Sun-Times;* it wasn't included when my column was syndicated to other newspapers.)

"This thing has taken over our office," Tom Schoenith told me by phone as the fax machine beeped and whistled in the background. "No one gets their work done. They're all reading the faxes." Schoenith had to hire an extra secretary just to deal with the reams of paper pouring out of the fax machine.

Without knowing what the response was, Paul Harvey read from my column on his syndicated radio program. Then, Detroit TV stations and newspapers got wind of what was going on over at the catering firm's headquarters. "Hohendorf may have invented the biggest new craze since the computer date," wrote the *Detroit News.*

Paul's story quickly went into media overdrive. He kept calling me in a panic: "It's out of control," he said at one point. For days, Paul talked about his fax operation to reporters and radio DJs around the United States, and the world. "After the wire services and the BBC picked it up, things just snowballed," Paul told the *Miami Herald.* He quickly topped three thousand faxed responses, including twenty from Australia.

Not everyone got the story straight. One newspaper reported that Paul had received twenty-three thousand photos from women. A supermarket tabloid quoted me as saying: "Paul is no Robert Redford, but the girls seem to love him." I'd spoken to the reporter, but never uttered anything resembling that quote.

Paul became a regular on TV. He brought his fax machine on Phil Donahue's show, and women sent him their photos live on the air. (Women in the audience, however, lambasted him as a sexist opportunist.) *Hour Magazine,* the syndicated TV talkshow, flew him to L.A., *Geraldo* to New York. And *People* magazine printed a large cheesecake photo of Paul, his machine, and a giant blowup of one of his prettier fax mates.

Paul told every interviewer that he appreciated the patience of his boss, Tom Schoenith. Tom never complained about all the fax costs. Still, by week's end, the escapade was beginning to wear on Tom. "He's laughing," Schoenith said, "but wait until he gets the bill."

As a caterer, Paul decided a party was in order. So he made plans to fly to Chicago with a few of his friends and throw a champagne and hors d'oeuvres reception for one hundred of the women—"Chicago's most eligible bachelorettes." He faxed invitations to the one hundred wittiest, sexiest, or most interesting women.

The ball was rolling. A Chicago hotel offered to spring for the party. Southwest Airlines gave the men complimentary seats and christened the flight "the Casanova Express." TV crews came to the airport to shoot Paul's departure. It was a textbook case of media hype, and, for the moment, everyone wanted a piece of Paul's action.

On the day of the party, Paul was the lead story on the front page of *USA Today*. Under the headline JUST THE FAX, *USA Today* described Paul as a wealthy bachelor who owned an Alfa Romeo, a Jaguar, and his own five-acre island in Lake Michigan.

With that kind of buildup, it's no wonder that so many of the partygoers showed up in their slinkiest dresses. Most were young and attractive, and said they'd faxed their photos to Paul just because it seemed like a novel thing to do. A few admitted they were on the prowl for men and they'd try any new technique. They came from all walks of life: There was a commodities saleswoman, an electrician, a limo driver, a lawyer, a telephone operator—even a sergeant in the U.S. Army. "I faxed him a very demanding letter," the sergeant said. "I demanded him!"

Eight TV camera crews showed up at the party, all elbowing each other for space in the crowded room. "The party turned into a media orgy, as local and national camera crews scrambled for interviews," wrote Richard Roeper, who reported on the event for the *Sun-Times*. "The expression on the women's faces was not unlike that of deer caught in the glare of a car's headlights."

I was there, too: I wouldn't want to miss it. As Paul made his way from woman to woman—shaking hands, thanking them for coming, hello, good-bye, next woman—the cameras and bright lights from NBC, CBS, *A Current Affair, Inside Edition,* etc., were in tow recording it all. It was a strange scene. The room was aglow with "the aura created by modern-day neo-celebrity techno-weirdness," wrote Roeper. So what did these women think of the fax flirt?

"How should I know if he's a nice guy," a woman told one of the TV reporters. "I talked to him for all of two seconds."

Said another woman: "He seems nice, but for all I know, he could spend his weekends wearing a raincoat and flashing people."

Sensing that some of the women felt ignored, several male members of the media put down their pads or TV cameras and began sweet-talking the ladies. "The odds are great," one TV cameraman told me. "There are hardly any men here, and all these women love me because I'm going to put them on TV."

I found the whole scene both exciting and disconcerting. "You created a monster," Paul called out to me as still photographers took his portrait surrounded by fifteen of his beaming "dates." He had a giant smile on his face and a glass of champagne in his right hand, a blonde on one arm, a brunette on the other.

Well, yes, I had created a monster. I suppose it was all good clean fun. But was it getting out of hand? Not content with his fifteen minutes of fame, Paul was making plans for fax forays into other cities—Dallas, San Francisco, Boston. He also confided that a fax machine company had agreed to make him its spokesman. They'd already given him two fax machines—including a traveling fax to fit in his briefcase.

When the party was over, Paul picked one of the prettiest women, a blond model, and asked her to dinner at a fancy restaurant. A camera crew asked to come along. Both Paul and his date thought that was a great idea.

As Paul and his entourage left, I couldn't help thinking about how, in the modern world, what's novel and unpredictable soon becomes passé and very predictable. "I'm getting my own fax machine," one woman told me as she was leaving. "You'll print the phone number in your column and I'll have twenty-nine hundred men to choose from."

I told her I wasn't sure a lot of men would reply to this sort of come-on. And I doubted she'd get any media coverage. She smiled. "Even if just five hundred men and one or two TV shows respond," she said, "that would probably be enough for me."

Striking a Chord

IN MANY CASES, the best columns are the ones in which I tell a simple story and then readers respond with theirs. The advice comes in the sharing of experiences. Often, we can learn the most by taking a new look at what's most familiar.

I don't always know which columns will strike a chord with readers and generate an avalanche of mail. But I'm finding that the most potent columns are the ones that lead readers to say: "Yes, that's me, too. That's my family, my friends."

Columns that set off such a response often come to me by accident.

For instance, one spring day I was riding bikes with my nieces, ages seven and nine. They live in the suburbs of Philadelphia and they had asked me if I wanted to take a bike tour of their neighborhood.

Kids on front lawns called out their names as we rode by. We raced down the local hill a few times, laughing. And my nieces pointed out landmarks: so-and-so's house. The school bus stop. The streets they're not allowed to cross.

Then we came upon a baseball field where a Little League game was going on. The weather was perfect, the stands were full, and the umpire was suitably theatrical. It was the Mets versus the Reds.

I hadn't seen a Little League game in years—when you live downtown and have no children, that's what happens—so I convinced my nieces to watch a few innings with me.

For a while, my nieces were taken in by the crowd's enthusiasm. We happened to sit on the Mets' side, next to the pitcher's grandmother, mother, and aunt. They all shouted encouraging words to their boy. My nieces joined in. The pitcher's name was Calvin, and, for a twelve-year-old, he had quite an arm. He kept retiring Reds batters in order. From the dugout, his coach issued a running pep talk, pacing furiously as he did.

After a couple of innings, my nieces began asking me when some homers might be hit. They were bored, but I was captivated by the wholesomeness of this suburban scene, and the nostalgic images it conjured up.

And then something happened that brought me back to reality in a troubling way.

It was the fourth inning and the Mets were ahead 4–0. Like I said, young Calvin was quite a pitcher. He was self-assured, tall, serious about his job.

There were two outs, and the Reds sent a boy to the plate who looked like he could hardly hold up his bat. He was frail, with glasses, and his demeanor was as tentative as Calvin's was confident. He took a few weak swings of his bat and looked like, well, a stereotypical wimp, as he stepped into the batter's box.

Just then, the Mets' coach screamed to his boys in the field: "Outfielders, move in, move in!"

Obviously, the kid at the plate couldn't hit the ball out of the infield.

And so all three outfielders jogged closer. If the poor batter could somehow make contact with the ball, he would deliver it into an infield crowded with eight Mets. The chance of a base hit was almost impossible.

I don't know whether I actually saw a grimace of pained embarrassment cross the batter's face, or just imagined it, but I felt tremendously sorry for him. I remembered all the nonathletes from my youth who struggled to perform in ways they never could. And at that moment, I decided to pay close attention: Here was a scene worth discussing in the column.

In the movies, of course, the kid at the plate would have taken a mighty swing and sent the ball sailing over the heads of all those outfielders playing him shallow. He would have skipped around the bases, his theme song playing in the background, a knowing smile on his face. And that special girl in the stands who never before noticed him would suddenly be aglow with interest.

In reality, as you could have guessed, the kid never got his bat on the ball. Calvin dispatched him with a handful of pitches. "Strike three!" the umpire shouted.

The boy, head bowed, returned to the bench and got a drink of water. It obviously wasn't his first strikeout. And the season was young.

As my nieces and I pedaled our bikes home, several thoughts filled my head. I know children can learn certain values through competitiveness. I know coaches feel they're setting a good example by playing to win. And bringing in those outfielders was unquestionably smart strategy: It guaranteed an out.

I know, too, that the world beyond Little League is tough and unfair, and the sooner a kid learns this, the better. Still, something seemed wrong. And when I shared this story in the column, hundreds of readers wrote back to tell me just how wrong.

One of the most famous books about the underbelly of major league baseball was Jim Bouton's *Ball Four.* If an expose were written about Little League, it might be called *Strike Three.*

Consider these Little League vignettes sent to me by readers:

"I know I'm going to strike out almost every time," wrote an unathletic twelve-year-old Texan. "My team really hates me."

"I once had to throw both coaches out of a game for foul language," wrote an umpire from Illinois. "One was our police chief, the other was the mayor."

I was even told about a Pennsylvania man's arrest for assaulting the ump at his son's game. "The ump provoked him," the man's attorney told me.

Readers' advice and comments ranged from angry observations about the downside of organized sports, to emotional arguments in defense of them. A sampling:

• "Face it, Zazz, what you describe in your column is what Little League is all about. Are you proposing that we give a kid four strikes?"
• "In 22 years of officiating sports, I've heard many parents yell at their kids, 'You stink!' Our society puts winning above all else. Many coaches and parents never 'won,' so they use children as their last chance to be 'winners.'

"There are youth leagues in which coaches get bigger trophies than players. I once watched a mother on the sidelines at a preteen football game grab her son's face mask. She twisted his head, yelling, 'You missed the tackle! You're not getting dinner tonight!'"
• "I know a boy who was so unathletic, that once, during recess, he found a big rock and dropped it on his foot—just so he could sit out the basketball game in phys ed that day."
• "As a coach, I've observed that unathletic kids, other than those with physical impairments, are the products of inattentive, self-centered parents. Healthy kids can do well in a sport if they receive

encouragement and assistance at home. Too many kids come to me not even knowing which hand their gloves go on. Too many parents use Little League as a babysitter."

• "My son is a star athlete and he makes me proud. But what makes me proudest is his compassion for less-athletic teammates. He's always reassuring them and boosting their egos. In the stands, I've heard adults shout cruel things at children. Our kids often have more sense than we do."

• "What should a parent say to an unathletic Little Leaguer? I know what not to say. Don't tell him it doesn't matter. It matters to him. Don't tell him 'he'll show them all someday.' He doesn't believe it and he doesn't believe that you do. And don't tell him it's OK because he's much better at, say, chess. If his peer group doesn't value chess, neither will he.

"What you can do is love and accept him as he is. Say: 'You're not a strong batter. That's OK.' And show him a way to turn his weakness into an advantage. Say: 'Let me tell you about bunts.' "

A good coach, I quickly learned, helps losing players feel like winners. A bad coach, without realizing it, can scar a child.

A father in Altavista, Virginia, wrote about his son's "cruelest lesson": "For the first time, my son found himself on a winning team. Though he was less skilled than his teammates, he was so happy and proud. At the final game of the season, the opposing team showed up one player short. So my son's coach made my son play for the opposing team, against his own team. The opposing team lost. This left my son crestfallen."

A mother in Texas wrote about the coach who called a time-out, then motioned his batter back to the bench. The youngster returned, dragging his bat, his eyes focused on the ground. The coach yelled, as the crowd listened: "Can't you remember how I told you to hold that bat? And look at me when I talk to you!" The boy began to cry. The coach screamed, "And we don't have crybabies on our team!" Naturally, the boy returned to the plate and struck out.

Not all the stories sent to me were so devastating. Some readers wrote to reassure me that Little League need not be humiliating for the unathletic. One woman sent me this marvelous anecdote:

Years ago, my father coached a team of 8-year-olds. He had a few excellent players, and some who just couldn't get the hang of the game.

Dad's team didn't win a game all season, but in the last inning of the last game, his team was only down by a run.

There was one boy on the team who had never been able to hit the ball—or catch it. With two outs in the last inning, it was his turn to bat.

He surprised the world and got a single!

The next batter was the team slugger. Finally, Dad's players might win a game.

This slugger hit the ball between first and second. As the boy who hit the single ran to second, he saw the ball coming toward him. Not so certain of baseball's rules, he caught it. Final out! Dad's team lost!

Quickly, my father told his team to cheer. With everyone cheering, the kid beamed. It hadn't occurred to him that he lost the game for them. All he knew was that he hit the ball and caught it—both for the first time.

His parents later thanked my dad. Their child had never even gotten in a game before that season: Other coaches always benched him.

We never told the boy exactly what happened. We wouldn't want to ruin it for him. And till this day, I'm proud of what my father did that afternoon.

THE WHITE PATROL

I like to use the column to fight for causes that we all feel strongly about, but rarely think about—or gave up long ago. One such "cause" came to me on a drive through Canada.

My wife and I were eating at a pizza parlor in Windsor, Ontario, and noticed that the restaurant's walls were decorated with old advertisements. While you wait for your pizza, you read the walls and get nostalgic.

One ad encourages you to buy a TV so you can watch the 1956 presidential conventions. Another compares clotheslines with the "more efficient" modern dryer.

But one ad in particular drives home how times have changed. Read this ad and you're reminded that the world was once more civilized, more considerate. The world was once cleaner.

The ad appeared in *The Saturday Evening Post* in the 1950s. A woman wearing white gloves is driving a convertible. Her three young daughters are in the backseat. They're approaching a Texaco station where a large sign announces: REGISTERED REST ROOM.

The copy at the top of the ad reads: "Something we ladies appreciate!" At the bottom: "You'll find Registered Rest Rooms wherever you drive in all 48 states."

I was captivated by this ad. Imagine a gas station in 1990 advertising clean rest rooms! These days, we take it for granted that public bathrooms are often filthy. We rarely complain or hold management responsible. A clean rest room is a lucky find, not an expected service. Somehow, our expectations for cleanliness have declined.

Ask a service station owner today if his rest rooms are registered. He'll surely look at you funny, wonder what you're up to, and deny you the rest room key.

So how did we get from the Age of Registered Rest Rooms to the Era of Rest Rooms from Hell? I called Texaco's headquarters to find out.

The public relations woman I spoke to recalled hearing that Texaco was once renowned for clean rest rooms. She did some research, and a few days later, mailed me a packet of old TV commercials, print ads, and Texaco annual reports.

Until the registered rest room program began in 1938, many stations had outhouses. That year, the company sensed the need to clean up its act. Dealers signed pledges to customers promising sanitary rest rooms. The pledge's last line: "You will confer a favor by giving me the benefit of your criticism."

Texaco sent "trained inspectors"—which the company called "the famous White Patrol"—out onto the highways to check things out. Clean rest rooms helped business boom.

But the program died during the oil shortage of the early 1970s. Efficiency became the priority over service. Stations went to self-service pumps and skeleton staffs, leaving no one to wipe down toilets or ride the White Patrol.

"The entire industry moved away from service," a Texaco vice president explained to me. With gas above a dollar a gallon, motorists wanted the station with the cheapest gas prices, not the cleanest rest rooms.

But times might be changing. Now, the Texaco VP confided, "there's a huge demand for an improvement in retail services. I think we'll see a return to that."

Well, we'd better. And I said so in the column. I gave advice to businesses: Quit underestimating your customers. We value things like cleanliness, for obvious reasons. That's why registered rest rooms were so successful.

I also had advice for motorists: a citizens' White Patrol. If any of us come upon a clean rest room, we should compliment the manager. And if we find a dirty facility, we should complain loudly.

A generation ago, Texaco said a rest room wasn't registered unless it had "a toilet in good working order, a washbowl, mirror, wastebasket, and an adequate supply of soap, towels and tissue."

Why should things be different in 1990? As Texaco said in those ads: "Any motorist has a right to expect these things."

Well, after my column ran, the mail poured in. Many people wanted to expose public rest rooms in their neighborhoods. One woman wrote: "A week ago, I spent $15 for lunch, went to the restaurant's rest room, and my food almost came back up. That's how filthy the rest room was! The place looked like it took years to get that dirty."

Another reader wrote: "I've complained to restaurant managers about their restrooms, and have been told, in essence, 'We don't make our money in our bathrooms.' If a restroom is dirty, I always wonder what the kitchen must look like."

Some people wrote to remind me that business owners aren't the only ones to blame for dirty rest rooms.

A retired couple had just traveled across the country, stopping in scores of rest rooms along the way. They wrote:

> We find that rest rooms are often cleaned several times a day, but the women's rooms are still filthy. Why? Because many women are horribly inconsiderate. They don't flush toilets, they throw paper on the floor, and the sinks are full of dirt and hair. We've even found women allowing their children to urinate in the sink. If we want clean rest rooms, we need to be cleaner ourselves.

After I printed the couple's letter, janitors wrote in to say it's true: Women are messier. But many women responded defensively. "Why are women's restrooms dirtier?" one woman asked. "One reason is obvious, but men never consider it. Who takes little kids into a restroom? Mothers."

The arguments went back and forth. The above letter generated these rebuttals:

- "If women can clean up behind their children in their own homes, why not in public?"
- "I was once a janitor at a factory. The women's room was always twice as messy. The cleanest item seemed to be the trash can. And guess what? Not one kid in the place."
- "I work for a cleaning company, and I'm tired of people telling their children: 'Leave it. The janitor will get it.'"

In the end, I was convinced, the public shares responsibility for America's dirty rest rooms. But that doesn't mean businesses are off the hook. When their lack of concern combines with some people's barbarous behavior, a rest room turns into a den of horrors.

Is there an easy answer? Readers offered many solutions—some less conventional than others. Consider the Neat Seat: Tucked in with my mail on the rest room issue was a package from a firm that makes plastic coverings for public toilet seats. You carry the small, sterile Neat Seat packet in your pocket or purse (it includes a "mitt," an antiseptic towelette, and a tissue seat-cover), and open it when you visit a public rest room. The company sent me four packets and suggested I try one.

In a pinch, I suppose, a Neat Seat might be handy. But the real answer to disgusting public rest rooms is this: There needs to be more diligence, respect, and common courtesy by all concerned—businesses and the public.

LOST WALLETS

The column can sure come in handy sometimes. Readers have helped me settle bets, win arguments, and, in essence, get the testimony of thousands of people at once. I don't need to hire the Gallup crowd to give me the pulse of America. All I have to do is put a note at the end of the column. Soon enough, the feedback pours in.

One evening, I was having dinner with my in-laws and we got into a philosophical argument. I was insisting that eight out of ten people who find a lost wallet will return it. Maybe I'm naive. I'm certainly an optimist.

Well, my brother-in-law insisted I was giving people more credit than they deserve. The consensus at the table: Eight out of ten people who come upon a lost wallet will keep it, even if it has identification in it.

I argued for a while, and then I thought: Hey, there's a way to get to the bottom of this!

That night, I wrote a column, and at the end of it, I explained my dinnertime discussion and tagged on this request: "If you've ever lost a wallet, please write and tell me if it was returned. Also, if you've ever found a wallet, write and tell me what you did with it. (OK, OK, I don't expect many thieves to write me and say they stole someone's wallet. Still, I'd like input, with or without signatures.)"

I admitted I wasn't conducting a scientific poll (I didn't want to be called the Shere Hite of lost wallets), but I promised to print the results.

When the mail started coming in, I quickly discovered that anyone who has ever lost a wallet has a story to tell about the state of honesty in America. More than six hundred people responded. For the most part, they told heartwarming tales of wallets found and returned. I learned, as I suspected, that the depths of dishonesty are overshadowed by all the unsung heroes who make great efforts to return our wallets, refusing rewards.

Fifty-eight percent of the respondents had their lost wallets returned with contents intact; 23 percent got their wallets back with money missing; and 19 percent never saw their wallets again. (Of those who found wallets, 87 percent said they returned them. I hadn't expected many thieves to write, so these statistics were obviously less accurate.)

Some readers wrote cynical letters about stolen wallets or finders who demanded rewards. But scores of appreciative readers saluted good-hearted people—cabbies, waitresses, cleaning people, garbage collectors, passersby—who found and returned their wallets. "I had to write you, Zazz, to help restore people's faith in mankind," explained one reader.

So many stories had happy endings. I heard from a man whose wallet was returned five years after it was lost—with nothing missing. And a clerk at an airport Traveler's Aid desk wrote: "Last month, a lost wallet was returned to my booth. I paged the wallet's owner. He had just arrived from India and he and his wife were crying when they reached my booth. As I handed them their full wallet, my only words were: 'Welcome to America!' "

Many finders were lauded as Lone Ranger types. "He wouldn't give his name. He wouldn't let me buy him a beer. He just smiled and disappeared into the crowd."

One woman whose wallet was mailed back to her found this note attached: "You look real cute in your license photo. I'd like to take you out sometime."

Of course, there were some heartless stories: A man wrote that he was swimming in the Gulf of Mexico when a wallet floated by. He checked the ID (the owner was from Iowa), took the one hundred dollars in the wallet, and tossed the wallet back in the ocean, feeling guilt-free.

I also heard from Wilbur Holmes, a retired superintendent at Chicago's post office. Every day, he said, the post office gets 40 to 50 wallets. If there's a parade in town (pickpockets' paradise), 125 wallets might show up on Monday morning. "Professional pickpockets can be what we call 'goodhearted thieves,' " Holmes said. "All they want is the money. So they throw the wallets in a mailbox and know we'll return them."

Since wallets are mailed back with postage due, some owners don't realize what's in a package and refuse to accept it. Thank-you notes, Holmes said, are rare.

For finders, returning a wallet can be aggravating. One woman found a purse on the subway and got so flustered running after the owner that she lost her own purse. A man who found a wallet tracked down the two addresses in it. Turned out, the wallet's owner had two women claiming to be his wife.

Then there was the couple that found $147 in a wallet. "We worried that the man's kids might go hungry without this money. We didn't have a car, so we walked to the address in the wallet, and were referred to another address miles away. When we finally found him, he said, 'Thanks, that was my horse-betting money.' "

Thirty-three readers wrote that they returned wallets, but kept the money as a "finder's fee." One man even listed his personal "ethics policy": "$50, I keep it; $500, I keep $100; $10,000, I keep $1,000."

Money isn't all that finders keep. I was told of a wallet returned with everything except money and a photo of Pope John Paul. And then there was the man who lost his wallet in Ireland and had it mailed back to him, with no return address, in the United States. "Everything was there except three condoms," he wrote. "I guess, being an Irish Catholic country, they didn't want them in my wallet."

Scores of wallet-finders complained about ungrateful owners. One example: "He grabbed it, leafed through it, asked, 'Is everything here?' and stormed off." Another: "I got a short letter, but no reward. It said, 'Thanks. I would have sent chocolates, but they melt in the mail.' Believe me, there had been a lot of money in that wallet, too."

One man found a wallet with $102.81 in it. Rather than send cash through the mail, he wrote a personal check for the amount and returned it with the wallet. He got the canceled check a month later, but never received even a short note of thanks from the wallet's owner.

Some finders had second thoughts about returning a wallet. A man wrote:

> I used to work for a car-rental company. One day, a man and his wife returned a car, and while he was at the counter, I found his wallet in the car. It contained $200, more than I was making in a week.
>
> I thought of keeping it but decided that would be wrong. I ran in and gave it to him. He thanked me, but offered no reward. I then carried their luggage to my van and drove them to the airport. I expected him to tip me when I dropped him off. But again, all I got was a thank-you. I felt cheated— like maybe I should have kept the wallet. Your thoughts, Zazz?

My response: Never regret being honest. As one survey respondent put it: "Honesty is its own reward." And some finders who were never rewarded figure there's a payoff down the road. "My hope is that somewhere on the big scoreboard of life, my good deed will be noted," one reader wrote. "Maybe someday the favor will be returned."

As you might expect, some wallet-finders were thanked profusely. "I still get Christmas cards from the lady whose wallet I found," a reader wrote.

A woman on vacation lost her wallet at Cincinnati's Riverfront Stadium. A man returned it to the lost and found, saying he didn't count the money (eight hundred dollars) because he didn't want to be tempted. He never left his name. "Cincinnati will always be my favorite city because of that angel at Riverfront," the woman wrote.

Several wallet-finders who kept money they found in a wallet said they remain haunted by what they did. One woman told of finding a wallet just before Christmas. It had ninety dollars in it. She wrote:

I'd always considered myself extremely honest, but it's difficult making ends meet in our family of five. I take home just $200 a week. I kept the money and returned everything else in the wallet.

It was a hard decision to make, and I only hope this person was grateful for having her other belongings returned. Well, Christmas has come and gone and so has the $90. But I still find myself questioning what I did. Am I still an honest person?

On a whim, to settle an argument, I had asked readers for some help. Their recollections and confessions came from the heart. Again and again, I'm reminded, what's most remarkable about having this column at my disposal is the access it provides to people's lives.

HAND-ME-DOWN GIFTS

Okay, I admit it. I've also used the column to stir up trouble. I'm no Morton Downey, Jr., but to keep the column entertaining, I'll sometimes do something devilish.

One slow day in June, I ended my column with this note:

Dear Readers: We're right in the middle of wedding season, so if you're a bride or groom, you're now going through stacks of gifts and saying, "Where on Earth did some of these things come from?"

Crystal bowls. Ceramic flower vases. Silver trays. Marble cheese-cutting boards. More silver trays. Brass picture frames. And then it hits you!

Some of these gifts are hand-me-downs! The gift-givers got the silver tray or cheese board for their wedding, didn't want or need it, and then gave it to you for your wedding. They saved money and cleaned house in one swoop.

If you could put a homing device on a silver tray, you might find that it makes its way into 10 homes in its lifetime—and isn't used in any of them.

I've gotten letters asking the etiquette rules for giving a gift that you have sitting around the house. Even if the gift is unopened, I say it's rude to pass it off on some poor, unsuspecting newlyweds. You didn't want it. What makes you think anyone else will?

Yet it's a pretty foolproof practice. The people receiving the gift never are quite sure they're getting a hand-me-down. They may be suspicious, but can they prove it?

Well, I'd like to get a handle on this phenomenon. If you've ever received a hand-me-down gift, or given one (and can justify the practice), drop me a line. Mail me only your letters, not your old gifts. I already have enough unused cheese boards and trays.

In the days that followed, I heard scores of incredible stories. I never realized how widespread the practice was. In my follow-up column, I had to change names so as not to embarrass recyclers or threaten friendships and family relations.

Betty's friend gave her a stylish apron as a bridal-shower gift. It was very nice, Betty said, "except for the gravy stain."

Debbie received a hair-curling kit from her sister-in-law for Christmas. When she opened the box, she found a long dark hair on one of the curlers. Debbie is blond.

Robert's mother-in-law gave him a bathrobe for his thirtieth birthday. Because he had three robes, Robert decided to return the gift. "The store clerk couldn't stop laughing," he wrote. "He said they hadn't stocked that robe for seven years!"

Dozens of readers wrote of opening a gift and finding a card addressed to the gift giver at the bottom of the box. Then there was Sue, who got a serving tray for her bridal shower that had initials engraved on it. "She held the tray up for everyone at the shower to see," wrote a friend. "To her shock, the initials belonged to the woman who gave the gift. The gift-giver was mortified. Obviously, she'd never opened the box and thought she'd just pass it on to some other bride."

Judy received three toasters for her wedding. She returned two of them, and had no choice but to keep the third. It had the name of a local bank stamped on the bottom: Evidently, it had been a free gift for opening an account.

Some readers wrote of getting back gifts they'd given years earlier. Follow closely now: Shelly gave a set of steak knives to her friend Wendy for Christmas. Wendy must have given the knives to their mutual friend, Laura, because three years later, Shelly got the knives from Laura for Christmas. "I knew the box, I knew the knives, I knew what happened," Shelly said.

Often, a gift is so strange that you know it wasn't selected especially for you. One reader explained: "When we pulled that electric pizza-maker from that old box retaped with masking tape, we just knew . . ." Another wrote:

> My husband and I got an electric potato peeler for our wedding. We got suspicious when we saw dried potato juice on it. And we had a good laugh when, in the box, we found a card addressed to the couple that gave us the gift.
> We plugged it in, flipped potato peels all over the kitchen, and decided that we, too, would recycle the gift. We gave it to my sister at her wedding, and she has since passed it on. I'd love to know where it is now.

Donna tried to return one of her wedding gifts: a mixing bowl set "in a box with age spots." At the store, she learned the item hadn't been stocked for five years. "They were able to find it on an old form and offered me 88 cents for it."

A tall, 175-pound woman wrote that her petite mother-in-law gives away her old clothes, and even pantyhose, as gifts: "My feet are size 10, but my mother-in-law has gifted me with her size-6½ slippers. At Christmas, I watch what gifts she receives, wondering if that's what I'll get next year. The topper was when I gave her a pin. I loved it when I bought it for her, and was thrilled when she accidentally gave it to me the next Christmas."

When Darrell got married, one gift he and his wife received was a tin tray that obviously came underneath a funeral fruit basket. "It was definitely a hand-me-down," he said, "but most of the gift (the fruit) wasn't even handed down."

Steve's Great-Uncle Bill died and his belongings were divided among relatives. When Steve got married, his aunt's gift was a thirty-year-old cobweb-covered warming tray. "Grandma knew right away," Steve said. "As soon as we opened it, she blurted out, 'That's Uncle Bill's!' "

Hand-me-down gifts can complicate the writing of thank-you notes. Don and Sherry received a useless serving plate from a friend for their wedding, and discovered a card from "Dorothy" inside the box. "There was no Dorothy on our guest list, but there had been such a guest at our friend's wedding. Our thank-you note contained the postscript 'Who's Dorothy?' but we don't think our friend ever made the connection."

Scores of readers wrote letters decrying hand-me-down gift giving. "People who recycle their old gifts think you want these things, but they're just kidding themselves," a woman wrote. "It's an insult to receive someone else's unwanted junk."

Still, dozens of people wrote defending the practice:

• "I have a special drawer where I keep unwanted gifts I've received. I'll shop long and hard for just the right present for a friend or close relative. But when I must get an obligatory gift for someone I care little about, I open up my gift drawer, wrap anything remotely appropriate, and recycle it. Remember, one man's trash is another's treasure.

"I'm not embarrassed, but please don't use my name. The people who unloaded that cranberry-sauce server on me last Christmas may read your column. I haven't given the gift away yet, but I will, I will."

• "Sometimes people can't afford to give a new gift. In the old days, a lot of people were poor, and gift-giving was the selfless sharing of what little they already had."

• "Go ahead and call me cheap, Zazz. I'm a single mother of twins and the babysitter gets more of my paycheck than I do. Hand-me-down gifts make gift-giving possible for me."

My recycled-gifts column led some readers to think of other cheap presents. My favorite letter:

Dear Zazz: Your gifts column brought back an old memory.

I once worked in a department store selling fine china. Among our markdowns was an $80 vase broken in three pieces.

A man bought the vase for $5 and paid another $5 to have it wrapped and shipped to California. He told me a relative there was "milking" him for a wedding gift. He said he hoped the relative would assume the vase broke in transit.

When he left, I carefully wrapped the pieces separately in tissue, enclosed a note naming a good glue to restore the item, and shipped it. That way, the recipient wouldn't blame the postman.

After that, every time the vase-buyer passed through the store, he gave me a dirty look. I wish I could have heard what his relative said to him.

Employees had a running gag at the markdown table. "If you think this stuff is cheap, you should see some of our customers!"

LETTERS TO SANTA

Every year, it's the same story. Santa Claus never makes it to the post office to pick up his mail. You can't hold it against him. The guy's busy.

But it's a shame for all the kids who write to him. They're so eager to get in touch with him—to tell him about their lives, their families, their wish lists. They'd be thrilled to hear back from him. Yet by the thousands, their loving, touching letters end up as undeliverable mail.

Luckily, over the years, Santa has had helpers—big-hearted citizens and postal employees who volunteer to respond on behalf of Santa, often sending presents to the neediest children. Still, these volunteers are never able to answer all the letters. Christmas comes and goes, and thousands of letters sent to Santa remain in the dead-letter office, unanswered.

That's why, a month after Christmas, 1987, I asked the U.S. Postal Service to send me a few bags of unanswered Santa letters. I figured readers might help out by playing Santa and writing belated responses to some of these kids. If a reader sent me a self-addressed envelope, I'd send him one of the kids' letters to answer.

I expected two hundred or three hundred readers to respond. But the outpouring of concern and generosity was astounding. I received more than seven thousand requests for letters to Santa—many with kind and touching notes attached. It was the largest response I'd ever received to a single column.

"My heart just aches when I think there's a child somewhere who never heard from Santa," one reader wrote.

"A child's unshaking belief in Santa is so short-lived," wrote another. "If I can bring a little joy to a needy child, maybe his or her belief could last a little longer."

Many readers promised to send toys or clothing. "Our young son has so much that it is almost a sin," wrote one couple. "He has more toys than he can play with in two lifetimes. We'd be happy to help."

Along with my assistants, Shelley Brown and LaVelle Allen, I spent two weeks sorting through thousands of kids' letters, separating the needy ones from the greedy ones. Through February, Advice Central looked like Santa's Workshop.

The Santa response taught me about the depths of people's generosity, and the loving innocence of childhood. It showed me that I should always look for ways to involve and motivate readers. (The Santa program also showed me the darker side of people, and of Christmas—but I'll get to that in a moment.)

The needy letters from kids were heart-tuggers. "My parents are behind in their bills and have no money for gifts," wrote Elizabeth, age ten. "I go to bed crying because it hurts me to see them so down."

Cindy, nine, wrote of how her parents have big hearts but no money for presents: "You're our only hope, Santa." Calvin, also nine, explained how his mother couldn't afford gifts because she had to pay "the rent and light bells [sic]." He asked for food, a winter coat, and something to wear to church.

Parents of needy children also wrote letters to Santa. Their efforts seemed calculated—they obviously hoped an adult would read their letter and help their family. Still, the fact that they were desperate enough to bring their troubles to strangers suggested that their needs might be great. Many asked for shoes or winter clothes. "I hoped to give my children a Christmas like they'd never had," wrote a poor, single mother. "They keep asking when Santa is coming. But every day, it gets closer to Christmas and I cry and pray because I have nothing to give them."

Then there were the letters from children who weren't necessarily needy, but would surely be thrilled to hear from Santa—no matter how late the date. A lot of these kids were the ultimate true believers. Bill wrote: "Santa, kids at school say you're fat, but I think you look good just the way you are." Joe wrote: "This year I have good news and bad news. The good news is the number of presents I want went down. The bad news is the price of presents I want went up." Jeff wrote: "How are your raindeers [sic]? Fine? Mine are fine, too. Ha! Ha! Just kidding!"

Lynn asked Santa to bring back Grandmom's dog: "If you don't find him, I'll understand." And Jessica wrote: "I want a kitten for Christmas because my cat, Trigger, died of old age. She was blind in one eye, had trouble breathing, and made a wheezing sound when she slept. God took her while I was at school. I'm heartbroken. I miss her so much. Can you help?"

So many of the letters were earnest, direct, or refreshingly polite—written just the way children think. A boy named Chris included a floor plan of his house, giving directions from the chimney to his room. James wrote: "Santa, I'm sorry about your hair." Billy asked for a small present because "Santa, you know how small my room is." And Missy asked for a husband for her divorced mother and a sister for herself. "If you can't do it," she wrote, "I love you anyway."

Steven explained: "I wasn't always a good boy, but my mother wasn't always good, and I still love her." Michael began his letter: "I've been pretty good. Now let's get down to business. I want . . ."

Several kids wrote Santa thank-you notes on December 26. "Thank you for the bicycle," wrote Sophie. "Today, after I was riding it, someone took it from my porch. Could you please send another one?"

There were strange letters, too. Jeremy's entire letter: "Dear Santa: How come we had a lot of rain on Dec. 20?" Mark, John and Mike wrote Santa a joint letter with just two sentences: "We hate tools. Give us toys."

Some letters were cute, if obviously calculated. Eleven-month-old Brittany explained that her brother, Chris, age ten, was writing the letter for her because she was too young to write. She proceeded to ask for a host of gifts for Chris.

Every letter from a loving, polite, or needy child was sent to a reader to answer. But what of the "other" letters? Well, we did sift through thousands of greedy letters. To satisfy readers who were thinking, "All kids can't be that sweet," I also shared some of these letters in the column.

Consider Jay. His letter didn't include the words "please" or "thank you." In fact, all he sent to Santa was a wish list—with eighteen page numbers (and forty-two product numbers) from the Sears catalog. Jay wanted nine items from page 273 alone. And he wasn't the greediest. Other kids asked for one hundred toys.

We came across more than a dozen letters from children recommending that other kids not receive gifts. Keith advised Santa that his friend, Chris, had been a bad boy and shouldn't get gifts or candy. A boy named Michael suggested that his brother Danny receive "rocks in his socks" because he's "a pain in the butt."

The oddest letters to Santa were the mean-spirited ones. Dylan wrote: "Santa bring me a TV or you're a dead man." Candy wrote: "Santa, I hate you—you're stupid!" and included her return address.

We can assume that Santa is a man of forgiveness and understanding. So were many readers. After I reprinted Candy's letter in my column, one woman responded:

> When I read Candy's remarks, my heart went out to her. Her letter was a cry of pain. That's why she included her return address. She was issuing a challenge.
>
> Her letter could have been the cry of a child in an unhappy environment who is lashing out at a symbol of joy. I know how Candy might be feeling. When I was a child, I was frustrated because I rarely or never received anything from Santa.
>
> I can recall trying to figure out what was wrong with me because Santa always skipped my house and gave gifts to my friends. It got to the point where I hated the Christmas season.
>
> Candy issued Santa a challenge she felt he'd have to answer. That's all she knew how to do. I know you didn't give letters from kids like Candy to your readers to answer. But I'd like to respond to Candy to tell her she is loved and to ask why she is mad. May I?

I passed Candy's letter on to this concerned reader, and she did respond, but her letter came back as undeliverable. Perhaps Candy's family had moved sometime after Christmas.

In some ways, the Santa program was more rewarding than anything else I'd done in the job. But there were disconcerting aspects, too.

Several suburban readers requested letters from "needy white children only." Others wrote back that they were disappointed in the letters they received. They had assumed they'd get letters from kids whose hardworking mothers and fathers were struggling to make ends meet. Instead, they got letters from the children of welfare mothers: In bastardized English, these kids wrote of living in grimy, fatherless households with six or seven siblings. For some readers, such images didn't jibe with their idealized notions of poor kids—modern-day Waltons. But unlike TV movies about struggling families at Christmastime, real poverty is more raw and disturbing.

"I'd rather not answer this letter," wrote one reader whose Santa letter came from the poorest of Chicago's projects. "Could you send another?"

Another troubling result of the Santa program: Many poor parents skipped Santa and wrote directly to me. "Dear Zazz: My kids are hungry. They need clothes. Send my letter to someone who can help me." Were they on the level? Were these letters drafted by the same people who devise elaborate welfare scams? Some adults were obvious in their tricks: They sent as many as forty photocopied letters to me or to Santa. But it wasn't always easy to determine who was sincerely needy and who was preying on the sympathies of the public.

Still, even though the Santa program was in some ways imperfect, I decided to do it annually. What convinced me? All the letters like this one from Susan, age ten: "My Mama always says there is a Santa Claus, but I don't know because he always forgets us. Please Santa, don't forget us this time again."

How's the Family?

OKAY, SO YOU can't pick your relatives. But you sure can complain about them. Everyone else does.

I receive more letters on family matters than on any other subject. Through my mailbag, I've been introduced to most every type of family squabble and every breed of family character. (I've changed some names so as not to embarrass those involved.)

There was Grandpop Howard—a depressed new grandfather. He was very averse to getting old, so he announced that his grandchildren should refer to him simply as "Howard." His family was horrified, but I tried to be understanding. "Some people adjust to the times of their lives more slowly than others," I told the family. "If Howard doesn't want to be thought of as just a grandfather, let him be. When the role feels right, the title will, too."

And what about Martha, the mother-in-law? Her son's wife wrote: "Every time she visits, she snoops around the house asking questions: 'How much does this cost?' 'How much does that cost?' It's like she's appraising everything we have. I think it's rude. How can I respond?" I suggested: "Next time your mother-in-law asks, 'How much does this cost?' politely respond: 'I'm sorry, it's not for sale.' "

Then there was Cousin Donna, the feminist. When she was pregnant, she and her husband agreed that if the baby was a girl, they'd give it Donna's last name. A boy would be given her husband's last name. This agreement would apply to all future children. Donna's cousin wrote to say this seemed mighty odd. I agreed, and replied: "Imagine the confusion if Cousin Donna gets divorced and marries a man who named his children using similar rules. You'd need a scorecard to keep track." I also wondered whether this name game would create unhealthy alliances. What if Cousin Donna had four girls and a boy? The lone brother might feel like a misnamed outcast. "It's hard enough growing up these days," I concluded. "Parents ought to try to make life as easy as they can for kids."

I get questions about every sort of relative (or ex-relative) there is—half brothers, stepfathers-in-law, ex–mothers-in-law, sisters who became Catholic sisters, ex-husbands who became brothers-in-law, great-uncles, lousy aunts, first cousins once removed, and second cousins who moved in and won't move out.

People are usually closest to their families, and are tied, for better or worse, to their spouses' families. So their concerns, animosities, and frustrations often run deepest with relatives, whether by blood or marriage.

Sometimes I find that the best way to deal with family concerns is to jolly folks out of it. A perturbed man wrote that his thirteen-year-old grandson kept talking about robbing a local bank: "He and his friends have it all planned out: how they'll do it, what they'll do with the money, etc. My grandson is a good kid. He's bright and respectful. He gets good grades. What should I do?"

I replied:

> Your grandson and his pals probably are just big-talkers. Kids that age are renowned for their great imaginations, not for their great bank heists.
>
> Remind your grandson of the legal and ethical improprieties associated with bank jobs. You might also point out the great risks. He'll be up against closed-circuit cameras, armed guards and money packets designed to explode in the getaway car. (Arranging for a getaway car will be yet another large obstacle for these boys. Tell them you won't drive it.)

Of course, a lot of family business is much more serious, and my responses must reflect this. Should a fifteen-year-old tell his mother that he's learned his father is having an affair? (He should talk to his father first, I advised.) Can a woman demand that her ex-husband take their wedding photos off the mantel in his apartment? (He has a right to display the photos in his own home, I replied. Though she may have adjusted to the divorce better than he did, she can't stop him from holding on to his memories.) Will a couple's "happy" open marriage be unhealthy for their child? "Our 3-year-old daughter is noticing that other men or women sometimes spend the night," the wife wrote. (I replied that the arrangement could be unhealthy for all concerned: "Be prepared for your daughter to someday question whether your husband actually is her father." I added that I'd heard from several readers whose open marriages fell apart when one partner became too enamored of the openness. The other then felt hurt and betrayed. I advised this couple to reconsider the whole arrangement.)

In my job, I am privy to the most horrid of family secrets. A woman wrote to say that she and her sisters were sexually abused as children by their older brother. "Now that his wife is pregnant, I'm afraid that if he has a baby girl, he'll abuse her, too. Should I talk to his wife? My sisters won't back me up because they don't want this secret out in the open." (I replied: "This is too important an issue to ignore. Consider approaching your brother and sister-in-law: They might have similar fears about his potential impulses. If he needs counseling, he must be encouraged to get it.")

The family troubles that follow cover the range from lightweight and amusing to shocking and hard-to-believe. Some of the problems have been in families for generations. Some are new to the nineties. Because all of us have family somewhere, we may see ourselves or our loved ones in the pages that follow.

A few of the major categories:

IN-LAWS

Dear Zazz: When my daughter got married a few years back, I encouraged her to show love and respect to her mother-in-law. Boy did my daughter take my advice!

She now dotes on the woman. She pays more attention to her mother-in-law than she does to me. I'm in my 50s. Her mother-in-law is 82. How do I tell my daughter I feel neglected?

—Sorry for My Advice

Dear Sorry: Women often seem to get along better with their grandmothers-in-law (the sweet old lady syndrome) than their mothers-in-law (considered witches until proven otherwise). The age of your daughter's mother-in-law probably makes her seem more like a grandmother, and thus more lovable and less troublesome.

Also, your daughter could be paying attention to her husband's mom because the woman needs more care than you do, or because such doting pleases her husband.

Your daughter has shown she welcomes your advice. This time, tell her that you might just be overly sensitive, but you

feel neglected. It's possible that your daughter already con-
siders the love between the two of you to be unshakable.
Maybe, for the first few years of her marriage, she'd like to
get to know and love the woman who raised her husband.

Question: "My mother-in-law doesn't allow smoking in her
house. But when she comes to our house, she doesn't want me
smoking either. Shouldn't I be allowed to smoke in my own
home?—Steaming Smoker"

Answer: "Your mother-in-law shouldn't write the rules in your
house. That's for you and your wife to do. But out of respect to her
(or any visitor), I suggest you refrain from smoking while she's
visiting.

"If that's too tough, smoke in a distant part of the house—or
outside. Of course, if she visits so often that it's as if she lives there,
you may have to establish a non-smoking section of the house—and
assign her a seat in it."

Q: "My mother-in-law gave me an expensive dress. I absolutely
don't like it. I don't want to hurt her feelings, but I know she expects
me to start wearing it. What can I do?—Haven't Worn It Yet"

A: "Let your husband take the blame. He might say to his
mother: 'Mom, I don't like that dress you got Judy. She really
appreciates the thought, but I don't think it looks right on her.
Maybe you two should go together to pick out something else.'
Your mother-in-law is less likely to get mad at her son. She may
figure he has no taste in clothes, but she won't question his taste in
women."

Q: "My mother-in-law won't come to our house alone. She
always brings along my husband's five sisters. It can be overwhelm-
ing to have to feed and entertain six people. How do I invite my
mother-in-law and politely tell her to leave the gang behind?—Too
Many Sisters-in-law"

A: "Be positive. Tell your mother-in-law that you'd like to
spend time alone with her and, besides, six guests can be over-
whelming. As for those Siamese sisters, invite them over one or two
at a time. If they show up in a pack, say, 'Sorry, we don't have
enough food for everyone.' And don't!"

Q: "Every Christmas, my mother-in-law lavishes gifts on my
husband's children from his first marriage and refuses to include my
children from a previous marriage. My husband has tried talking to
her, but it doesn't help. I hate seeing my kids' disappointed faces

when all the presents are opened. Your advice?—Hurting for My Kids"

A: "Your husband must inform his mother that all the children are equals in your family. If she's on a limited budget, she should use whatever money she earmarked for her biological grandchildren to buy less expensive gifts for all the kids. If she refuses, your husband should tell her to bring no presents at all."

Q: "My husband is an alcoholic and when he's drunk, my two sisters-in-law often come over and ask him for things around our house—furniture, artwork, anything that isn't nailed down. Because he's drunk and I'm not home, he gives them things!

"I'm not on speaking terms with his sisters, both of whom are in their 70s, so I've written them to demand everything back. No response. I went to see a lawyer and he said that the belongings are ours in common and my husband can do what he wants with them.

"His sisters are absolutely nutty. They tell him people with brown eyes are mean and rotten—and then he tells me. My husband and his whole family have blue eyes. I have brown eyes, as do our children.

"My husband is a generous man and he loves his sisters, but these problems are eating my insides out. What can I do?—Going Nutty Myself"

A: "Though your in-laws sound like certifiable looney-tunes, your biggest problem isn't with them, it's with your husband. He's the one giving away your belongings and telling you you're inferior because of your eye color. (The Nazis, too, had a fondness for blue eyes, you'll remember.)

"Your husband needs help for his alcoholism, and counseling for the marriage. If he won't recognize that his loyalties should be with you, not his sisters, you may have to consider leaving him."

SIBLINGS

Question: "I'm an 18-year-old girl with a 16-year-old sister. When I bring home a boyfriend, my sister is always a complete flirt. I've confronted her about this, but she says she's just being friendly. Now a guy I used to date has called to ask out my sister. What should I do?—Furious"

Answer: "If you no longer care for your ex, tell your sister she's welcome to him. Maybe with a boyfriend of her own, she'll be less of a flirt with yours. And from now on, there are two ways to keep your boyfriends off limits: (a) tell them to beware of your smiling sister, or (b) tell Mom."

Q: "My teen-aged brother always walks around the house in his underwear.

"He lives with me and my mother. I'm a few years older than he is, and I don't believe it's right. He doesn't see anything wrong with this. What do you think?—Half Naked's Sister"

A: "Tell him to put his clothes on. He's not the cute kid brother anymore, running around in Superman or Smurfs underwear, and he should know that his parading around in almost nothing makes you uncomfortable.

"His modeling of his underwear is no different from you wearing nothing but a bra and panties. Would he feel comfortable with that?

"Buying him a nice bathrobe might help him along."

Q: "My hot-tempered fiance hunted down his sister's ex-boyfriend. The man had punched my fiance's sister, and so my fiance avenged her honor. As a result, my future husband got his arms slashed, and his eye was almost cut out with a knife.

"I'm terribly upset. The incident has left a handsome man, the love of my life, with nasty scars and hefty doctor bills.

"Every day, I must look at these scars. He never realized that what would hurt him would hurt me, too.

"His sister doesn't seem too concerned. But I've lost weight and sleep over this. I fear he'll again get into trouble. It seems he thinks more of his role as his sister's bodyguard than his role as my future husband. Am I being selfish?—Unsure of His Loyalties"

A: "You're smart, not selfish. And you've been given a painful glimpse of your fiance's family dynamics. Before the wedding, you'd better establish ground rules for family responsibilities and loyalties.

"Your future sister-in-law may be the type who repeatedly gets mixed up with the wrong crowd or abusive boyfriends. There may be other situations that require a rescue by a fearless brother.

"Before you marry this man, make it clear that you're not asking him to give up his loyalty to his sister. You just want him to avoid the dangers, and to think how his actions might affect his safety, your peace of mind, and any children you eventually have."

Q: "I'm probably making twice my brother's salary, and he has two kids and a wife to support. Money is always tight in his household.

"I feel a little guilty and uncomfortable with my good fortune.

I'm starting to think I should spread the wealth—maybe find a way to give my brother's family some money.

"It's not that I feel an obligation to be my brother's keeper. It's just that I feel bad as a single man driving a sports car while he has trouble buying his kids clothes.

"I doubt he'd take my help, but should I offer it?—Oh Brother"

A: "You might embarrass your brother by making an outright cash offer. But there are ways you can help without hurting his pride.

"For Christmas and the children's birthdays, you can give substantial presents: clothing, bikes, savings bonds, college-fund money. You also can give big-ticket gifts to your brother and his wife on the right occasions.

"Also, you might at some point remind your brother that if ever there's an unforeseen catastrophe, you'll be there for him. If, God forbid, one of his kids gets sick and medical bills become a burden, your brother should feel free to seek your help.

"Meanwhile, enjoy your sports car. Only feel guilty about it when you drive too fast, race it through red lights, or use it as a tool to impress women."

Q: "I'm in love with a guy I've known for 20 years. We've dated for a year. The problem is that until seven years ago, he was married to my sister.

"Needless to say, my family doesn't approve of the relationship. My sister, whom I've never gotten along with, is especially upset. How can we have a happy relationship if everyone is dead set against us?—Feeling Alone"

A: "Steer clear of family gatherings and don't expect your family to be too understanding. It could take them a long time to come to terms with your relationship. They may never accept it.

"The best you can do is let the family know you two are together because of your love for one another, not because you wish to hurt your sister. If you're lucky, you will find your love is stronger than family difficulties.

"Of course, if you decide to marry, a big family wedding wouldn't be in order."

PARENTS

Question: "I'm a 14-year-old girl and I'd like to be a manager of the school baseball team. My parents don't like the idea of a girl riding around with a bunch of guys. I've told them that there are two other girl managers, but they still refuse to sign the permission slip. What can I do?—Striking Out"

Answer: "Ask the coach to give your parents a call to reassure them. Promise always to sit at the front of the team bus. And remind your parents that a girl who wants to accompany a player to first base—or beyond—could do so off the baseball diamond as well as on it. Let your parents know that their decision here will measure their trust in you."

Q: "My mother is 40 and I'm 14. She's driving me crazy. She thinks teens today are just like teens in her day. She even wants me to wear bell-bottomed jeans. I want to wear clothes like all the other 14-year-olds. How can I make her see this?—Up Against a Brick Wall"

A: "Your mother grew up in an age of startling generational differences. Because parents and kids today have such staples as rock music and running shoes in common, she may not recognize that generation gaps still exist. Invite her to observe what kids wear at your local mall. Explain your preferences. Depending on what she can afford, maybe she'll oblige your up-to-date tastes."

Q: "My father died five years ago and my mother constantly tells me that I look like him. I think she resents me because of the resemblance. I've explained to her many times that I'm not my father. What can I do?—In My Father's Image"

A: "Tell your mother how much she's hurting and upsetting you. Let her know that you loved your father and miss him, too. Both of you should consider your resemblance to your dad to be a happy reminder of him. If your mother can't cope with that, she probably needs to see a counselor."

Q: "Am I being unreasonable if I cringe every time my mother introduces me as her 'older daughter'? I'm 60 and my sister is 55.— Neither Young nor Old"

A: "To your mother, you'll always be the older daughter. But because you don't like the distinction, it's time for her to quit broadcasting that fact.

"Ask her nicely to cut it out. If she doesn't, I assume you can live with it. You have for 55 years. And besides, be thankful you've got a mother on this earth to introduce you."

SPOUSES

Question: "I was married for 25 years and have two children. My first wife died and I've remarried. A major problem in our marriage is where I'll be buried when I die. My kids want me alongside my first wife. My current wife, naturally, wants me buried with her. What's a solution?—Torn"

Answer: "How about cremation? You can even have your ashes placed in two urns—with one buried alongside your first wife, the other by your second. Also, remind your children and current wife that your devotion to them shouldn't be measured by where you opt to be buried. You're alive and you love them. That's most important."

Q: "I have three children, ages 8, 6 and 3. My husband is cheating on me and takes the kids to his girlfriend's house. It's uncomfortable for me and I don't want my children brought up that way. What can I do?—Very Upset"

A: "Tell your husband the situation is unhealthy for your kids. But your marriage may be beyond repair, in which case you'll need to consider divorce. Understand, though, that your husband can seek joint custody of the kids or at least visitation rights. If that happens, he's sure to take them to his girlfriend's. Like so many families wounded by divorce, you all will have to learn to adjust to the awkward situation."

Q: "When I got married, I was a registered Democrat, as was my husband. Now he has decided to run for a local office as a Republican. He wants me to switch parties as well, though I'd rather remain a Democrat. Your advice?—Not So Eager"

A: "You shouldn't be pressured, but out of loyalty to your husband, you might want to change your registration. What if his opponents learn you're a Democrat? They may use this against him, which could hurt his chances of election. No matter how you're registered, the decisions you make in the voting booth are your own. So for the sake of appearance, consider making the switch."

Q: "When my husband and I married six years ago, he was a professional weight-lifter and model.

"Because of the flimsy briefs he had to wear, he was asked to shave his pubic hair. Sex with him when he was clean-shaven was heavenly.

"The problem is that he now works as a gym instructor, and because he uses the common showers in the locker room, he felt compelled to let his hair grow. As a result, sex is no longer as exciting for me.

"If his old boss at the modeling agency could demand that he shave, don't you think that, as his wife, I'm entitled to make the same demand?—O.J."

A: "You can make the request. But your husband's body is his property, and if he'd feel uncomfortable being clean-shaven in a crowded shower, he's entitled to wear hair.

"If he ever quits working at the gym, encourage him to get a job where he remains clothed and showers in private. Most desk jobs fit this description. That way, maybe he'll start shaving again for you."

Q: "I'm a very attractive 28-year-old woman. My husband likes me to walk around the house nude. He says I am beautiful and he enjoys looking at me. I like the compliments.

"What I don't understand is why he sometimes encourages me to remain naked when his friends come over. He says I'm too beautiful to cover up and hide. He also says it is nice to hear from others who admire my beauty and figure.

"Are many husbands like this?—Maryland Wife"

A: "As you may know, I'm an advice columnist who often makes house calls. I think it's more appropriate, however, if I handle this question without making a visit.

"Yes, your husband is a rare one. And so are you.

"If you're not bothered by his requests, then you're entitled to do your own thing in your own house. Many people have exhibitionist tendencies, and you obviously have yours.

"If you're uncomfortable being undressed around his friends, don't be forced into it. And out of respect, your husband shouldn't pressure you.

"Consider this, too: Because your husband seems to need verification from his friends that you're attractive, he may indeed have insecurities about the marriage. Why does he need an audience to appreciate your beauty? Perhaps you need to look at your total relationship for some answers."

Q: "My husband of 21 years wants me to have sex with other men. This has become an obsession with him, and it is destroying our marriage.

"I have absolutely no desire to do this, but my husband says it would enhance our marriage. He says he'll get turned on by listening to me talk about my adultery. In fact, when he and I make

love, he is most satisfied when he fantasizes about guys having sex
with me.

"He says I'm just old fashioned (I was a virgin when we married), and he keeps saying he'll bring home friends to have sex with
me. He even wants me to flirt with the husbands of friends and
relatives. I won't jeopardize friendships just so he can get turned on.

"I think about killing myself every day. I've even told him that,
but he persists. I should also mention this: My husband feels very
inferior about his ability to satisfy me in lovemaking. But he's very
good as a lover.—Minneapolis Wife"

The answer I gave this last woman was an obvious one: Her
husband's requests were unhealthy and he was abusing her emotionally. For the marriage to survive, they'd both need marriage
counseling. If he refused to go, I advised her to go herself. Many
readers supplemented my answer with their own letters of support
and warning. A Chicago lawyer wrote:

> **Dear Zazz:** Minneapolis Wife is in a no-win situation.
> She may think giving in to his demands will satisfy him, but
> it will probably only make things worse.
>
> My husband and I have had several friends who were
> "swingers." One of them, a psychologist, says that it is very
> common for a man to drag his reluctant wife into "swap-
> ping," and then to become obsessively jealous of her lovers.
>
> A couple we were once friends with—Carl and Terri—
> were the most egregious example of this scenario. She was an
> old-fashioned woman, but he kept suggesting she have sex
> with his old Army buddy, Dan. Finally, she gave in. After a
> while, she and Dan got very fond of each other. Carl then
> refused to let Terri see Dan. Eventually, they got divorced
> and Carl sued for custody of their son. His grounds? Terri's
> sexual activities made her an unfit mother. (He lost, but it
> cost Terri a lot of time and money.)
>
> The psychological mechanism at work here seems to be
> that when a man lends his wife to another man, that empha-
> sizes his "ownership" of her. But when she "lends" herself
> to somebody else, that undermines his power over her. Un-
> less Minneapolis Wife likes being a possession, she had bet-
> ter either renegotiate the terms of her marriage, or get
> out.—Chicago Lawyer

Off the Wall,
On the Mark

I'LL CONSIDER ANY question. I'm almost dangerously curious, and readers know it. So they send me whatever oddball questions pop into their heads. I can picture them at home saying, "Send it to Zazz, he'll answer anything!" It's an inescapable cycle: Weird questions beget more weird questions. But I don't mind. Unpredictability is what makes the job fun.

Consider the woman who wrote: "My husband is a very special man, and I would love to see his face on Mt. Rushmore. I know this is a big request, but how might I go about getting this idea in motion?" She signed herself "His Biggest Fan."

For an answer, I called the folks in South Dakota who tend to Mount Rushmore. A spokeswoman didn't question or dismiss the qualifications of this woman's husband, but she did say the couple was out of luck: Mount Rushmore has no more carvable rock. "There's no way another head could be carved up there," the spokeswoman said. "I'm sorry."

So I told the letter writer: "Should Washington, Jefferson, Lincoln or Teddy Roosevelt ever fall out of favor, I suppose their likenesses could be recarved to resemble someone else—your husband, perhaps. But I don't want to encourage unattainable pipe dreams. I suggest you find a more modest way to honor and glorify your husband. Maybe your local luncheonette could name a sandwich after him."

Then there was the young Chicagoan who wrote that his girlfriend spent a week vacationing in Dallas. When she returned, her head was partly shaved, she wore strange clothing torn in several places, and she even spoke differently. "Is this normal behavior for people in Dallas?" the young man asked.

I shared his letter with the Dallas Convention and Visitors Bureau, which denied that shaved heads and torn clothing are the norm there. (Their tourism brochures supported their contention.) A spokeswoman did, however, allow that "like any big city, you'll find a variety of dress and styles here." While she admitted that she wears giant "stylish" shoulder pads, the spokeswoman assured me she'd never shaved her head.

Plenty of letters mailed my way read like they've been post-marked in the Twilight Zone. I try to encourage these letter writers to come down to earth. Consider this one:

> **Dear Zazz:** I've been told by several psychics that throughout my life, a bad spirit will follow me. The spirit doesn't want me to be happy in romance because he and I were married in a previous life. The psychics say I cheated on him in this other life, and he now seeks revenge.
>
> At first, I didn't believe it. But now I'm 33 and I'm won-dering if it's true. I've been a failure at all relationships.
>
> I thought I'd beaten the curse last winter, when I married a wonderful man. But a few months later, he told me that even though I was caring, loving and sexy, he was not sexu-ally attracted to me.
>
> I know my story sounds bizarre. But could it be true?
> —Haunted

> **Dear Haunted:** Romances fail for a variety of reasons: bad luck, bad chemistry, bad communications, bad breath.
>
> Bad spirits? Only Shirley MacLaine can say for sure, but I'm doubtful. A lot of people have a string of failed romances and a bad marriage or two, but they pick themselves up again and again and keep trying. Don't spook yourself out. Don't allow yourself the "I'm haunted" excuse. Just try your best to make the next relationship work.
>
> Also, consider dropping psychic consultations from your life. You've already heard what they've got to say. You're paranoid enough without them. Concentrate on your future, not on your past.

I have no doubt the distraught letter-writer above was sincere. But every so often, someone sends me what I classify as a "Well, maybe" letter. Well, maybe the problem is on the level. And maybe not. Either way, I sometimes can't resist sharing it in the column.

Such a letter came from a man who said his wife, Sandra, was a big Elvis fan. The husband wrote:

I didn't mind. I liked Elvis, too. But then my wife's sister saw someone contact Elvis's spirit on the TV Show "A Current Affair." She and my wife decided to use a Ouija board to try to talk to the King beyond the grave.

Zazz, what happened next is so crazy; I just couldn't make it up. My wife lit candles in a dark room and soon began screaming. The Ouija board had worked, only not with Elvis. It seemed she'd connected with one of Elvis's friends from the fifties—Eddie Cochran.

Sandra figured this was some sort of sign. So she packed away her Elvis stuff in boxes and started going to record shops all over town, looking for Eddie Cochran albums. Now she plays his music over and over again. If I hear "Summertime Blues" one more time, I swear I'm going to go out of my mind!

The man said that except for his wife's Eddie Cochran obsession, his marriage was fine. He signed himself "All Shook Up."

Eddie Cochran's life story, it turns out, is a sad and ironic one. He was something of a boy genius. "Summertime Blues," for instance, featured Eddie playing every instrument. One of Eddie's last songs was called "Three Steps to Heaven." He recorded it with the surviving Crickets after Buddy Holly died in a plane crash. A few months later, in April 1960, Eddie died in a taxi accident near London. He was twenty-one.

Anyway, I told this letter writer that as long as his marriage was fine in other respects, he should indulge his wife's newfound fanaticism by ignoring it:

Since Eddie had a limited repertoire, she might soon tire of him without your intervention. Then, on her own, she could return to her Ouija board in search of other early rock stars: Holly, Jackie Wilson, Marvin Gaye, Bill Haley, Richie Valens. If she tracks down some of these fellows and heads to the record store in search of their music, you'll at least have some diversity on your home stereo.

Actually, the strangest letters I receive may be the ones asking personal questions. Often, these letters sit on my desk for a few days while I mull them over. Do I really want to reveal my private life in print? Usually not. But there was one time I couldn't resist. The letter:

> **Dear Zazz:** My name is Robert and I'd like to know if there is anything wrong with masturbation. We men keep quiet about it. We'd like to know what you think. Thanks, Zazz, and we'll be waiting to hear from you. Also, if you do it yourself, please let us know.
> —Wondering

Obviously, this was as personal as a question can get. And yet, I had an appropriate answer for this man and I figured, what the heck, I might as well share it with him, and with others readers, too. I replied: "Dear Wondering: Done in private and in moderation, masturbation is natural and normal. As for myself, I have a commuter marriage. I live in Chicago. My wife lives in Detroit."

Even though there were no dirty words in the man's question or my answer, both the newspaper syndicate and the *Sun-Times* chose not to run the letter or my answer. "We want your column to run in family newspapers," one editor said to me. "By the way, you ought to take the rest of the week off and go see your wife."

THE REGULAR JOES

Most advice columnists lean on experts—psychologists, professors, authors, sex therapists. Of course, I also consult know-it-all types from time to time. They like to talk and flex their brains. I like to listen and observe brains in mid-flex. We get along.

But experts are often too busy running tests in the lab or collecting business cards at a trade show or telling Donahue, "You're right, Phil, and that's why I wrote this book!" So experts can be ignorant when it comes to many problems the rest of us live with every day.

That's why, for commonsense advice, I established my Regular Joes Advisory Board. I put out a call for cabbies, bartenders, barbers, and the like—all named Joe, Josephine, Joanne, or some logical variation thereof.

I wanted people with smarts but no Ph.D.'s; people who have seen it all and have the photos to prove it; people who love to give advice, don't mind taking it, and have plenty to say when someone asks, "Hey Joe, whatta ya know?"

I looked for Joes with open minds, big hearts, too many opinions, and a free night once in a while to come to my Joe meetings and help answer questions.

I didn't want Joes with presidential aspirations (most of them are only concerned about people's problems during an election year) or Joes seeking control of *Fortune* 500 companies (they tend to call themselves Joseph and use a middle initial. Too pompous.)

I wanted the Joes you meet in the lunchroom, the ones who tell you how to sweet-talk your way out of the house for a poker or mah-jongg game. I wanted Joes who sweat to give their families a home, and like to remind them of that fact; Joes who learned so much from their first divorces that their second divorces came off without a hitch; Joes who are always saying, "Jeez, I could write a book"—but never will.

In my mind, Regular Joes are people who always offer you a beer—no need for a coaster—when you come over to their house. They like to hug you, yet they're not reluctant to tell you how your kid misbehaved in the carpool, the little brat.

Well, when I first put out the call for Joes, I got a lot of applications from well-meaning folks with names like Tom, Dick, Harry, Sue, Betty, and Fred.

I asked for Joes, I heard from Freds. Go figure!

But I was determined to hold out for people with the right name and the right stuff. It was the only way to make the shtick work.

Soon enough, hundreds of birth-certificate-authentic Joes and Jos sent in applications. I was overwhelmed by their enthusiasm and charm. One Joe said he'd carry a pager to be on call for emergency advice. I heard from a woman who said her name was Jomama—as in "Jomama wears army boots!" And I met two Chinese artists, the Zhou (pronounced "Joe") brothers, who explained how Confucius's advice is outdated.

The twenty-six board members I finally picked were a great mix of Joes: black, white, Hispanic, straight, and gay, with all sorts of ethnic variations. They ranged in age from sixteen to seventy-nine. All of them were sharp, witty, and eager to get started. (I also found a guest spot on the board for comedian Joe Piscopo, who plays regular Joes in TV commercials.)

The first board meeting, in August 1987, set the tone. "Hey Joe!" I said as I entered the room. All heads turned my way at once. Perfect! I called the meeting to order and everyone introduced themselves. A sampling:

Retiree Joe Berger, then seventy-nine, was the Chicago White Sox batboy in 1925 and 1926, and later managed a gas station and sold men's clothing. "I'm the most regular Joe you'll ever meet," he said. "Joseph? Forget it. I won't acknowledge that name."

Cabbie Joe Curtis, sixty, said he hails from a clan of Joes: grandfather, father, mother (Jo), son, and grandson.

Hairdresser Jo Grech, thirty-nine, said she "takes care of people's heads and sometimes their brains." Her advice: "Whenever you're blue, get your hair fixed."

Joe Kelbus, forty-four, said he's been called Joe College, Sloppy Joe, GI Joe (in Vietnam), and Zipper Joe (after open-heart surgery.)

Jo Mitchell, assistant director of the Illinois Department of Financial Institutions, described herself as "female, black, a high school dropout and runaway at sixteen" who went on to get a masters degree and a gubernatorial appointment.

Payroll clerk Jo Reconnu said she knows she's a regular Jo when she sees all the big-number paychecks at her company. She had one long-term marriage (fifteen years) and one short-term marriage (six weeks). She brought the short-term ex to the Joes meeting.

Mailman Joe Sorce, thirty-four, said he gives advice to people on his route. License plate on his car, "The Joemobile": JOE-3001.

Teacher Joe Strauss, forty-four, said he has seen it all: "Seven ex-students are dead; eighteen are or were in jail." Plus, he said, he has "an overly hormonal fourteen-year-old daughter."

Ever since that first meeting, I've turned to the Regular Joes with one reader's letter every two or three weeks. And many readers even solicit the Joes' advice. A common postscript: "Zazz, could you please run my letter by the Regular Joes?" The Joes are like having an instant Gallup Poll at your service. Should you leave your husband? The Joes advisory service allows you to put your question to a cross-section of average Americans. (And even if the Joes vote 21 to 5 in favor of dumping your husband, you're under no obligation to abide by their verdict. So it's no risk.)

The Joes offer a fresh and personal perspective that I wouldn't get from experts. For instance, a frantic male newlywed brought this problem to the Joes: "I've been married for seven months," he wrote, "and, sadly, what everyone predicted has come true: Our sex life has taken a dive.

"Before my wife and I got married, we made love four times a week. Now, I'm lucky if we make love twice a month. Is this common? I don't know how much less I can take!" He signed himself "Not Enough."

"Welcome to the club!" responded steelworker Joe Barry, one of many married men on the Joes Board.

Engineer Joe Catina added: "You say you're lucky to have sex twice a month. Well, you're right. You are lucky. I know married guys who'd consider it a significant improvement to make love that often."

Now if I'd brought Not Enough's question to a sex therapist, I'd likely get advice backed by research and sex-frequency studies. Very useful, maybe. But the Joes responded from the gut and from experience. They've been there.

Also, they know what works for them. Joe Seifrid, an interpreter for the deaf, advised Not Enough: "Stop being so concerned about your needs and start considering your wife's needs. Communication is the best foreplay. Who knows? If you start scratching her back, you may be surprised by what she'll do for you."

The Joes are most often called upon to tackle domestic disputes. A man wrote:

> I'm 5-foot-7 and my wife is 5-foot-10. The height difference doesn't bother us. We're used to people staring— especially when we're dancing.
>
> The problem is my mother-in-law, who is also 5'10". She always encourages my wife to wear high heels. She says, "A tall girl looks best in heels."
>
> I wish my mother-in-law would shut up! I'd like to saw her off at the ankles, unless you or your Regular Joes have a better idea.

He signed himself "Short of Patience."

At the next Joes meeting, everyone agreed: The man and his wife needed to inform her mother that she'd given her suggestion, and nothing more needed to be said. "In so many words, tell her to keep her nose out of your wife's shoes," suggested Joe Seifrid.

Joe Kelbus advised: "The next time your mother-in-law tells your wife, 'a tall girl looks best in heels,' your wife should reply: 'This tall girl looks best with her husband.' "

"In any case, the height difference is an attribute," said Jo Reconnu. "Whenever I see a tall woman with a shorter man, my reaction is: 'There's a guy who knows who he is and likes what he sees.' The enhancing difference between a man and a woman is his masculinity and her femininity, and those intrinsic qualities have nothing to do with height."

GI Joe Bulkowski said sawing off the mother-in-law at the ankles would be a touch strong: "Instead, the next time she visits, get your power saw and take an inch or two off her heels. She'll get the hint."

Finally, legal secretary Jo Biszewski recommended that "Short" take it all lightly: "Mothers always give advice. Just give your mother-in-law a big smooch (be careful where it lands, in case she's wearing heels) and be happy that you and her daughter have a happy, loving marriage."

Some readers use the Joes input to take stock of their own feelings. "What's the difference between love and infatuation?" asked "Not Sure in New Jersey." "I don't know whether I'm in love or infatuated. What are the signs?"

"The only way to force the issue is to get married," Joe Mitchell replied. "Then you'll find out."

"My second ex-husband said that if you're infatuated after 20 years, it must be love," said Jo Reconnu. (FYI: That was the husband she was married to for just six weeks.) Reconnu also had her own very apt definition: "Infatuation is an appreciation of assumed qualities in a person. Love is an appreciation of someone's known qualities."

Then there was hospital worker Jo Marasovich, whose answers tend to be the most unpredictable on the board. She replied: "Love is something wonderful 85 percent of the time. Infatuation is spending one crazy summer with your gynecologist."

Marasovich isn't the only board member with an odd sense of humor. Joe Piscopo has also been playful with his answers. Asked if a guest can wear white to a wedding without overshadowing the bride, he advised: "Yes, if the guest is a virgin."

Many of the letters addressed to the Joes beg for tongue-in-cheek responses. For instance, a sixty-two-year-old California woman asked me to poll the Joes Board for her. She wrote: "Don't you and the Joes agree that older women with long hair look silly? The long hair only accentuates the age factor and usually doesn't look very good. An older woman shouldn't pretend to be a teenager. I say, if an older woman wants to wear long hair, she should at least pin it up. I assume you and the Joes agree."

"You mustn't assume anything about Joes' opinions," replied Jo Almaney.

Indeed, virtually all the Joes said people have a right to wear their hair any way they choose. "As long as it's well-groomed and doesn't find its way into my coffee cup, it's none of my business," said Jo Marasovich. Cabbie Joe Curtis added that women can look good with long hair at any age "whether 18 or 80! If it's clean and not dragging on the ground, it's OK by me. Short hair looks good to me also. In fact, as long as you gals leave the crew cuts to the guys, I have no complaints."

Age needn't be a factor, either, said the Joes. Hairdresser Jo Grech recalled that her grandmother had hair down to her knees. "She put it in a tidy bun each morning. It was like a work of art."

Finally, Joe Creek, a TV producer in Chattanooga, Tennessee, reminded the letter writer not to be quick to judge others: "For every person who looks silly to you, there's probably someone else who finds that you look silly to them."

The Joes often read between the lines of a letter—and respond quite bluntly. A high school girl wrote:

> I don't want to sound conceited, but I'm kind of the All-American teenage girl. I have a lot of friends. I'm a student council officer. I'm the number one singles player on the tennis team. I'm a reporter for our school paper. And I'm an honors student.
>
> The problem? No guys like me. Are guys intimidated by an overactive girl? Do all of my activities turn them off? Should I cut back?

Teacher Joe Strauss responded: "Rather than overactivity, your problem may be your focus on yourself. You used the word 'I'm' six times and the pronoun 'I' four times."

"If you blow your horn to everyone as you did to us, it's easy to see why guys might back off," said Joe Curtis. "What looks great on a resume can fall flat on a social calendar. Don't drop activities—but try to downplay the ego trip."

The Joes and the Jos rarely disagree by gender lines. All had similar responses to "Expectant Mother" whose letter asked: "Why is it that men can name their sons after themselves—Don Smith Jr., Bill Jones Jr.—but women can't honor their daughters in the same way? Don't you think that if a woman wants to name her daughter Mary Smith Jr., she ought to be able to do it?"

All the Joes and the Jos were cautious of the idea. "Obviously, you can do what you want when it comes to your daughter," said nurse Jo Cavaliero. "But inevitably, a child named after a parent gets called 'Little So-and-So,' and I can't think of any woman who would enjoy being referred to as 'Big So-and-So.'"

Jo Almaney said that people who give offspring their own name are usually honoring themselves, not the children. "And usually, the 'Jr.' is nicknamed Bud or Curly or Moose or just Junior to avoid confusion."

And what if Mary Smith, Jr., grows up to marry Bob Jones, Jr.? "Would she choose to keep her entire own name?" asked Jo Reconnu. "And if she decided to hyphenate it, where would the Jr. go?" (Betty Smith-Jones, Jrs., perhaps?)

Then there was Jo Marasovich, who suggested that it's beneath women to discuss this issue: "Men have overinflated egos. In the backs of their teeny-weeny minds, they want immortality. Junior—a male extension of themselves—satisfies this illusion. Women, on the other hand, cut the umbilical cord."

To be honest, not all readers are sold on the idea of the advisory board. Some just don't see the point. "Now that you've got your Regular Joes, who needs you?" asked Mrs. K.M. of Worth, Illinois. "I thought you were an advice columnist, not an advice collector." Another reader, who signed herself "Irregular K," wrote: "You call yourself an advice columnist? People don't write to you to have their problems answered by your Regular Joes or anyone else. If you can't handle this job, quit!

"They're not paying your Regular Joes. I think they should call your column 'All Those Joes (with occasional help from Zazz).' Unless this nonsense stops, I will not read your column!"

I gave K's letter to the Regular Joes to answer. I couldn't resist. But they took the attack in good spirits and did their best to explain the rationale behind the Joes Board.

"We're ordinary people," said Jo Marasovich, "and our problems may be the same, or closely related, to yours."

Jo Mitchell explained: "My experiences are unique to anyone else's on earth. The Joes bring myriad perspectives to a single problem, enabling an advice-seeker more options than just Zazz's."

"The Joes come from all walks of life," said homemaker Jo Owano. "We're blue- and white-collar, children, parents and grandparents. Our strength is in the combined experience of the group."

"We represent you and your neighbors," said Joe Curtis. "We don't appear that often, so bear with Zazz and with us. I think we'll grow on you."

Since the Joes are only human, a few admitted to feeling put off by K's letter. "Cool your jets," said Jo Biszewski. "Zazz is the meat and potatoes. We're the optional mixed vegetables."

Jo Reconnu's reaction: "You sound like one of my exes."

And Joe Kelbus gave Irregular K's problem full consideration. "Have you tried eating 'Regular K' cereal or eating more fresh fruit?" he asked. "You might want to see a doctor about your irregularity. If that doesn't work, then there are other advice columns you can read."

REGULAR EXPERTS

When I do use traditional experts, I try to give them questions that the average advice columnist might not throw their way.

One such request for expert input was on behalf of Nikki Edwards, age eleven, of New Castle, Indiana. She was the girl who had front row seats at one of Michael Jackson's concerts on his 1988 tour. Not only did the singer pull Nikki up onto the stage, he gave her a kiss on the cheek, too. It was the thrill of her eleven-year lifetime, and Nikki made a vow: She would never wash her face (or at least that cheek) again. "Every time I take a shower, I put a washcloth over my face so it doesn't get wet," she said.

Assuming the fifth-grader would stick to her plan, I wondered what would become of her. I figured readers might be interested, too. So I asked several experts: "What would happen to a girl who didn't wash her face for a year or longer?"

"Her parents probably wouldn't give her any dessert at the dinner table," Dr. Richard Lucas responded. But then the good doctor got serious. Humans shed skin very quickly, he explained, so the dirt that would accumulate on the top layer of Nikki's skin would be shed as well. "She'd be cleaner and healthier if she washed her face," he said. "But it's not essential for survival."

However, Nikki's pores would become clogged, there would be an odor from bacteria, and she'd surely develop bad acne, Lucas added. Needless to say, if Jackson's kiss was never washed off Nikki's face, her social life would be ruined. She might never be kissed again.

After consulting with the experts, I knew what advice to give. I told Nikki to wash her face.

* * *

Certain questions beg for certain experts, and I make it my mission to track down these experts—even if they're hard-to-reach celebrities.

"I'm a single guy in the blue-collar industry," a man wrote. "I occasionally bring fresh flowers to put on my desk at work. As a result, some of my male co-workers are casting aspersions on my character and sexual preferences. Is it possible to be a Renaissance man in a blue-collar world?" He signed himself "Mum's the Word."

One true mark of a Renaissance man is someone who ignores the small-minded and does his own thing. Still, I wanted to give this man moral support. So I took his question to former pro-football star Merlin Olsen, the spokesman for FTD florists. Merlin is a giant tough guy. And, predictably, he was on this flower lover's side. His message for the man: "Tell your co-workers that if they don't lay off you, I might have to come down to where you work and have a talk with them." Enough said.

Celebrity experts can be quite spirited when they help me give advice. I had no trouble coaxing two dueling experts to answer this question:

Dear Zazz: I am an usher at a six-screen movie theater. People waiting in the lobby often ask me what I think of the movies that are playing. I'm no critic, but I have my opinions and I've always tried to be honest.

Well, the other night, this couple asked me for my thoughts on a movie, and I gave it a rather negative review. The manager overheard me, and later said that if I can't say something nice about a film, I should fake it or say nothing.

Whatever happened to freedom of speech? And if I don't like a movie, should I fake it to keep my job?
—Opinionated Usher

Dear Usher: I brought your question to famed film critics Siskel and Ebert.

Roger Ebert observed: "Obviously, you are a movie lover and the manager is a bureaucrat."

People go to movies because they're in the mood to be movie buffs, he said. "A bad movie doesn't stop people from going to the movies. It just gives them something to talk about when they're there."

Ebert assumed that because you love movies, you also recommend good films to moviegoers. And that entitles you to your negative views. "People appreciate an honest usher," Ebert said. "It makes them feel more positively about the theater. So you're doing the theater a favor by being honest."

Gene Siskel was also on your side. "Because of your honesty," he said, "you probably should be booking the movies for the theater, rather than hauling pre-popped bags of popcorn around the lobby."

Ushers are never paid what they're worth, Siskel added. "You couldn't pay me enough to walk around in the dark telling people—whose size I couldn't see—to take their feet off the seats or to stop talking. Therefore, I suggest that you get a new job.

"Film critics can make significantly more money than ushers. You are welcome to have my job in 25 years."

Assuming you want to keep your ushering job until Siskel's job opens up, my advice is this: Couch your criticism of bad films when the manager is within earshot. In a normal voice, you might say, "I give it five stars!" Then whisper, ". . . on a scale of one to 50."

CONTESTS, QUIZZES, AND UNSOLICITED ADVICE

By writing an interactive column, I sometimes feel like I'm a pen pal to the universe. That can be a lot of fun—and a lot of work stuffing envelopes.

A reader asked if I knew of a hearty chicken-soup recipe. "I know that Jewish people are renowned for their chicken soup," she wrote.

I replied that she'd come to the right place: My mother makes wonderful chicken soup from a simple recipe passed down by my grandmother. I offered it to interested readers, and was startled to receive nine thousand requests for it!

Many of the requests had little notes attached:

"Have cold: Please send quickly!"

"I'm told my chicken soup is awful. Please send your mother's recipe ASAP."

"Zazz, I would send you a copy of my mother's Italian equivalent of Jewish penicillin, but I don't have it. The original copy is the subject of a property settlement in my divorce proceedings."

Another mail barrage got under way when a reader suggested I get involved in the White House greetings program. The President sends a birthday card to anyone eighty years old or older, and anniversary cards to couples celebrating fifty or more years of marriage. So I told readers that if they sent me their loved one's vital statistics, I'd forward all requests to the White House. Thousands of readers took me up on the offer (requests were still coming in a year later), and many wrote back after their loved ones received cards.

One man said his eighty-six-year-old mother looked bored and unconcerned when she opened her card from President Reagan. She snapped, "It's about time these Republican presidents realized what I've done for them! My daddy's daddy, my daddy, and my husband and I always voted Republican. I'm glad they're finally showing some appreciation!"

There were a few foul-ups. The White House sent a graduation card to one woman, rather than a birthday card. "I think President Reagan must be getting old and forgetful, because I graduated high school 70 years ago," the woman said.

Good reader-participation contests can be born from a simple question. To kick off my annual "I Owe You One" contest, I asked: "Who gave you such great advice that it changed your life?" In hundreds of touching letters, readers nominated relatives, coworkers, newfound friends, and long-dead mentors.

A woman who had weighed 225 pounds cited "a man I met on a late-night train who advised me to dust off my dreams and quit wallowing in self-pity." In the months that followed, she lost eighty pounds.

A woman whose ex-boyfriend helped her cope with the aftereffects of her childhood rape wrote: "We are no longer going out, but maybe his purpose in my life was to get me over this—and give me courage."

And then there was Claire Metzger. She nominated author Studs Terkel, "a man who has made a career of speaking up for those whose lives have taken a bump or two."

Claire told of the day she was fired from her secretarial job and, in tears, was walking across a bridge over the Chicago River. She happened upon Studs.

"Why the tears, kid?" he asked. She told him her story, and he responded, "Do you like the theater?" Claire nodded.

"I can't give you a job," he said, "but I'll leave a couple of tickets for a show I'm in at the Goodman. Bring a friend, have a laugh or two, and things will brighten up."

This incident took place about thirty years ago, and things did work out for Claire. Her encounter with Studs gave her a new motto: "No matter how bad life seems, there's always the theater." Ever since, she has passed Studs's advice—and a free ticket if she can—to others getting a low blow in life.

I've run whimsical contests, too. The "All That Zazz" version of *Jeopardy!* is played just like the hit TV game show. I give the answer and readers must provide the question. My answers require readers to use their imaginations and draw on their experiences to come up with entertaining questions.

One *Jeopardy!* answer I offered: "It's up to you, of course. You should decide what you want out of life. What other people think is less important than what makes you happy. To me, it sounds like you want to go for it. Well, be sure. Be brave. Be careful. And good luck."

A lot of readers sent in questions that employed more imagination than personal experience. No matter. It was just fun trying to figure out which letters were real and which were, well, less real. My favorite response to the question above was:

> **Dear Zazz:** I'm strongly attracted to two life-styles. In the first, I see myself leading a "Suzy Homemaker" existence—baking bread, waxing floors, and vacationing in Yellowstone with my husband. For excitement, we'd eat Chinese food. Needless to say, my parents like this idea.
>
> But I have this craving for a more adventurous life. I want to be a Greenpeace guerrilla. In my spare time, I'd raise albino kangaroos and become a concert bagpipe player. For vacations, I'd bring POWs out of Vietnam.
>
> I've prayed to God to help me decide, but he told me to write to you. What should I do?
> —Vanessa Ferrell

I also like to design quizzes that might help people better understand themselves and their loved ones. With a little help from a few psychologists, I devised a test to determine how likely readers were to keep their new year's resolutions. Almost half of the 247 respondents vowed to lose weight—a total of more than thirty-five hundred pounds. However, if they lost their resolve and followed past patterns, the tests showed they'd collectively gain more than eight hundred pounds.

The other big vows: to stop smoking, stop drinking, and "improve my love life." Six people resolved "to never make a new year's resolution again."

I also devised a quiz to help readers determine whether their spouses have a sense of humor. The quiz asked fifteen questions, such as:

• If you said, "Knock, knock," your spouse would respond: (a) "Someone's at the door"; (b) "Quit bothering me"; (c) "Who's there?"; (d) "Honey, stop repeating yourself."
• A comedian comes on *The Tonight Show.* Your spouse would: (a) smile at funny lines; (b) take notes in order to repeat jokes to friends; (c) deliver the punch line before the comic does; (d) switch channels to watch Ted Koppel interview contra leaders.
• After someone tells a joke, your spouse: (a) laughs along with everyone else; (b) laughs first; (c) laughs last, proving the old adage: "He who laughs last doesn't get the joke."
• Some previous generations considered humor unimportant— even sinister. The Bible hardly mentions laughter. Your spouse: (a) calls the Dark Ages "the good old days"; (b) thinks the Bible is funny as it is; (c) would be more receptive to the Bible if it had better punch lines.

The quiz also had questions like: "When you tell your spouse's jokes at a party, does he or she call you a thief, or laugh along as if he/she never heard it?" I gave a higher score to spouses who laugh along. As the old saying goes: "A sense of humor is the ability to laugh at your own jokes when your wife tells them."

Spouses who don't mind being the butt of jokes scored well, too. Many psychologists say a sense of humor is best defined by a willingness to laugh at oneself. Also, an ability to laugh at jokes is just as important as the ability to tell them. That explained this quiz question: "Does your spouse have good hearing in the left ear?" I asked this because studies show people find a joke funnier when they hear it with their left ear. Information goes from the left ear to the right hemisphere of the brain, which may be better at processing humor.

More than a third of my respondents said laughter during lovemaking is "frequent and uproarious." The other answers: "My spouse is so serious you'd think someone died" (30 percent); "I make a request in bed and my spouse responds, 'Don't make me laugh' " (18 percent); "We make love so infrequently it's nothing to joke about" (13 percent).

A woman from New Jersey took the quiz twice: One set of answers related to her husband, the other to her boyfriend. She wrote that lovemaking with her husband "is so infrequent—it's nothing to joke about." And with her boyfriend? "Uproarious!"

Rich and famous people aren't perfect. They need good advice to help them through life's rough spots, and big-dollar therapy doesn't always do the trick. So from time to time, I make a point of giving unsolicited advice to celebrities. Readers do, too.

Sometimes the unsolicited advice is subtle. One reader suggested that actor Sean Penn drink decaffeinated coffee. Readers can be blunt, too: Actress Susan Dey was urged "to splurge on a day at the beauty parlor" because she looked like she had a six-buck haircut. Michael Jackson's plastic surgeon was advised by a reader to "give the guy a rest. He barely looks human anymore. It hurts to look at him."

Two women wrote in to offer advice for Elizabeth Taylor regarding her "heavy-handed use of cosmetics": "She wears eye liner above and below her eyes, shadow from eyelash to eyebrow, and heavy Cleopatra-like eyebrows. Where are her real eyebrows? C'mon Liz, the '60s are over!

"Now that she has written a diet book, *Elizabeth Takes Off,* she ought to consider a sequel, *Elizabeth Takes Off Her Makeup.*"

Because readers are often terrific at giving advice to celebrities, I turned to them for guidance on how I might deal with a certain celebrity: David Letterman.

When I first got this job, some friends were only mildly impressed by the publicity and TV appearances. "If you get on David Letterman's show," they said, "then you'll know you made it."

Well, at first, Letterman's people called to say they were interested. They told me to leave a certain Tuesday open. They'd phone again with details.

But they called back with bad news. My personality, they said, "wouldn't mesh well with David's." In a follow-up letter, they added, "The chemistry between Jeff and David would not be right."

Now what did that mean? Am I somehow inadequate? I decided to ask readers: "If you're a regular viewer of Letterman's show, give me some advice on how to go about 'meshing' with that guy. Or tell me it's not so important to mesh around with him and I'll go on with my life." I promised to ask Letterman's producers to let me bring along a reader or two who taught me how best to behave on his show.

Scores of Letterman fans lent a hand. Among their tips:

• Willingly become the butt of Letterman's jokes, wrote John Bialas. "No one is above ridicule. If you think you are, he'll find your weakness—improper dress, a weight problem, an unusual name—and exploit it mercilessly."
• Several readers suggested I tell Dave about a "brush with great-ness." He likes hearing celebrity-brushing anecdotes. (My brush? Because I'm in Ann Landers's old office, I often use the bathroom she called her own for all those years.)
• Don't flatter David. "It really makes him nervous," wrote Marcia Weiszmann.
• Be prepared for bizarre questions. (Tom Ryan suggested several Dave might ask about the advice biz, such as: Is this a good way to meet chicks?)

Many readers told me not to worry about Letterman's snub. "Who made Dave the guru of meshable personalities?" asked Beth Kujawski. "Maybe he should try to mesh with you!"

Well, after I printed all this advice in the column, a Letterman staffer called and left this cryptic kiss-off message with my assist-ant: "Thank you, but there is nothing we can do at the present time."

I called back the staffer for some insights into unmeshableness, so I could explain my rejection in the column. I thought I was polite; I knew I wasn't wanted, so I didn't want to seem pushy. "I don't know what to tell you," the staffer said, "and if you quote me, I'll sue you."

I then decided to leave well enough alone. It's not for me to mesh with trouble.

THE LANDERS LEGACY

Written in pencil on the base of one of my office telephones is this statistic: "85 million readers."

No, I don't have eighty-five million readers.

The telephone is a remnant from the Landers era. Maybe that statistic was written on the phone to help Eppie's secretaries field calls from the media. ("How many readers does she have? Eighty-five million daily.") Or perhaps it was there to remind Eppie's staff of the power, scope, reach, and importance of her column. I can only speculate.

There aren't many other clues as to what life was like in this office before I moved in. When Eppie bolted from the *Sun-Times,* she left the place totally empty. I arrived to find rows of bare filing cabinets. A few still had subject headings on them: I've tried to guess what she kept in the others.

Starting my own filing system—keeping track of experts, pertinent news clippings, self-help books, thousands of readers' letters—was a daunting task. At first, I had the urge to call Eppie and ask, "So, how did you do it?"

What a great resource she could be for me! She could point out the pitfalls, the shortcuts, the best ways to attend to dozens of readers at once. If I needed advice, who better to turn to than the Advice Queen herself?

Even though we'd become competitors, I thought it appropriate to ask Eppie to a friendly lunch. I phoned her office at the *Trib* three times in the fall of 1987, asking if we could set up a lunch date. Eppie never returned my calls. Finally, I told her assistant that I was surprised Eppie hadn't gotten back to me.

A few days later, I received a short don't-call-me-I'll-call-you letter from Eppie. She was very busy traveling and giving speeches, she said: If ever she had time for lunch, she'd get in touch. She never did, but my calendar remains open. . . .

Actually, I probably should have known better. Though Eppie was very pleasant when I interviewed her for my *Wall Street Journal* story about the search for her replacement, I knew she found the whole matter distasteful. When I won her job, that was it. In her mind, I assume, I went from a friendly young reporter covering the story to a coconspirator.

After Diane and I were selected, Eppie issued a flurry of "no comment" comments to the media. Some folks said they'd expected her to give a simple, classy statement: "I wish them luck." After all, we were no real threat to her: She's solidly entrenched in twelve hundred papers. We began in twelve. But as her biographers and associates point out: She and her sister Popo are driven by their competitiveness.

I soon learned, from several newspaper editors who buy the Landers column, that Eppie was making no secret of what she thought of my column: Unsolicited, she told them she didn't like it.

In her own column, on several occasions, Eppie took the initiative to "set the record straight." One day she led her column with a letter asking if she had retired. "You were rather abrupt with the woman who wrote to say she thought you had retired," wrote one of her readers. "Let's be fair, Ann. Several months ago, there was a great deal of publicity about a worldwide search for your replacement. The finalists received a lot of coverage. Will you please explain exactly what happened so those of us who read about the contest to replace you will not feel like morons?"

Eppie responded that when she left the *Sun-Times,* not one word was said about retiring. She went on to write:

> The *Sun-Times* ran a contest to replace me. Keep in mind that my column is syndicated around the world and the only paper I pulled out of was the *Sun-Times.* Every one of my 1,200 additional clients remained in place. Moreover, not a single paper dropped me to take on the winner of the *Sun-Times* contest. . . . I intend to keep on doing what I'm doing as long as you, my readers, think I'm doing a good job and the good Lord grants me the strength to do it.

In my mind, her answer didn't exactly set the record straight. It may have even confused the issue by making it seem as if the *Sun-Times* selected one winner (not two), and that no newspapers picked up our columns.

After Eppie learned that *Woman's Day* magazine planned to feature her advice for Christmas, 1988, alongside advice penned by me, Diane, Judith Martin, Sally Jessy Raphael, and Letitia Baldridge, she withdrew her answers. And when the *Minneapolis Star and Tribune* announced that it planned to ask readers to vote for their favorite advice columnists, Eppie called the paper to complain. The *Star and Trib* runs Ann, Abby, Diane, and me. (Eppie won handily, but Diane and I were pleased that after just a year on the job—compared to three decades for the twins—we garnered almost as many votes as Abby.)

It's understandable that Eppie wouldn't want me or Diane compared to her professionally: She worked hard to get where she is, and might now view us as new kids bent on stealing her thunder. (Popo seems less concerned about the competition. I met her briefly at an AIDS fund-raiser and she was friendly and supportive. She told me she'd been reading my column and thought it was fun.)

Though Eppie might not want me in her life, she remains part of mine. For one thing, I still get mail for her occasionally. (I forward it on.) Also, wherever I travel or whenever I give a speech, I am invariably asked what I think of her, or how I differ from her. People always want to know if I ever wrote to her for advice. (I didn't.)

I answer these questions by first complimenting Eppie: She has developed a tremendously loyal following by writing a topical, engaging, sensitive column. I truly feel she helped turn advice giving into an art form.

And how am I different from her? Well, here's just one example: In 1988, Eppie got a letter from the mother of a teen who had gone to a rock concert. The parent was very upset. She'd heard so much about drug use and violence at these shows. She wanted Ann Landers to address the dangers of rock concerts.

Eppie replied that she might not be the best person to deal with this issue, since she'd been to just one rock concert in her life. She asked her readers to lend a hand and respond to the woman's letter.

When I read that column, I wondered who had performed at the "rock concert" Eppie attended. Was it Jerry Vale? Bobby Sherman? Wayne Newton? I then realized this: Here was a perfect example of how Eppie and I differ. I've been to scores of rock concerts. I wouldn't have to throw that question to readers. Though Eppie brings to her column the wisdom of experience and the confidence of longevity on the job, she comes from a different spot on the timeline than many of her readers. Unlike Eppie, I've never been a grandparent, and I didn't live through World War II or the Depression. But there are many other more current subjects that I may be better equipped to handle, if only because of my youth and gender.

Readers seem to enjoy the advice rivalry. I often get letters comparing me favorably or unfavorably to Ann or Abby. Sometimes, letter writers offer good-natured ways to stir things up. One reader wrote me to say he'd read that Ann Landers has the photo on her column changed every few days. "I have an idea for you," he wrote. "Why not change the name of your column on a regular basis? I even have some suggestions: All This Zazz, Some of that Zazz, Don't Zazz Me Buster, Di-zazz-ter Control, All My Zazz, None of That Zazz." (I replied that the input was appreciated, but changing the name of the column could be very confusing. As it is, many people still haven't adjusted to the column's name. I get mail every day addressed to "All That Jazz"; I've also been called All That Zap, Zazzboy, My Man Zazz, All That Jeff, All That Sazz—and worse.)

I read Ann and Abby almost every day. Sometimes, people send the same letter to all of us—they're hedging their bets, I suppose—so it makes sense to keep tabs on what letters the twins are printing. I try to approach my rivalry with Ann and Abby as good-natured fun. I've never mentioned them in the column by name, but I've alluded to them a couple of times. For instance, after Eppie printed the words to "The Star-Spangled Banner" in her column, I felt this devilish urge to somehow get involved.

A reader had written to Eppie to complain that when the national anthem is played at ball games, too many people move their lips and fake it. So as "an act of patriotism," he asked Eppie to provide the lyrics and encourage her countless millions of readers to clip her column and memorize the words.

Well, I told my readers that reprinting lyrics isn't merely an easy way to fill a lot of space in a column. It is not necessarily lazy. No, it can be a real service to readers. Americans sing many songs without knowing the words.

I decided to steal Eppie's clip-these-lyrics idea, but I wanted to offer a more current, yet still legendary song that millions of us have faked our way through. What's number one on the mumbler's hit parade? Of course: "Louie Louie."

So in my column, I offered the first stanza. I'd reprint it here, but I'm afraid you might feel obliged to tear the lyrics out of this book and, in the tradition of Ann and Abby, attach them to your refrigerator. I wouldn't want this book to fall apart at the seams before you're finished reading it. So I'll refrain from printing the refrain.

Recurring Themes

THERE ARE A handful of recurring themes that are the foundation of any advice column. Most of the letters I receive, and most of the columns I write, fit into one of the categories in this chapter.

It is not always easy to take a fresh approach to these subjects. Nor is it always necessary. Sometimes, people want to read about the same old problems because that's what they have.

And yet, from time to time, I strive to give readers an unexpected way to look at a familiar subject. I like to write essay columns that are off the beaten track, about people and events that are sometimes far from the norm. I know I've succeeded if readers respond by saying they identify with the emotions I've written about—if not the experiences. I know a column was worth writing if readers send letters admitting, "I learned something I didn't know" or "I've got a different outlook now."

All of the stories that follow generated just this sort of reader response.

MOTHERHOOD

As a mother, her devotion to her offspring was all-encompassing. She gave them life. She nurtured them. And when her lack of foresight left them near death, saving them became her only thought.

The mother I'm writing about is a duck that lived on the grounds of an apartment complex in Farmington Hills, Michigan. She had created a nest and laid thirteen eggs under a tree outside Susie and Marty Rosenzveig's bedroom window.

Susie and Marty are friends of mine, and at the time they first noticed the eggs, their daughter was one year old. Observing the incubation was akin to waiting for a miracle, Susie told me. "We felt like expectant parents again."

Soon enough, on a bright Saturday morning, Susie and Marty heard a chorus of chirping outside their window, and amid scattered eggshells, saw thirteen tiny ducklings. Then, on Sunday, Susie woke up and found the nest empty. She'd been told it would happen this way: The ducklings would line up behind their mother, and off they'd march to start their lives.

But a few hours later, as the sky filled with storm clouds, Susie realized something was amiss. She saw the mother duck across the street running around in a frenzy.

Susie went to investigate, and, to her horror, discovered that all thirteen ducklings had fallen between the bars of a sewer grate. What happened was obvious: Leading her babies to a nearby pond, the mother had walked across the sewer, and one by one (plop plop plop), all thirteen of her tiny offspring had fallen in. By the time she turned around, her babies were stranded in a pool of muck eight feet below.

"We didn't know how many were alive," Susie said. "We called the fire department, the humane society—no one would come. They said they don't do this sort of thing, and, besides, it was a Sunday. We felt so helpless."

Finally, someone recommended Harry Markham, a chimney sweep who traps raccoons living in chimneys, then releases them in the wilderness.

Though Harry had never rescued ducks, he agreed to try. By then, it was 4:00 P.M., and the mother duck was still holding a vigil by the sewer. In her own failed rescue effort, she had cracked her beak by jabbing at the grating.

Harry and his partner, Frank, first had to chip off all the tar that sealed the sewer grating to the street. "Then we had no idea how deep the water was," Harry later explained. "The only way to reach the ducklings, we decided, would be for me to hold Frank by his ankles and lower him in."

For Frank, a 170-pounder, the sewer opening—two feet wide— was a tight squeeze. And for Harry, the weight of his partner seemed to increase by the minute. As Frank grabbed at the ducklings, they swam about helter-skelter. It was a tedious process, made more tense by the approaching storm: The ducklings would likely drown once rainwater gushed into the sewer.

In some ways, the scene was reminiscent of the rescue of young Jessica McClure from a well in Texas. But at the sewer in Michigan, there were no TV cameras, no cheers for the brave—just a few people doing all they could for thirteen vulnerable ducklings.

Eventually, Frank grabbed the ducklings, one by one, and handed them up to Susie, who waited with a cardboard box. "They were so wet and helpless and beautiful," she said. As each duckling was brought up, Susie counted: one, two, three . . . and finally, happily, thirteen.

When Susie let the ducklings loose, the mother ran for them. "It was an emotional reunion," Susie said. "We could see their relief and happiness." Within minutes, the ducklings lined up behind their mother and completed their journey to the pond. The threatened downpour soon followed.

Susie offered Harry and Frank money for their work. They refused. "Seeing those ducks march away was enough of a reward," Harry said.

Susie never saw the duck family again, but as a new mother, she had trouble shaking her fixation on the incident: "That mother duck was so protective. Her babies were her life. Then, due to forces beyond her control, she almost lost all thirteen of them. It seemed so tragic. I couldn't help thinking: Life is pretty unfair, even at the duck level."

I found several lessons in this story, which I shared in the column. It helps us realize that a well-meaning parent can unintentionally lead us to danger. It shows us the depths of a mother's love. And it teaches us, too, that sometimes all of us—whether fowl or human—can depend on the kindness of strangers.

FATHERHOOD

The man from Madison, Wisconsin, had let a piece of his life slip away, and now he wondered if it was too late to get it back. He signed his letter to me with only his initials: "D.W." He was embarrassed to sign his name. A man shouldn't run from fatherhood, D.W. felt, and that's exactly what he'd done.

He had gotten divorced shortly after his son's birth. He later allowed his ex-wife and her new husband to adopt the boy. Years passed. Now his son was eight years old.

"My ex-wife and her husband don't mind if I visit him," D.W. wrote, "but they live 150 miles away, so I don't get there very often. I'd now like to move closer to them so I can see my son regularly. Am I unrealistic to expect a relationship after almost abandoning him for all these years?

"I feel good seeing him and we get along pretty well. We play ball and talk. Should I move closer and try to be a father again, or is it hopeless?"

I brought his question to my Regular Joes Advisory Board. Several of them have been divorced. Almost all of them have children. They suggested that D.W. shouldn't expect too much, too soon. Nor, they said, should he immediately move into the neighborhood and disrupt his ex-wife's family environment.

"It's never too late to start a relationship with your son," said hairdresser Jo Grech. "As for being a father to him, the man he lives with is his dad."

"Always keep in mind what is best for your son, not just what you, as a born-again father, want now that the boy is eight and fun to play with," said Texan Jo Catalano.

"If you feel you abandoned him, how do you think HE feels?" asked civil servant Jo Mitchell. "You may have a lot of explaining to do."

I thought the Joes were on target. I told D.W. he should proceed with caution.

Well, a fifth-grade class in Edina, Minnesota, read the column and asked if they could lend D.W. a younger perspective as Junior Joes.

"This type of problem is all too familiar to many children," teacher Ellen Swanson wrote. "My students' letters are surprisingly insightful. They empathize not only with the child but with the feelings of adults as well."

Many of the fifth-graders wrote from their own experiences. And almost all of them suggested that D.W. pull up stakes in Madison and move closer to his son. "I've been through a divorce and my dad moved away," wrote Megan. "He has changed, and it seems like I don't know him anymore. I would do anything to have him move closer so I could know him again. He means so much to me."

Theresa wrote: "The boy probably wants to get closer to his real father. I'd like to get closer to mine. My dad lives 520 miles away, and I wish he'd move closer so we could get better acquainted."

"I've been in the same position as the boy," wrote Rusty. "What the father should do is see the boy as much as possible." Kacey concluded: "Personally, I love my father and don't know what I would do without him."

"In the winter I live with my mother in Minnesota, and in the summer I live with my father in North Carolina," wrote Kelly. "I think D.W. should try to work something out, sort of like what I do."

Almost all of the children encouraged D.W. Asked Ryan: "What's the worst that can happen? He'll know his son a lot better, and they'll do things together." Ingrid even suggested that D.W. "move a block away from his son so the boy can visit his father as he would a friend."

A few students had reservations. "If I were the boy, I'd be confused," wrote Molly. "I'd have questions like, 'Why did my dad leave and why does he want to be with me now?' I'd be scared to ask him. So that's why the father should get together with the boy and talk it over. That's my opinion."

Most of the students, however, were adamant that D.W. must move closer. "It means more than anything to a kid to know his parents," explained Elisabeth.

Megan even made a prediction: "If the boy never got to know his father, it might lead to frustration and bad grades. The boy will probably lead a happier life by knowing his real dad. Knowing that your family loves you is an important thing in life."

Advice can come in many forms from many sources. These ten-year-olds wrote from the heart, and their insights offered courage to other absentee fathers. Several readers asked me to pass on their thanks to the class. One man wrote:

> I am a recovering alcoholic, and my wife left me when my daughter was two. It has been five years since I last saw my daughter.
>
> I'm feeling better and really want to see my child again. I've always wanted to see her, but when my life was in shambles, I knew it was best if I didn't.
>
> Some people have advised me not to get in touch with my ex-wife and daughter just yet. They said the results might damage my sobriety. So I've taken their advice and lived with the pain of not seeing my child, of wondering how she is, what she looks like, and what she thinks of me.
>
> But then those precious fifth-graders helped put my mind at ease. I just wanted them to know how much faith and hope they've given me.

CHILDHOOD

In 1971, when Joe was thirteen, he spent six months by the ocean in Atlantic City, but never made it into the water. He lived on his back or his stomach, locked in a cast from his belly to his toes.

At the Children's Seashore Home, many residents spend their childhoods belted onto gurneys. They're wheeled onto the boardwalk each day to taste the salt air and endure the stares of passersby. "People would offer me money," Joe recalls. "When you're in a body cast, people assume you'll never walk again."

But Joe prayed that his painful operation and endless months in a cast would make him a regular kid. Though he was miserable, the idea of walking normally kept him going.

Joe never was a regular kid. After he was born, a staph infection lodged in his blood, eating away his hip socket. His right leg was shorter than his left. He walked funny.

I went to school with Joe in the suburbs outside Philadelphia. I remember him as a tall, serious kid forever branded by a bad limp. He had friends. But some kids—especially his neighbor, Bruce—teased him and imitated his limp.

"Bruce was the neighborhood bully, hassling me from the time we were little kids," Joe says. "He saw me grow up with one leg shorter than the other. He had to be pretty small-minded to pick on someone like me."

Joe always was told to be strong. Smile when you limp, Joe. Ignore cruel kids like Bruce. But there were so many setbacks— "times when he needed luck and it didn't come," says Joe's mother, Rita.

I lived in Atlantic City in the summer of 1971 (I was twelve), and twice visited Joe at the home. He worked up a smile, talked about a TV sportscaster who had visited, and introduced me to other kids. But I mostly recall being uncomfortable and eager to leave. I also remember riding my bike past the home later that summer—and not stopping to say hello.

Maybe the home didn't belong in "a happy-time place," Joe says. "When you're in a body cast, watching everybody live it up in the surf, you get depressed."

Yet maybe it was all worth it. For once out of the cast, Joe's legs were the same length. Over time, his limp began to fade. His smile became genuine, not forced.

Then one morning the following year, Joe stepped out of class into a crowded hallway. For those of us in the hall that day, what happened next is remembered in slow motion—like the shootings of Kennedy and Oswald.

Bruce approaches and sticks out his leg. Joe falls, terror-stricken. Bruce runs. Joe is on the ground, writhing.

His doctors were blunt. Joe would have to repeat the whole process—the surgery, the body cast. He successfully sued Bruce, but that was little consolation. "For years after that, Joe was bitter and depressed," Rita says. "He lost some of his spark."

He needed many more operations. (Today, when he's wearing just swim trunks on the beach, "he looks like he's been cut up by a shark," says Rita.) In fact, Joe was in a hospital on that day in 1982 when a face from his past appeared on the TV news. Police finally had caught a multiple rapist who had been terrorizing Philadelphia for weeks. The alleged rapist was a truck driver. It was Bruce.

Joe turned to the patient in the next bed. "I know that guy," he said, and thought to himself, "His time has come."

Many people write me about insurmountable handicaps and cruel people they can't forgive. Their letters remind me of Joe and his childhood courage. I told his story in the column, thinking he might inspire some readers.

Until I called Joe to write the column, we'd been out of contact for eleven years. But I was glad to find him in good spirits. Though he was laid off from his print-shop job, he was optimistic.

"I wasn't fortunate growing up," he told me. "I'd ask, 'Why me?' a lot. Now I try to be positive. Some people can't walk. I can."

Though Joe said he can't forgive Bruce (who ended up with a long prison term), he does feel some good came out of the tripping incident. "I had a lot of time to think after that. And I taught myself not to dwell on the past."

Sometimes, Joe walks around the old neighborhood, from his house to Bruce's. "I was always the kid inside, looking out the window at other kids running around," he told me. Now he's comfortable with that memory. "I can't change how I was born or what I've been through. It was fate. I learned to accept that."

He hadn't lost hope. "You know," he said, "somehow, something will come through for me."

BROTHERHOOD

One day in the fall of 1987, the LaPorte brothers, Victor and Tony, checked into neighboring rooms at the hospital.

They had always been inseparable—palling around together as boys, coowning a bowling alley as young men, counseling each other through the troubles and joys that defined their adulthood. It was fitting, then, that they would share the most traumatic moment of their lives.

The story that follows is their love story. I learned about it after Victor entered my "I Owe You One" contest.

I had asked readers to name the person to whom saying "I owe you one" would be the ultimate understatement. Victor, forty-five, nominated Tony, his forty-year-old kid brother.

He wrote his entry letter from his bed at the University of Illinois hospital: "All the words in the world couldn't express the love and gratitude I'm feeling . . ." he began.

For three years, Victor had been terribly sick. His kidneys were failing. He would pass out. His arms were black and blue. Infections made things worse and dialysis wasn't a cure. He was dying.

Doctors said a kidney transplant would help and Tony kept offering his kidney. Victor refused. He didn't want to put his brother through the pain of an operation or the risk of living with one kidney.

But Tony insisted. "Hey, I love you," he kept saying. "It's something I want to do."

Tony never thought twice about his offer. "If I needed the transplant, Victor would be there for me," he said. "No doubt in my mind."

Transplant doctors say the reason God gave us two kidneys is so we can donate one. It took them a long time to convince Victor of this. Tony would likely be fine with just one kidney, the doctors said. In a moment of weakness, Victor agreed to the transplant. Tony was thrilled, but the process wouldn't be easy.

Several times, the brothers went to the hospital, only to have the operation postponed because of Victor's infections. Tony never thought of backing out. After each disappointment, he announced: "We're coming back!"

Tony got Victor a T-shirt that read I'M NO QUITTER, which Victor wore each time to the hospital. And Victor gave Tony an ORGAN DONORS MAKE BETTER LOVERS T-shirt. "I couldn't quit," said Victor. "Tony wouldn't let me."

The operation was hardest on Tony. Doctors had to remove part of his rib to get the kidney out. His recuperation took longer. He had more pain.

Victor felt guilty. It was tough facing his brother. They spent a lot of time in their separate rooms, clutching their guts to hold back the pain, hoping the transplant miracle would take hold.

One day, Victor's wife brought him my column asking for "I Owe You One" entries. "It was like fate had directed us to the contest," she said.

Victor wrote: "Because of Tony's unselfishness and love, I have a chance to see my four children grow up. Already I'm feeling better. . . .

"I'll never know my brother's pain, fears and feelings. All I know is the love we share. How can I tell him thanks? Maybe by letting everyone know that I have the greatest brother in the world." When Victor finished his letter, he couldn't see it through the tears.

Tony was reluctant to accept the award: a plaque, and a limousine ride with his brother to a complimentary hundred-dollar dinner. "I don't feel like a hero," he said. "And I wasn't Victor's only support. He had his wife, his children, our mother."

"This is how I want to repay you," Victor said. "If you don't like it, take back your damn kidney!"

When I told Tony how Victor called him "my inspiration," Tony said, through tears, "My brother had a hell of a lot to live for. He didn't need me."

After some prodding, Tony agreed to accept the award on behalf of the thousands of kidney donors. He said he hoped his story would inspire more donations. "It's the most rewarding thing I've ever done. I saw my brother laugh the other night. I've never seen him laugh so hard. That's all the reward I needed."

SISTERHOOD

Down in Texas, Evelyn dropped everything. She told friends she had a meeting in Chicago. She told her husband and kids to fend for themselves for the weekend. And she told herself that, after fifty years, this was a trip she had to make.

"There was no way I'd miss my reform school reunion," she said.

And so there she was on the night of the big reunion—reminiscing with 130 other "girls" who once were locked up at the House of the Good Shepherd.

I'd heard about the reunion from a reader, Geri Cieck, who wrote:

Shepherd was once home to thousands of Chicago's most troubled teenage girls—myself included. We were sent there because the courts saw something in us worth saving—some redeeming quality, however small.

It was up to the Good Shepherd nuns to take street-smart girls and give us purpose and direction. The sisters helped so many of us become happy, productive young women. Twenty-five years ago, they turned my life around.

We are now trying desperately to organize a first-ever House of the Good Shepherd reunion. After all these years, we've found some "girls" who lived in the House as long ago as the 1920s. But other sisters or graduates, many of whom moved across the country, have been harder to find. Could you help get the word out, Zazz?

I was glad to mention the reunion in my column. That's how Evelyn learned about it: She read my column in the *San Antonio Light.*

I was also invited, and I found it to be a remarkable evening.

The reunion took place in a cloud of smoke. The nuns didn't seem to mind that so many grads were chain smokers. They were just thrilled to see the girls—grown up and prospering.

Most who attended were the success stories, with good jobs and secure families. They were proud of themselves and of one another. They'd made it. "We were as close as sisters," one graduate said. "We leaned on each other, learned from each other, and cared for each other. It's like a family reunion, not a school reunion."

Some who didn't show up, I was told, never rebuilt their lives. They remained troubled, involved in crime. And a few stayed away out of embarrassment. "One girl married someone very wealthy and prominent," said Marilynne. "She said the reunion would remind her of a part of her life she doesn't want to remember. That's okay. We never liked her anyway."

Marilynne had stolen a car as a girl and would have gotten into further trouble, she said, if not for Shepherd. At the reunion, she reminisced with "girls" she hadn't seen in decades. Most were runaways from awful home situations until they were sent to Shepherd in the early 1960s. "We were locked up," one said, "but it felt comfortable to finally have restrictions."

These were tough girls—nicknamed Fox, Dwarf, Elephant. Over the years, many tried to escape from the house. "I chased a lot of runaways," recalled Harriet McNamara, who began working in the Shepherd laundry in 1930 and stayed on the payroll for a half century. "They'd climb over the wall and I'd run after them. I had my first heart attack chasing one girl. She's not here tonight."

Several nuns told me that the girls' toughness often masked low self-esteem and a desperate need for love. The sisters gave advice most had never heard at home. "We told them to aim high; they were worth it," said Sister Mary Jane.

Mary Forsythe was Mother Divine Heart at Shepherd. "The girls felt like nobodies," she said. "Most weren't bad. They were just teary-eyed girls who needed to talk. Our remedy: A great deal of love."

Love wasn't always enough. "Some kids were so disturbed, they needed more than we could give," Mary said. "One girl who'd been sexually abused by both parents tried to drown another girl. We had to send her away. She needed serious psychological help. But she got down on her knees, grabbed my legs, and begged me not to make her leave. To this day, I wonder what became of her."

A few grads had some bad memories of Shepherd. Marilynne still resents that she wasn't allowed to attend her father's funeral. And the sisters wouldn't permit girls to reveal where they were headed when they were released. "They didn't want us to stay in touch," said Dolores. "They were afraid of bad apples getting together" on the outside. As a result, the reunion committee wasn't given access to lists of graduates.

Mary Forsythe worried that because she was harsh when she ran Good Shepherd, some at the reunion might be bitter. But every woman she met was glad to see her. "They threw their arms around me and said thank you."

"We had discipline, but we also had love," explained Evelyn, who left Shepherd in 1939.

When the grads presented Mary with a plaque of appreciation, many had tears in their eyes. So did Mary. "You are the most fantastic girls on earth," she said. "I love you, I've always loved you, I'm proud of you."

Even though it was a room full of adults, many of whom now have grandchildren of their own, for that moment, they were again Good Shepherd girls. I looked at their faces. Positive reinforcement and loving words could still make them glow.

LONELINESS

Ray was bored and lonely and there was nothing good on television. So he picked up his phone and, as usual, dialed 221-8192.

At that very moment, I was walking down Fifth Avenue in New York City with Fred, an old college buddy. A pay phone was ringing. Always curious, I answered it. Ray was on the other end.

"Hello, how ya doin'?" he asked.

It was about 5:30 P.M. and scores of people were hurrying by on the sidewalk. Ray seemed relaxed.

"My name's Ray," he said. "I just thought I'd call."

I introduced myself. When in area code 212, I do as the natives do.

Many people would have hung up on a guy like Ray, dismissing him as some "crazy weirdo." But like I said, I'm curious. So I fumbled for my notebook and proceeded to ask him so many questions that he soon thought *I* was the crazy one in the conversation.

Ray said he was twenty-five and didn't have many friends. Though he was employed as a newsstand clerk, he said he reads very little and watches a lot of TV. He began calling this phone at the corner of Fifth Avenue and Forty-second Street (across from the library) six months earlier. A coworker turned him on to the idea. "This guy is really addicted," Ray said. "He calls every day."

Same phone booth, too. Ray's only explanation: "It's an easy number to remember." In fact, sometimes, when Ray calls and gets a busy signal, he assumes his coworker is on the phone. "I'm not as into it as he is," Ray said. "I only call a few times a week."

But why call at all? Why talk to strangers? And why do strangers talk back? "Not everyone in this world is too busy to have a little conversation," Ray said. "You get to know a lot of interesting people this way. And they get to know me. There are so many nice people in New York."

I looked back at the swarm of New Yorkers speeding by on the sidewalk. How many of them would take the time to answer a pay phone and converse? "You'd be surprised," Ray said. "A lot of people just hang up, and that's fine. I understand completely if they're too busy for me. Sometimes I'm too busy for them."

Ray told me the phone usually is answered after twenty rings. When he's got a voice on the other end, he tries to sound friendly, harmless, and outgoing. Three out of four people hang up immediately. "But I get some real talkers. Everything from businessmen to drunks to lonely people—a lot of lonely people—to people looking for jobs. I can't give them a job. But I can talk to them about it."

Women rarely answer, Ray said. "I guess they're afraid. They shouldn't be. All I want to do is talk."

Ray stressed that he's not a pervert or a criminal. He's just a guy with a boring job and no social life. The pay phone is a lifeline of sorts. "I'm a normal guy," he said. "I do normal things. In a few minutes, I'm going to watch *Family Ties.*"

By contrast, some of the "talkers" are quite strange. One man offered him three hundred dollars to make a sex movie. Others propositioned him or asked him for money. "One gentleman wanted me to fulfill his fantasy by picking him up and leaving him in the street—nude. That's weird, very weird." Others have babbled on so much that Ray had to hang up on them.

Ray said he lives ten blocks from the phone booth and has visited it "just to see where I'm calling." He has met only a few talkers in person. "It's strange. We never seem to hit it off. I haven't made any long-lasting friends."

About fifteen minutes into our conversation, my friend Fred, who'd been standing by impatiently, shaking his head at me, suggested that we move on. "Enough already," he said.

Before saying good-bye, I asked Ray to call right back. I wanted to see who would answer. I stepped twenty yards back and soon the phone was ringing. Thirty times. Scores of people walked by. A young woman was about to pick it up, but her friend pulled her away, giggling. A businessman answered, listened for a moment, then hung up. Ray called again. Forty-two rings. A woman answered and hung right up.

Then the phone was quiet. Fred and I stood there waiting—"I feel foolish," he told me—but Ray didn't call again. Figuring *Family Ties* had started, we headed down Fifth Avenue.

In my job, I get a lot of mail from lonely people. The closing line in a letter I once received sums up the sentiments in many: "I don't want much; just someone to talk to."

No, I wouldn't advise lonely readers to start calling pay phones. But Ray was doing okay for himself. He'd found his way to cope. I give him credit.

I wrote a column about Ray, and ended it by telling readers: "If you're ever at the corner of 42nd and Fifth in New York and Ray calls, give him my regards."

GRIEF

In the same instant, Marc Goldberg watched his daughter come into this world—and leave it. Throughout his wife's eighteen hours of labor, he knew it would be this way. Doctors had said the baby would be stillborn. And yet, in the horror of the moment, Marc felt a tinge of joy.

"Despite my grief," he says, "I couldn't help but marvel at the miracle of life. Two people blend themselves and create a child. It's magical."

Much of society tells Marc and his wife, Colleen, that they lost a fetus, not a child. "We will tell you differently," Marc says. "This was a real person. We bonded with her as surely as if my wife had breast-fed her and I had diapered her. But we lost her before we even got to know her.

"To the outside world, we lost a pregnancy. Colleen was pregnant. Then she was not. But Colleen had carried our child inside her. It was an amazing experience. By feeling our baby move, I felt bonded to her, and more bonded to my wife."

The pregnancy, Colleen's first, had progressed perfectly for five and a half months. Then, on August 31, 1987, she realized she hadn't felt the baby move in twenty-four hours.

Marc had read that sometimes a baby will take the day off. But Colleen was hysterical. She knew her body, she said. She knew what was happening inside her.

Marc drove her to the hospital. "I'm not a religious person, but I prayed all the way there," he says.

At the time, Marc was thirty, Colleen twenty-four. They hadn't prepared the baby's room with furniture or toys. In Judaism, tradition dictates that you wait. This had made sense to the Goldbergs. "We wanted a healthy baby, then we'd celebrate," Marc says. And yet, in many ways, it was as if the baby had already moved into their suburban Chicago home and turned two people into three. "We loved that baby. We had plans," he says. "We'd chosen a boy's name, a girl's name."

At the hospital, a nurse tried in vain to find the baby's heartbeat. Sensing the Goldbergs' terror, the nurse allowed that maybe the battery was dead on her electronic stethoscope. It was a kind remark, but the couple saw through it.

After more testing, Colleen and Marc were left alone. For forty minutes, they cried and hugged one another, waiting for a miracle.

A telephone rang. "It was the doctor," Marc says. "He was very clinical. Cold. He said the baby was dead. I couldn't believe it. He was right in the hospital, and yet he couldn't face us.

"Obstetricians deal with life. Maybe some are unnerved talking about death."

Marc told his wife the news. "It was the hardest thing I've ever had to do. It was devastating."

To induce labor, Colleen was given a drug with intense side effects: vomiting, diarrhea, painful contractions. Because the baby's health was not a concern, she was also given strong pain-killers.

After eighteen hours, her water broke and a baby girl was delivered. She was twelve inches long and weighed two pounds. She would have been named Elizabeth and so she was.

When Elizabeth was taken away, an anesthesiologist arrived to prepare Colleen for a D and C (dilation and curettage). Marc, nervous that his wife was already heavily drugged, began asking about the procedure. This offended the anesthesiologist. He said, "Listen Dad, would you like me to do it without anethesia?"

"He knew what we'd just been through and yet he called me Dad," Marc says. "He wasn't some young resident. This guy was fifty years old.

"The nursing staff was very caring. But some of the doctors were incredibly insensitive. At a time when we needed them the most, they gave us the least."

The Goldbergs had Elizabeth cremated, and buried her remains under a small gravestone.

In the weeks that followed, some of the couple's friends suggested that it was time they "got over it." Why did they seem to be in mourning? people wondered. "We feel we lost a child," Marc says. "That put us at odds with society."

One happy note: Exactly a year after the stillbirth, Colleen gave birth to a healthy girl. "We love Samantha so much," says Marc. "But I still think about our other baby every day."

The Goldbergs belong to a nationwide support group for bereaved parents. Called the Compassionate Friends, the group helps parents resolve their grief together. There are no dues. Members often have just one thing in common: All have lost a child.

Some are mothers and fathers of teen suicides and accident victims. Others are parents as old as eighty-five who want to come to terms with the deaths of fifty- or sixty-year-old children.

The death of a child has been called the ultimate grief by psychologists. Of all sorrow, it may be the hardest to overcome. One explanation is that parents see themselves in their children: their smiles, their eyes, the way they think or laugh.

Parents who survive their children often suffer alone. Friends and family can't always understand the depths of their grief. It is natural, then, for bereaved parents to turn to each other.

At Friends meetings, members break into subgroups. The Goldbergs' subgroup is composed of parents who lost children as infants or in stillbirth. These are the parents who often feel most alone. The parents of a teen who dies can be consoled by people saying, "He was special to me, too" or "I also loved him." But parents of a stillborn have no one else to mourn their loss. No one knew that baby.

The Goldbergs and others in their subgroup helped me write a column outlining how they'd like their friends and loved ones to deal with their grief. Among their requests:

• Don't tell us, "It's God's will" or "It's all for the best" or "There was probably something wrong with the baby, anyway." Why would God choose our children to kill?
• What can you say? Simply this: "I'm sorry." No words can make our grief disappear, so you needn't try so hard. A sympathetic "I'm sorry" goes a long way.
• Don't be surprised that we're depressed, and don't expect us to quickly snap out of it. Surveys show that most people assume it takes no time at all—between forty-eight hours and two months—to deal with the grief of a stillborn or infant death. This is a terribly wrong assumption. Experts say it actually takes two to five years to recover emotionally. Please give us time to grieve.
• Let us talk about our children. Acknowledge them. Say their names. Sometimes, their names are about all we have, and we hold on tight. We don't have home movies or school photos. Our only recollections are of an infant. Try to help us preserve that memory.
• Recognize that in some ways, our grief may be more painful than that of a couple whose older child died. We not only lost our child, we lost all our dreams for him. Also, some of us can't have more children. This intensifies our hurts.
• Acknowledge fathers as well as mothers. You might be more inclined to ask a husband, "How's your wife doing?" Those of us who are fathers wish someone would ask, "How are you doing?"
• If you are a grandparent, recognize that you lost a grandchild. The father of one woman in our group vowed to plant a tree in his yard for every grandchild. Yet when her baby was stillborn, her father didn't plant that tree. He should have. The tree would have acknowledged both his grandchild and his daughter, who brought that child into the world.

NEIGHBORHOOD

One day in the winter of 1985, a new neighbor appeared at a busy street corner in the affluent Chicago neighborhood of Lincoln Park. The man sat down on a bus stop bench, folded his hands, hunched his head, and there he remained—in the worst rains and the bitterest cold.

Whatever brought the homeless man to that particular bench at Clark Street and Deming Place, he wouldn't say. He talked to almost no one, and he refused spare change or offers of help. He just sat, filthy and disheveled, day after day, stirring community unease and resentment.

He told a priest his name was Jim, but in his tattered poncho and gray beard, he looked more like an unwashed Moses. He warily guarded his piles of junk, stacked beside him in rusted shopping carts. To residents, he was an eyesore who tested compassion—and prompted frequent complaints to the police.

Even on subzero days, Jim was seldom invited into nearby stores; shopkeepers said his odor drove customers away. He shocked passersby by urinating into plastic antifreeze jugs that he pulled under his poncho. And he infuriated bridal parties by showing up uninvited for weddings at a nearby church.

One night in the summer of 1986, Jim and his belongings were mysteriously set on fire. He survived and retreated to an alley in another neighborhood a few miles away. But his bench still bore an angry charcoal-black burn—a reminder to Lincoln Park of its limitations and frustrations regarding the homeless.

At the time of the fire, I lived a block from the bench and was still working for *The Wall Street Journal*'s Chicago bureau. Many of us in the neighborhood were disturbed by Jim's plight, but felt helpless. I wrote a *Journal* article about the growing backlash against the homeless, and used this unknown man to illustrate the problem. Only later did I learn the secrets of Jim's life. By then I was already working at the *Sun-Times,* so I shared his troubling story with readers of my advice column.

People everywhere fear the crime, panhandling, and unsightliness associated with the homeless. As the ranks of the homeless swell and lap against the doorsteps of the affluent, actions against them have increased. Shopkeepers in some cities douse discarded food with bleach to prevent "dumpster-diving." Upscale New York neighborhoods have used barbed wire to keep sleepers off heating grates.

"Street people have become like nuclear waste. Everyone screams, 'Not in my neighborhood!' " Philip Walters told me. A Lincoln Park resident, Walters witnessed his neighbors' indignant opposition to plans for an emergency shelter.

The shelter wasn't built, but Jim's plight became Lincoln Park's problem anyway. And this community's struggle with his presence said a great deal about society's failures in dealing with the homeless. To write about Jim, I talked to many of his "neighbors."

"He's a modern parable," said the Reverend Robert Oldershaw of St. Clement's Church, just down the street from Jim's bench. "His story disturbs us, shocks us, and keeps us searching for some kind of further meaning."

At the busy corner of Deming and Clark, Jim sat on a bench emblazoned with an advertisement trumpeting SELF STORAGE in large orange letters. He wasn't welcome. "No one wants a vagrant camping by your door," said the manager of the Greek restaurant across the street. "It's like someone pitching a tent on your front lawn."

On the coldest mornings, young professionals would awkwardly keep their distance from Jim as they waited to board warm buses heading downtown. Although few even acknowledged his presence, Jim was unavoidable. "I felt so guilty," said Jerry Zucker, a resident. "I would walk behind him instead of in front of him. I didn't like making eye contact."

The shops within view of Jim's bench—a sushi bar, a beauty salon, a record store, a hat store—provided a striking contrast to the old man. "This is a neighborhood of rich yuppies eating 'designer' ice cream," said Rod Stasick, the manager of Dr. Wax Records. Record buyers rarely mentioned Jim, except to joke about him. "Customers asked if he was Dr. Wax, keeping an eye on the place," said Pete Nathan, a clerk at the store.

Jim didn't drink or panhandle, and he seemed intelligent, even compassionate. At his bench, he'd read newspapers left behind by commuters and write in a little notebook. And each day, he'd rise from his bench to walk a young blind man across the street.

"He had a sort of Christmasy face," said Fred Strauss, executive director of the Lincoln Park Chamber of Commerce. "If I were casting a Santa Claus, he'd be a good choice." Added Pete Nathan: "He looked like an old philosopher, as if the bench was his alternative life-style."

Jim often attended mass at St. Clement's but never took communion or went to confession. The first time he arrived, Father Oldershaw told him to leave his bags of junk outside. When Jim refused, the priest said he first locked him out, but then "had a conversion" and invited Jim in.

Jim became a regular, if unwanted, guest at the church's weddings, hunched near his bags at the side of the ornate, Byzantine sanctuary as bridesmaids in their finery glided down the aisle. "Fathers of brides would demand that I 'get rid of the bum!' " the priest said. "I'd say, 'He's not a bum, he's a parishioner.' "

Jim rarely spoke, though he once yelled at a group of boisterous children for "disrespecting the house of God." The children dismissed him, and told Father Oldershaw derisively, "He's just a bum."

Jim told Father Oldershaw only that he was born in Kentucky of German descent, and that he carried an ice pick under his poncho for protection. Did he ever work? Did he have a family? Though many street people will tell their life stories for a cup of coffee, Jim refused to answer questions. Some residents, myself included, would try to speak to him or give him money, only to be rebuffed with an angry wave of the old man's hand.

Most residents speculated that, like an estimated one third of the homeless, Jim had a mental disorder. "I'd like to know what went on in his head," said Raymond Hudd, the hat store's owner. "We all need something to hold on to. For him, maybe it was the trash in his shopping carts."

Whatever the case, Jim was among the hardest of the homeless to help. Enigmatic and antisocial, he offered no last name and no history. With no address, he got no public assistance. Unwilling to accept money, he got no aid from overburdened social agencies.

Residents grew desperate to rid their neighborhood of Jim, angrily calling the police, hospitals, their alderman—"everyone but the animal shelter," said the manager of the Greek restaurant—all to no avail.

Jim couldn't be kept in a mental hospital unless he was deemed a threat to himself or others. And he couldn't be sent to jail for safekeeping. Police in Chicago may not force people into shelters involuntarily. "People say, 'Look at this poor guy sitting there and the police won't do anything.' But we can't just hijack a guy off the street," said Richard Adamski, the policeman who handled Jim's "benevolent arrest" after he was burned.

Lincoln Park probably demonstrated as much charity toward Jim as most affluent neighborhoods would. "Lincoln Park isn't heartless," said Fred Strauss of the chamber of commerce. Older residents took Jim leftovers from their senior-citizen lunch programs. Young people tossed him cookies as they walked by. Residents regularly donate to canned-goods drives at their health clubs. And two blocks from Jim's bench, they lined up by the hundreds in the spring of 1986 for Hands Across America, the nationwide benefit for the homeless.

But a few months later, on a workday just before dawn, Jim was set ablaze, and no one called the police until noon. That's remarkable, since scores of rush-hour commuters saw Jim and the charred remains of his junk strewn across the parking lot of the sushi restaurant. Jim survived, police said, because the flames didn't eat through his many layers of clothing. Neighbors suspected young hoodlums or nearby businesses, which denied any involvement. "It was a concerted effort to get him out," figured Pete Nathan, who had received anonymous calls at his store demanding that Jim be removed.

A fingerprint check showed that Jim had no criminal record. Police released him the day of the fire, and he soon turned up in an alley beside St. Alphonsus, a church just north of Lincoln Park. On Election Day, workers at a polling place in the church complained that Jim and his bags got in the way of voters. Police arrested him for disorderly conduct, couldn't get him to talk, and released him without charges to a mental hospital under the name "John Doe."

A week later, doctors at the hospital still hadn't determined what to do with "John Doe." "We haven't even gotten a first name out of him," a spokesman told me. In mid-November of 1986, Jim was released back to the streets, and he returned to the neighborhood near St. Alphonsus.

In Lincoln Park, the mood about Jim after the fire was a mix of pity, sadness, and relief. Father Oldershaw said he will always consider the intersection of Deming and Clark to be "Jim's corner." But the sentiment wasn't widely shared.

Neighbors told me of a man who witnessed Jim burning from his third-floor apartment overlooking the bench.

The man didn't go to the police, and he refused to come to the door to discuss the fire when I visited him. His wife spoke through a crack in the doorway, without unhooking her safety chain. "We never," she said, "saw any man on that bench."

When I first wrote about Jim, his only identity to most of us was his homelessness—and the stir he caused. But then a man named

Glenn Andersen read my *Journal* piece and saw something familiar in the limited description of this homeless man. Andersen, a retired Chicago Transit Authority supervisor, suspected he'd finally found his old friend, Jim Northcutt.

Andersen went to the alley where Jim was living. Jim shooed him away. But even though Jim's face looked so old and weathered—he was fifty-eight but appeared to be twenty years older—Andersen knew that his hunch was correct.

In the early 1960s, it turned out, homeless Jim was a respected engineer who helped introduce computers to the transit authority. "For months, they couldn't get the computer to work," Andersen recalled. "Jim stepped in, reprogrammed the thing, and became a hero."

Always a pack rat, Jim was a rail buff who filled his apartment with train memorabilia. He was intense, religious, and "always eccentric," Andersen told me. "He liked to eat just one meal, every few days." In 1968, Jim disappeared. "I never would have guessed he was in Chicago, right under our noses," Andersen said.

After finding his friend, Andersen contacted Jim's sister, Gail, a Detroit teacher. (She'd been searching for Jim for years—through the Internal Revenue Service, her senator's office, the Veteran's Administration. She even ran advertisements offering a reward to anyone who knew his whereabouts. The one response: "How much?")

Gail flew to Chicago, but Jim wouldn't talk to her. She kept coming back. She learned of his history of mental illness, sensed that he was physically ill from all his time in the streets, then became his guardian and had him hospitalized. The doctors' diagnosis was that he had leukemia.

On February 29, 1988, Jim died. Luckily, unlike many homeless people, he was buried with a last name, under the care of a loved one.

In the months before he died, Jim did speak to his sister. "I resolved to let him know he was loved and searched for," she said. "I'm proud, not ashamed of him. He had a strong sense of spirit and compassion."

Gail asked that I write a column offering advice to people with relatives like Jim. "We're afraid of mental illness, especially in our siblings, because we're most like them," she said. "But we can't be frightened. We have to help."

Thrilled that she got to see her brother before he died, she talked of feeling a new kinship with the homeless. "I look at street people and I wonder, 'Who has been looking for you for ten years?' The homeless are precious to someone. It's sad that they don't know it or can't return that love."

I went to Jim's funeral. It was held in the basement of St. Clement's—in the same room where the homeless congregate each winter night.

For a man who lived in self-imposed isolation, there were a lot of people there: a hundred or more. Some were shelter workers or church members. A few were homeless themselves. But many were ordinary folks who saw the information about the service in my column, and decided they wanted to be there. One man brought his children. Perhaps they could learn something, he said, from knowing Jim's story and hearing the priest's thoughtful sermon.

Jim's mother, a woman well into her eighties, had come up from Kentucky. She carried a photo of a young, handsome Jim in a World War II army uniform. She told stories of how bright and loving he was as a child. She hadn't seen him in forty years.

I got many letters about Jim. One woman wrote:

> Like you, I lived in Jim's Chicago neighborhood and saw him often. My most vivid memory of him is from five years ago on a cold, windy winter night. He was in the park, howling in the wind, his coat open and blowing around him.
>
> Here was a man who refused to speak to others, and yet the pain of the cold and wind forced him to use his voice. He was a survivor, despite the indignities and hardships he suffered.
>
> I am the mother of a 28-year-old mentally ill son. He has spent years in mental hospitals and on the street. When I looked at Jim, I often wondered if I was looking at my son, years from now.

Another letter writer wrote:

> I remember Jim. For a while he lived on the bench across from where I worked. A co-worker and I would periodically bring him blankets and hot lunches. He'd accept food from us, but not money.
>
> I'm not looking for recognition for my good deed: This is

between God and me. It's just that I'm tired of hearing people say that people like Jim ought to take care of themselves. This is not possible in all cases.

Goodbye Jim. I'm happy for you. You're no longer home-less.

Matters of the Heart

ROMANCE AND LOVEMAKING issues are the backbone of traditional advice columns, and they are certainly a staple of mine.

Almost all relationship questions fall somewhere within the six basic journalistic questions—Who? What? When? Where? Why? and How? Some examples:

WHO?

Suspicious spouses have the most Who? questions, and they are usually frantic when they contact me.

"Something is up," a man writes. "I don't know if my wife is sleeping with another man or another woman (knowing her, it could be either, or both), but I'm certain she's cheating on me. I want to find out who it is and I want to find out now."

A woman writes: "I know my husband is having an affair. The evidence? (1) I saw a note to 'April' saying 'Sorry about Wednesday.' (2) I called his office and there's an April who works there. (3) One day I pressed the automatic redial button on our telephone and a woman answered. I said, 'Is this April?' She said yes. In shock I hung up."

Another woman writes: "I think my husband is involved with someone else. I've found blond hair in his car and on his jacket. He and I both have dark hair."

I advised all three letter-writers to confront their spouses. Maybe there are explanations. The first letter-writer might just be paranoid. The second might be relieved to learn that her husband's relationship with April is all business. And the third might discover that her husband has lent his car and jacket to his new male colleague—the blond, long-haired Norwegian.

Okay, Okay, so maybe these letter-writers' spouses are sleeping with who-knows-whom and are making things worse by flaunting their affairs. But in any adultery situation, Who? is not the most important question. The more vital questions are: Why? and Where do we go from here?

WHAT?

These are often the cosmic What is love? questions.

A male reader calls the hot line: "I've been dating a woman for four months now. She says she loves me, but when I ask her why, she says, 'Love cannot be explained.' I disagree with her. If she loved me, don't you think she'd be able to put her feelings in words?"

My reply: "Trite phrases or gooey greeting-card sentiments do not necessarily guarantee that love is genuine. If you ask me, love means never having to say, 'Love means never having to say you're sorry'—or other 'love' cliches. I agree with your girlfriend: Love needn't always be explained. Let it be enough if she says she loves you."

Other What? questions deal with an endless variety of What should I do? dilemmas.

A man writes: "I've been happily dating Bette for six months. But now we've learned that her old boyfriend will soon be getting out of jail on parole. He went to prison for stabbing a guy he thought was seeing Bette. I don't want the same thing to happen to me. What can I do?"

My response: "Look at the bright side. Maybe Bette's ex is no longer jealous, or even interested in her. Maybe he's reformed. Maybe he bought a one-way ticket to Guam. Or maybe he'll get out of the pen and meet a train, head on. You might feel better sharing your concerns with the police and his parole officer. And just to be safe, don't neck in public."

Then there are the What am I getting myself into? questions: "My girlfriend and I are planning a rafting trip and invited an old friend of mine along. My girlfriend has told me she thinks he's attractive. Now I've learned that he says the same thing about her. I'm starting to think it's not such a great idea for the three of us to go away together."

My reply: "Tell your girlfriend about your concerns. So she finds him attractive. That doesn't necessarily mean she's interested. Then again, if you've seen "Deliverance," you know bodies can be left behind on rafting trips. So play it safe. If you question anyone's motives, consider canceling the threesome. But recognize, too, that your girlfriend and pal don't need a vacation with you to find each other."

A man writes that his fiancée returns to her hometown in South America several times a year. There's no room at her parents' house, so she stays with her ex-boyfriend, whom she sleeps with. The man continues:

> She says that if she goes to bed alone, she always stays awake, feeling scared and lonely. She assures me that her boyfriend is just a friend to her now and that nothing happens—no lovemaking—when they sleep together.
>
> She thinks I'm making a big deal over nothing. But I'm going nuts!
>
> I won't tolerate such behavior after we're married. I'm especially worried because I'll soon be leaving for the Army. What should I do?

I replied:

> Be careful. You'll go into the Army and she'll call in the Marines—to read her a bedtime story and tuck her in.
>
> Tell your fiancee that she'd better find another solution for her insomnia—or another guy to marry.
>
> Before you enter the service, you might reconsider this marriage. Are you sure you want a wife who can't tell the difference between a night light and an ex-boyfriend?

A forty-year-old man writes to say that his girlfriend borrows his car to drive her kids to her ex-husband's house: "It's far and she spends the night. She gets all dressed up and fixes her hair to go there. When she's out with me, she looks like a bum! What should I do, stop lending her my car?"

I advised: "Talk to her about your feelings. Perhaps she gets dolled up to visit her ex to prove to him that she's doing swell and looking great now that you're in her life. Or she could have unresolved feelings. By talking this through, you'll learn her emotions, and she might decide to fix herself up for you, too."

Finally, there are the What do you think? questions:

"My boyfriend and I have been going out for more than a year.

The other night, while we were making love, he called me by his ex-girlfriend's name. I got very upset, and he said I was overreacting. He said he made a mistake and I have to forgive him. What do you think of this?"

I answered:

Yes, he made a mistake, but look at it this way: He's yours, not hers. Would you rather he made love to his ex and called out *your* name? I say forgive him. And recognize that the brain behaves in strange ways during sex, often sending unpredictable impulses to many parts of the body—tongue included. Indeed, there are many "foot in mouth" positions in lovemaking.

WHEN?

These questions often come from people on treadmills ("When should I give up on this rotten guy I've been dating for 14 painful years?") or from people on cloud nine ("When can I tell Bob I love him? This weekend, we're going out on our first date.") My answers: "Soon" to the first question, and "Not yet or he might run" to the second.

People who ask When? questions often want a concrete timetable, and that's not always possible. A mildly retarded woman who works in a hospital wants to know when she could marry her boyfriend, who is also retarded and is a part-time janitor. "We've been dating for five years and love each other very much," she writes. "His parents say we shouldn't get married until he is more settled. And they think he should be the breadwinner, not me."

I replied:

Couples, whether handicapped or not, often decide to postpone marriage until their lives are more settled. There may be wisdom in the suggestion that you wait a bit.

However, his parents are sexist to presume he ought to be the breadwinner. If both of you contribute in some way to the upkeep of the household, and if you're able to maintain a loving and mature relationship, then marriage makes sense.

Set a goal: a date by which you'd like to be engaged. And

discuss your plans with a social worker, employer, relative or someone else whose judgment you trust. They'd know your needs and abilities better than I would.

WHERE?

The biggie in this category: Where can I go to find someone to love?

A woman writes: "I'm a single woman in my mid-30s. I'd like to meet nice men, but my ventures into the extracurricular world lead me only to women. I took tennis lessons and met lots of athletic women. I took a night course and met lots of intelligent women. I joined a health club and met lots of fat women. Where can I go to find single men?"

I replied:

You'll find single men at a strip club, but you probably wouldn't like the show. Single men go hunting, but you might not look good in a fluorescent orange vest. Single men play poker, but they might not be overjoyed to have you in the game unless you're a chump.

My point is, there's no magical gathering place where you can meet single men. As many happy couples attest, you often meet the right person when you least expect it.

This doesn't mean you should go home each night, crawl into bed, eat junk food, watch garbage TV, and read trashy novels. Go on with your life, doing things you like. Keep putting one foot in front of the other, whether strolling down a pretty street or walking in the mountains with the Sierra Club.

The important thing is that you do what interests you. If you don't like tennis, stay off the courts. If you don't like birds, don't join the bird-watching society no matter how many hunks you've seen around town with binoculars and bird encyclopedias.

Circulate at parties, pick activities that appeal to you and keep your eyes open. There are no guarantees Mr. Man-of-Your-Dreams will show up. But chances are, if he's doing what he likes and he meets you, doing what you enjoy, you'll be that much more compatible.

The other frequent Where? question: Where is my spouse when he/she is out of my sight? A man writes: "I've been married for 12 years. My wife works in a restaurant until 2 A.M. and goes out after work, often until 8 A.M. She says she's a big girl and where she goes at night is none of my business. Where does she go and don't I have a right to know?"

My response, in part: "It doesn't take an all-night disc jockey to know what's playing between 2 A.M. and 8 A.M. And yes, you have a right to know where she is all night and she has a responsibility to tell you."

WHY?

These are often the hardest questions to answer definitively. From the Why? mailbag:

Question: "Why do women give out their phone numbers to guys they never intend to date?"

Answer: "Giving out a seven-digit number is easier than giving a speech. Some women would rather give their numbers than have to say, 'I'm sorry, I'm not really interested.' Or: 'I'm not really attracted to you.' Or: 'I've got a boyfriend'—which could be a lie they'll have to embellish. Many women don't realize they'll have to give a speech anyway—when the man phones."

Q: "Why do unmarried adults always get asked, 'Why have you never been married?'"

A: "The answer to this is simple. People are nosy. The way to respond? Answer this personal question with a question: 'Why do you ask?' or 'Why have you never been divorced?'"

Q: "Why does my husband buy pornography, even though I know he loves me and we have a healthy sex life?"

A: "Men are drawn to pornography, some experts say, because it satisfies their primary fantasy: access to beautiful women without risk of rejection. Looking at unattainable naked women allows a man to remember his masculinity and indulge in his fantasies without threatening what he cherishes most—his real life. At least that's what some experts argue."

HOW?

How-to questions are endless. How do I approach him/her? How do I ask him to wear a condom? How do I tell my wife I want to divorce her to marry her sister?

Question: "There's a very attractive man I see every morning at the bus stop. We've never spoken, and I don't really know anything about him, but he's on my mind every day. I'm trying to get him to talk to me and ask me out. How do I do this?"

Answer: "The best way to get a person to talk to you is to talk to him. Start a conversation: 'Do you have the time?' Or: 'Is it 8:30 yet?' Or: 'What time would you guess it is?' (You needn't be original to be successful.) There's no reason to expect him to make the first move. Show some initiative. And, of course, if you discover he's married, show some restraint."

Q: "I'm a white man married to a black woman. Every time we're walking down the street, we get terrible stares. How can I stop this from happening?"

A: "You can stop the stares by walking on opposite sides of the street, or walking 15 paces behind your wife, or divorcing her. Short of wearing bags over your heads (people would stare but you wouldn't know it), I see no other solutions in a society that remains so perversely race-conscious. So I say, smile, grab your wife by the hand and ignore the people rude enough to stare."

Q: "All my boyfriend wants to do lately is sit home and watch public TV. Sometimes he'll sit there for five straight hours. How can I tear him away from the TV?"

A: "At least your boyfriend is upscale in his viewing addictions. But the best time to drag him away is during the frequent and monotonous public TV fund-raising drives. Even diehard fans can't sit through too many hours of guys in tuxedos pleading for cash. After your boyfriend makes his contribution, invite him out to dinner, the opera or an in-person appearance by MacNeil and Lehrer."

Q: "I'm very much in love with my girlfriend, but her house is crawling with cockroaches. I'm extremely uncomfortable when I'm over there. Now she wants me to move in. How can I politely tell her why I'm declining?"

A: "Just be honest. It's very 'in' to hate roaches—always has been. If housekeeping is the problem, help your girlfriend clean up her act. If her house is infested, call an exterminator. And if nothing helps (and she can't or won't move), remember this: Roaches love the dark. If you're going to make out with your girlfriend, do it with the lights on."

AN AIRBORNE MR. LONELYHEARTS

Wherever I go, I carry a duffel bag of mail and my portable word processor. I get a lot of work done on planes, especially if I'm alone in a row, with no seatmate to second-guess my advice.

Well, on one particular flight from Phoenix to Chicago, I was leafing through readers' letters and eating airline peanuts when a flight attendant recognized me from my photograph in the newspaper. She asked if I had a few minutes to spare.

A young woman back in 16-C was crying, the attendant said, and had told a fellow passenger that she needed advice. The attendant overheard her and immediately thought of me. (I know flight attendants are trained to ask whether a doctor is on board if a sick passenger needs help. Pressing an advice columnist into service is a somewhat broader application of this policy.)

Anyway, I headed to 16-C and met Sissy, a beauty-salon receptionist. That flight, routine for most of us, signaled a crucial moment in her life. After living in Phoenix for eight months with her boyfriend, Robert, she had left him and was on her way to Chicago, where her mother lives. As our plane hurtled through the clouds between Arizona and Illinois, Robert had no idea that Sissy was gone.

Sissy was scared and depressed. Though very pretty, she looked drained. She was trying to be brave. She felt in her heart that leaving Robert was necessary and healthy. Yet a large part of her wanted to turn the plane around so she could try again to make a life with the man she still loved.

In the skies above America that night, surely there were thousands of people like Sissy. They were fleeing their pasts and jetting to new homes, torn by the still-fresh memories of old homes. If it's any consolation, I told Sissy, many others shared her sense of upheaval, maybe even on our very airplane.

But I did more listening than talking. Sissy told me how the relationship began beautifully, but collapsed into a well of distrust and disharmony. They fought every day. She felt addicted to him. "I was so attached to him, so insecure," Sissy said. "I went through his phone book and called every female name in it."

Was Robert unfaithful? "Probably." Did he love her? "Yes." Could he make a commitment to her? "No. That was impossible for him." When he'd find her gone, would he try to lure her back? Sissy paused. "First he'll be in shock, and then, I don't know."

In the plane's belly, Sissy's eight boxes and suitcases, her wordly goods, were proof that she meant business. She had left Phoenix. She had made her statement. And yet she asked me: "If Robert wants me back, should I go?"

From ten minutes of conversation, I couldn't make that decision for her. But I told her this: She decided to pack up those bags, to travel thousands of miles to get away from him. She should trust her instincts, at least at first.

Then I asked: If Robert would come to Chicago to get her, what would she do? She took a breath, perhaps for strength, and said, slowly: "I won't go back. Not yet. I'll tell him to think about us for a few months. Then we'll talk again."

She smiled meekly. It's so hard to be brave. I wished her well, asked if I could share her story in my column, and headed back to 5-A, where I started writing her story on my minicomputer.

I often hear from readers who are afraid to end troubled relationships. Maybe, I decided, Sissy could be an inspiration to them. Yes, changing your life or leaving a lover can be terribly painful. But if it's healthier in the long run, people must find the courage to do it.

GETTING DUMPED

There have been a couple of occasions when I thought that sharing a personal memory might lend some perspective to a lovelorn issue. Once, it was after a young man wrote with this story:

Dear Zazz: I met Judy at a friend's party and felt I was falling in love. The next day, I asked my friend for Judy's phone number.

Judy and I went out twice, and for me, those dates were magical. I told friends that no woman had ever captivated me so completely. She was smart and beautiful, with this terrific laugh. People said I glowed when I talked about her.

When I called her for a third date, she was hesitant. I tried again two days later. Again, she gave excuses.

I soon learned that Judy had met another man at the same party where she met me. I remember the guy: tall, with round "John Lennon" glasses. Judy began seeing him the week of our first date. In fact, she told her friends that she was crazy about him!

I felt humiliated. I'd been proclaiming my feelings for

Judy to anyone who'd listen. Judy was falling in love, too—
only I wasn't the guy in her head. I felt hurt, betrayed, angry.

I might be overreacting, but I think it'll be a while before
I can pursue another woman. Why didn't I see this coming?
—Dumped

I told Dumped to go easy on himself. "When we're taken in by
someone's charms, we don't always see clearly," I replied. "If it's
any consolation, almost everyone who has ever had the courage to
fall in love has, at some point, been hurt and embarrassed. All we
can do when we're dumped is move on."

I then told him that I had a humiliating story to top his.

In the first week of my senior year of college, I met Beth, a very
sweet, very pretty freshman. I was infatuated by both her beauty
and her wide-eyed view of college. She was intent on getting
beyond her small-town roots. I was fascinated by her fascination
with the wider world. And, okay, maybe I was most fascinated by
her good looks.

I had just broken up with my longtime college girlfriend, and so
I asked Beth out. We went to the symphony and I thought we had
a wonderful time. We went on two more dates, and I told everyone
about my infatuation.

I knew, of course, that other guys on campus would be interested in Beth. After all, at my college, the male/female ratio was
four to one. Even if girls like Beth wore ski masks, they couldn't
keep the guys at bay.

Well, I asked Beth out a fourth time and she said, "We'd better
talk."

We met in the lobby of her dorm. She was nervous, businesslike.
I remained smitten, but I knew something was up.

"I want to be honest," she said. "Since I've been on campus, I've
been interested in three guys."

I took a long breath, unable to conceal my disappointment, and
asked, "Who are the other two guys?"

"The other three," she answered.

I'd never had a brick thrown at my head, but in that instant, I
knew what it felt like.

Needless to say, the relationship died right there. Beth had a list,
I wasn't on it; there wasn't much more to talk about. We shook
hands, I tried to smile, and I got on with my life. What choice did
I have?

After telling Dumped this story, I advised: "Don't let your experience with Judy make you gun-shy. Romance is always a risk. I've found inspiration in a marvelous song called 'If You Don't Want My Love,' by J. D. Souther. He sings: 'If you don't want my love, well, the road goes on without you . . .' That's the best attitude to take."

FORMULAS FOR ROMANCE

The early days of a romance are marked by the sweetness of discovery, and the sharing of new adventures and passions. But as time passes, and couples get married, they often settle into their routines, take each other for granted—and forget.

I sometimes get letters from readers I call "romantics with a cause." They believe that many marriages could be saved by well-intentioned smiles, some kisses here or there, and a few shared recollections of how great things were. From time to time, I print their letters because they're absolutely right. Here's one:

> **Dear Zazz:** I've got advice for married men. My message is for my husband, but I know it could apply to thousands of your male readers, Zazz. Here goes:
>
> Bring back that romance, that spark, that thrill. Be spontaneous. Pull over to the spot where we used to neck in the beginning. Let me know you still remember.
>
> Do something wild. Kiss me in an elevator when the doors close. Let me know you still think I'm sexy. Sometime when I'm washing the dishes, come up from behind and give me a big hug like you used to. I'll do the same for you when you're on the couch watching football on TV.
>
> Tell me you love me. Call me in the middle of the day to say it. Whisper something sexy in my ear when we're in a crowded room.
>
> Take the time to listen to me. Don't make me have to cry just to get you to listen. And let's laugh together. You used to always try so hard to make me laugh. Keep trying. That's one of the reasons I fell in love with you.
>
> For all these little things you remember to do for me, I promise to do for you 10 times over in return. You have my heart and soul in your hands. Please cherish them, as I trusted you with them when I gave them to you. I love you.
> —Donna R.

On behalf of husbands everywhere, I replied:

Dear Donna: Beautifully said. Maybe more than a few husbands will be inspired next time the elevator doors close, or when the dishes are being washed.

But such advice works both ways. And many husbands could give a message to their wives that might go something like this:

Honey, I still love you, and I know you love me. But let's bring back the romance we once had.

Remember how you used to get dolled up to see me? You'd put on your favorite dress, your best perfume, that locket I gave you. Now, sometimes it seems you don't care how you look when we're together. And what happened to that locket?

I keep suggesting that we exercise and go on a diet together. You're never interested.

And when I'm over on the couch watching the game, be patient. Don't stand in the kitchen, fuming. Come over during a commercial or time-out, give me a hug, and I'll hug you back. I try to give you space for activities that interest you: talking on the phone to your mother, for instance. Indulge me a little, even if the game goes into overtime.

Try not to shake your head when I tell variations of the same old jokes. Those very jokes used to make you laugh so hard when we first met. I'm sorry my sense of humor has gotten so predictable. But if you'd at least smile, I'd be reminded that you love me.

And, sweetheart, baby, try to loosen up. If I whisper something sexy in your ear, don't roll your eyes like you usually do. Whisper something sexy in return. You know the words. Use 'em!

I love you, honey. I gave you my heart and soul. I know you still have them. But where'd you put my socks?

THE DILEMMA OF OLD LOVE LETTERS

"I'm about to get married," a man wrote. "For sentimental reasons, I'd like to hold on to my old girlfriend's love letters. Is that a bad idea? Should I throw them away?"

This is a frequent question, and I feel strongly about how I answer it. "Those letters are a record of your past, your emotions, your youth," I told the groom-to-be. "Throwing them away would be like tossing out a part of yourself. There's no need to do that, especially if you're in a trusting relationship. Tell your fiancee that holding on to them in no way diminishes your devotion to her."

When readers write to me with concerns about their old love letters, I've written back and shared with them a story from my past. In its fleshed-out version, it goes like this:

One Wednesday in the fall of 1984, I received 237 letters in the mail. All were originally sent to my college girlfriend between 1976 and 1981. By me. With her wedding just weeks away, she thought it best to box them up and return them.

Was there no longer any room for my letters in the farthest corner of her deepest closet? That wasn't the point, said my friends. She was embarking on a new life with a new love. Someday, when her husband enters their shared closet in search of a bowling ball or a lost scarf, he needn't stumble upon proof of my onetime affection for his wife.

So why didn't Ilene just throw the letters out? Well, she knew I'd find them invaluable. In the earliest, I had just turned eighteen. In the last, I was twenty-two. And rereading them reveals a maturation more pronounced than the improving grammar or diminishing innocence. The letters mirror my thoughts at a tender time when many of my contemporaries and their lovers were on the phone. They can only recall past love from memory. I've got mine on paper.

I first wrote to Ilene in my freshman year during history of Western civilization class at our college in Pittsburgh. My note offered sarcastic comments about both history and Western civilization. "Dinner?" was my postscript. She accepted.

Within ten days, we'd traded "I think maybe I might love you" letters. A week later, the declarations could have been written in concrete. We were certain.

The letters enhanced our romance in ways the telephone would have inhibited. I rambled on with sappy clichés, devoting entire essays to such subjects as her eye shadow. And Ilene's perfumed letters kept her in my thoughts by stinking up my room. I fell for her because she was delicate, caring, and ambitious. She was also awfully pretty. And so the poetry: "Your wondrous looks befuddle me, 'til I want you silly puddily."

I went home to Philadelphia each summer to be a hot-dog vendor at Phillies games, and we'd admonish each other for writing less than once a day. Struggling for letter-fodder, I'd describe inning-by-inning action—in the stands. Many of my tales of hot-dog sales, written after nights at the ballpark, still have yellow traces of mustard on them.

One summer, Ilene got a job at a bank in Tromsø, Norway. At first, she wrote naively of white-blond Nordic bankers who seemed more interested in her jet-black hair than her views on Norwegian economics. The sun there doesn't set all summer. "Stay out of dark places," I wrote her. She soon figured out what I was talking about.

By senior year, though, our letters were less frequent, less passionate, less truthful. She wrapped herself in career planning. I had wandering eyes. We broke up, got back together. Then, on Valentine's Day, I wrote: "Roses are red, / Violets are blue, / Had I nine lives, / I'd spend three with you." It wasn't nearly enough of a commitment.

After graduation, I headed to Florida to be a newspaper reporter. She ended up at Harvard Business School. The letters continued, there were visits, but she found someone else, I was tantalized by Florida and its women, and Ilene and I became just warm memories to each other.

Then in 1982, for a Valentine's Day newspaper article, I asked readers to send in copies of love letters they'd sent or received. Voyeuristically, I read about five hundred correspondences. There were the long-married couples ("Nobody in the world except you can remember certain things I remember"); the long-distance romances ("I watched as you crossed the street for the last time, trying hard to memorize you"); the marriage proposals ("I ain't got nothing, ain't had nothing, don't want nothing, 'cept you"); the doomed adulterers ("I didn't even know your favorite color"). And there were the lovers caught by war—the World War II pilot who wrote of "leaning across 6,000 miles to kiss you," and the kid in Vietnam who penned clumsy poems to his high school sweetheart and later died in battle.

These letters convinced me that love, despite our audio and video age, may still be best expressed and best remembered in writing, however awkward or inarticulate. And old flames are hard to forget, even if a new love is satisfying. Many happily married people said they had long hidden away old lovers' letters because, well, because.

Naturally, all of my perusing made me miss Ilene, who by then was in Manhattan to be near the man she would eventually marry.

"Follow your heart," my mother suggested. And so I sped to see her, feeling not unlike Dustin Hoffman chasing Katherine Ross in *The Graduate.* I could almost hear Simon, Garfunkel, and my mother harmonizing in the background.

I called Ilene from the skyscraper where she worked. "Guess where I am." I said.

"Florida?" she guessed.

"The lobby," I answered.

When we met for lunch, we realized it was over. We blamed maturity and circumstances. We talked about our jobs, our ambitions. Then we reminisced about our letters. We pictured ourselves as octogenarians, keeping the past alive in bags and boxes.

But that's not how it turned out, of course. Out of the blue, she felt compelled to mail me back my letters. And then what to do with them was up to me. I was left with two large boxes: her letters to me and my letters to her. Everything.

Well, my decision was easy. I didn't expect to read any of the letters but once or twice more in my life, but I had room in my closet and I wanted to keep them.

When I packed the letters away, I realized that I might eventually marry a woman who wouldn't want those boxes resting by her boots and shoes. I assumed I'd agonize over the dilemma. And then, I feared, like many good husbands, I'd decide it best to get rid of them.

Luckily, when I married my wife, Sherry, our commitment to each other was beyond question. We knew we'd each had experiences and relationships, good and bad, before we arrived in each other's arms. That's part of what prepared us for our life together. We're both pack rats of sorts. So she saves her old boxes of letters. I have mine. And what's most important, we have each other.

A LIFETIME OF LOVE

In May 1944, when Ralph Illion was a sailor stationed in the Pacific, he wrote a love letter to a girl named Gloria back in Chicago. He also wrote to his wife, Lillian.

You can imagine Lillian's surprise when she opened her letter and found Gloria's included.

Dear Gloria: It's about time I introduced myself to you. We haven't met, yet I have heard so much about you that I must confess I've fallen in love with you.

This confession might come as a shock to you, since you know nothing about me except what other people have told you. Don't take them too seriously. I'm really not a bad guy once you get to know me. And I can assure you that my feelings for you will never change as long as I live.

I hope this makes the proper impression and you won't think me too ardent or bold. Send me a picture of yourself soon that I may cherish and look upon while we are so far apart.

Please keep my love for you locked in your heart, to be opened only when I call for it in person.

In January 1989, I received a photocopy of this letter. It came from a reader. In an encore of my send-in-your-love-letters solicitation idea, I had asked readers to send me old love letters so I could write a column about them on Valentine's Day. This letter to Gloria was one of the sweetest I received. Have you figured it out?

Gloria was three months old when Ralph, her father, sent it to her. He'd been on a combat vessel for ten months and had never seen her.

Gloria, now in her mid-forties, also mailed me the letter her dad wrote in May 1944 to her mom. He ended it: "Oceans of love and a kiss on every wave to my sweetheart." Gloria told me her dad was seventy-nine years old and still happily married to Lillian.

Readers sent many other beautiful love-letter stories, and I filled my column with them. Their love notes ranged from cultivated eloquence to awkward, ungrammatical scribbles. But whether a letter was inspired prose or a singsong poem smothered with clichés, one thing was obvious and touching: The person who shared the letter with me was either thrilled to receive it or proud to have written it.

Perhaps the most touching story came from Alice Aubele of Woodridge, Illinois. In the 1920s, she explained, her parents worked for the same company and sent love notes by interoffice mail. Her dad once wrote to her mom: "Honey, you know it isn't bright out today, but it seems to me as if the sun is shining and the birds are singing. I am so happy that I can't sit still—all because of you."

Wrote Alice: "Zazz, I know these notes are not earth-shaking, but they are a prelude to a love story that lasted 50 years."

Alice's parents, Harriet and Richard, got married in 1926. They raised four children through the Depression, and went on to experience the familiar struggles, sorrows, and triumphs of middle-class lives. "Through it all," Alice wrote, "Dad never ended his day without telling my mother, 'I love you.'"

In 1974, Harriet got sick and went into a nursing home. When she came home ten months later, "Mom and Dad were like kids at Christmas!" Alice wrote. But their joy was shortlived:

> Five days later, a despondent young man who lived in the apartment below them ended his life by filling the place with gas from his oven.
>
> The first explosion destroyed the front of the building. Dad could have escaped, but Mom was trapped and he refused to leave her. The second explosion took both their lives. We buried them together in a single grave.
>
> After the funeral, I drove past the site of the fire. In the parking lot stood my mother's dresser. It was battered and burned, but was still in one piece. In a drawer, I found a box tied with a satin ribbon. It contained about 30 love letters. Most were short, mundane notes in which Dad might ask Mom to meet him after work. But every note ended with a declaration of Dad's love for her.
>
> These are the only things of value, real or sentimental, that survived the fire. They are my treasured heirlooms and will be passed on to my daughter. They are, after all, a testimony to a love that was the reason for my coming into existence.

The Wisdom of Age

SENIOR CITIZENS MAY be the most loyal readers of advice columns. Newspapers are often more central to their lives than, say, television is. TV is pervasive, but older folks often feel more comfortable with their morning paper.

Also, the older generation is used to writing letters. So, unlike many younger readers (who prefer the instant appeal of calling our hot line), senior citizens are more apt to be writers: Their correspondences routinely reach five or ten pages. And if they forgot to include something, they're not bashful about sending follow-up letters. (Some write me once or twice a week.)

Their problems? Loneliness, illness, boredom, inattentive children, a sense of helplessness. Their strengths as writers to the column: Their letters (commenting on society, today's ethics, and the people, good and bad, who populate my column) lend perspective and wisdom to each discussion. In their lifetimes, they've seen most of the problems I deal with in the column. They're a big help to a young advice man.

All generations are tied to one another. This chapter is about old people, yes. But no matter what your age, you're sure to see yourself somewhere in the pages that follow.

Senior citizens are not immune to love troubles. And often, I find, their ages are irrelevant as I formulate my answers.

A seventy-nine-year-old widower wrote to tell me that his eighty-three-year-old "ladyfriend" was pushing him to marry her. He was very reluctant. He liked Betty's company, but figured he was too old to marry again. "My kids are in their fifties and they're encouraging this marriage," he explained. "Betty's kids are even older than mine, and they like the idea, too. Now Betty and all the kids are ganging up on me, pressuring a proposal."

My response:

I'll give you the same advice I'd give to someone decades younger. If you don't want to get married, don't give in to pressure.

Tell Betty that you care for her, but she'll have to live with your terms. She can have you in the current, very pleasant arrangement—and quit pressuring you. Or she can risk losing you completely.

As for the kids, tell them to stay out of it or you'll send them all to their rooms.

Children often have quite an emotional hold on their elderly parents. Many senior citizens are curious about when their parenting responsibilities end. One elderly couple wrote to say that they're retiring and moving to Florida, leaving behind unmarried children in their thirties. "As a result, we feel incredibly guilty," the couple wrote.

I advised:

Relax. Your kids are old enough to find their own way in the world. What if every retired couple in America waited to move until their unmarried children were hitched? States like Florida and Arizona would be short quite a few golf partners and card players. Then you'd have another reason to feel guilty.

Call your kids and visit often. Send postcards. But you're entitled to hit the road, guilt-free.

Often, questions from and about the elderly focus on death and dying. Consider this letter: "When my father died 20 years ago, my mother wrote his obituary, claiming all sorts of academic achievements that weren't true. Now she's 85 and has written her own obit with equally false claims. If the paper runs it, everyone will know it's a lie and think I wrote it. I'm an only child. Should I honor my mother's last wishes?"

My answer: "Remind your mother that through you, she will live on. Tell her you will perpetuate her memory every time you tell a friend how much she meant to you and how much she added to the lives of those who loved her. But also tell her that obituaries are written to comfort the living. Your father's obit was written for your mother. And your mother's will be written for you. Tell her you won't lie in her obituary."

TILLIE AND ALEX

I'll sometimes devote my entire column to the story of one couple or family. In fact, the very first column I wrote after starting this advice job was a look at the love, strength, and struggles of one elderly couple: Tillie and Alex.

Tillie, I explained, was well aware of the prevailing opinion. Everyone—doctors, social workers, her children—said it was time to put her eighty-seven-year-old husband, Alex, in a nursing home. She didn't. Fate did. And if a certain joy can be found in tragedy, I suggested that readers might find it in the story of Tillie and Alex.

Starting in 1982, Alex began asking very odd questions. Sitting in their living room, he'd wonder, "Do you have a bathroom here?" He complained about hair in his ice cream and bugs in the carpeting. He was soon seeing crowds in his bedroom and singers on the porch.

Eventually, he was diagnosed as having Alzheimer's disease, a degenerative disorder that steals your lucidity, thought by thought.

For a while, Alex still drove his car, with Tillie as navigator. "I'd say go left, go right, go here, go there," Tillie, who never owned a driver's license, told me in an interview.

But Alex's abilities kept deteriorating. He spoke haltingly. Then he whispered gibberish. Then he hardly spoke at all.

Tillie became his nurse—dressing, bathing, and shaving him. He ate slowly, often unwillingly, but she'd spoon him dinner for as long as it took.

When she wasn't watching, Alex would put Vaseline on his head or do something equally unpredictable. But when she was watching, he would often smile at her, reminding her that he loved her once. That kept her going. "My joy was having him in my life. Period," she said. "He'd sit across from me and I'd go and kiss him on the cheek."

They had met on Halloween, 1918, and at first, Tillie didn't like him. "He would come to my house and I'd run away," she said. Her mother felt sorry for Alex, an orphan, and encouraged the romance. The couple married on Halloween, 1922.

Alex, a real estate salesman, was strong yet gentle. He could walk forty yards on his hands and swim a half mile out to sea. He was stubborn—during early fights with Tillie he'd disappear for two days, usually hiding out at his sister's. But Tillie prefers to remember his finer moments. Several times, he talked people out of jumping off of bridges, and he often wondered whether he was somehow meant to be on those bridges at those particular times.

But that was all long ago.

In recent years, some people told Tillie that it might be better if Alex passed on. They didn't understand. "He was worth something to me," Tillie said. "He was my companion—someone breathing in the house. He still had life because he added to my life. I talked to him as if nothing was wrong and it felt good.

"People said I was his slave. But I was willing to sacrifice. After sixty-four years, he was like a part of my body."

Alex gave her life purpose. And even when her tasks got harder, Tillie persevered. By late 1986, she was diapering him and lifting him into bed. At age eighty-three, her stamina was remarkable.

Then one bright morning, standing in her basement, Tillie collapsed without warning and broke her hip. She crawled to the hallway, screaming. Alex, in the living room and in his own world, couldn't help. Eventually, the mailman arrived, heard her, and rescued her.

She spent four weeks hospitalized. Alex was taken to a nursing home ten miles away. In their only contact during that time, a nurse placed the phone against Alex's ear and Tillie talked and cried. At one point, he said, "Hello." That was all.

Doctors said Tillie might never walk again, but, using a cane, she does. She saw Alex only another dozen times. Because the nursing home staff didn't have time to feed him the way Tillie had, he died, malnourished, on April 5, 1987.

There are many spouses of Alzheimer's victims whose courage and devotion compare with Tillie's. And for the 1.5 million families dealing with the disease, Tillie offers hope and advice.

"You need love and patience," she told me. "The job isn't for everyone. But it was right for me. I loved my last years with him and wish he were at my table right now." As she spoke, for the first time in our conversation, she was teary-eyed. "He'll be in my heart for as long as I live."

I told this story in my column for a few reasons. Yes, it is inspirational. But I thought it made another point, too. You see, when I took over for Ann Landers, reporters asked how a young man could advise the elderly. I answered that I'd enlisted experts like George Burns, Maggie Kuhn, and my grandmother. Some reporters suggested I was looking for laughs by mentioning my grandmother.

To the contrary. I'm pleased to have her as a consultant. I ended my column by telling Tillie Zaslow that I'm very proud of her.

THE EIGHT-DECADE MARRIAGE

Often, the best resource for a young person with a question is an old person with answers that come from experience. A young new-lywed wrote the letter that follows:

> **Dear Zazz:** I've been married just 18 months, and I'm already a little bored with my wife.
>
> We get along fine and rarely argue, but there's not much excitement. We make love twice a week or more, so I guess we're OK in that department. But we often don't have much to say to one another.
>
> I know we're still in love, and I can't picture living without her. But I'm worried I'll get so bored in the years ahead that I'll climb the walls.
>
> We're both 24, so it looks like we've signed on for a long life together. How do people do it?

How, indeed? As a newlywed myself, I didn't think I was the most qualified person to answer his question. So I took his letter to Calvin Dunmire of Kittanning, Pennsylvania. He's something of a matrimony expert. At the time I called Calvin, he and his wife, Mina, had already logged eighty-one years of marriage to each other.

Having one of the longest marriages in the history of the world meant 106-year-old Calvin could offer a unique perspective to this young man's problem. In the phone interview, I found Calvin's hearing good, his mind sharp, and his advice worth considering.

He said boredom is a natural part of marriage. Talk too much and you might run out of things to say, or you might find reasons to quarrel. "If you mind your own business and keep employed, you won't have time to quarrel at home," he said.

He worked construction after their 1906 marriage; there was little time to be bored. "I'd come home tired and hungry. I'd eat a good meal and we'd go to bed. We were getting along fine."

When Calvin and Mina finally found a moment to converse, "we never ran out of things to talk about," he said. "Certainly not. I enjoyed my wife's company and she enjoyed mine." (Mina, only 101, was sick and didn't come to the phone, but Calvin said he'd vouch for her.)

Don't idealize marriage, Calvin advised. "You don't have to go to shows all the time to have a good marriage."

Calvin said that more "exciting" marriages sometimes fizzle faster. "We always observed how other people went about things and determined not to go that route," he said. "We had neighbors. They used too much liquor and took too many vacations."

The Dunmires' son, Paul, eighty-one, agreed that a laid-back, routine marriage might work best in the long run.

"My parents' relationship wasn't bubbling over all the time," he said. "They weren't overly romantic. They were busy with day-to-day activities—housework, kids, my father's job. But they loved each other."

Marriages go through cycles. At different stages, things occur to rejuvenate a relationship and prevent boredom. "When my parents had grandchildren, that added a spark to their lives together," said Paul. Then, of course, there were the great-grandchildren and the great-great-grandchild. Each generation gave the Dunmires a new role, a new reason to be involved with each other and their family.

"I don't see any evidence that they're getting tired of each other," Paul said.

Using Calvin's input, I suggested that the twenty-four-year-old letter writer and his wife decide together how they might add spice to their relationship. But they need to recognize that marriage, like life, is made up mostly of ordinary moments.

A time comes in most every successful marriage when the husband and wife know that they're stuck together, happily, despite the dull aspects.

Calvin Dunmire, for one, said he was comfortable with his decision to stick with Mina. "I'm not making plans for the future," he said. "We get along fine and I suspect we will to the end."

TEACHING THE YOUNG

A lot of older folks write me with "used-to-bes": It used to be a gentler, friendlier, kinder, less expensive, more hospitable world. Their letters usually end with warnings that I call "gonna-gets": It's gonna get worse unless we instill some values in our young and take "a good, hard look" at our declining morals. (I'm not sure what a good, hard look looks like, but I recognize that it means business.)

Some of the more pessimistic letters get on my nerves. At least once a week, a certain angry Chicagoan in her eighties writes me a seven- or eight-page letter in a tiny scrawl. "America has gone to hell," she writes. "It is beyond salvation." Her basic message seems to be: Don't trust anyone under eighty.

Not all the "used-to-be" letters are so fanatical. Many are worth considering. Our society certainly has flaws worth noting and repairing. And often there are answers to be found in a review of the good old days.

Of course, the best older-people-taking-issue-with-younger-people letters are the ones that offer solutions rather than just complaints. One such letter came from a seventy-four-year-old Texas grandmother named Wilma Wheaton. She wrote:

> **Dear Zazz:** I have 17 grandchildren and two great-grandchildren, and I buy each a Christmas gift. Even though my immediate family numbers 35, I see that each one is remembered.
>
> For years, however, the problem has been that most of them haven't remembered me. It was rare that I would get a thank-you note, or any acknowledgement that these kids had received my gifts.
>
> Well, this Christmas, I decided to buy 19 boxes of thank-you notes and a roll of 22-cent stamps. Along with each grandchild's gift, I included a box of thank-you notes with the top envelope stamped and addressed to me. (The ones who didn't respond, I decided, would be dropped from my gift list next year.)
>
> So far, 13 children have returned the thank-yous. And what fun it was to get the stationery back with their letters written on it!

As soon as I finished reading Wilma's letter, I called to congratulate her on a brilliant idea.

She explained the genesis of her inspiration: "I just got so disgusted sending gift after gift and never hearing from them. This year, I figured, I'm going to fix them."

Wilma reported that by the time I called, 16 of her 17 grandchildren had sent thank-yous. "The response was totally positive," she said. "Some of the kids had never written me before in their lives. I'd been afraid that the thank-you notes might have boomeranged or that the children would be insulted and hate me."

Her grandchildren are scattered around the country: Idaho, California, Texas, Wisconsin. I called them, too, asking permission to embarrass them in print.

"I was always a bad boy," admitted grandson Ross Wheeler, twenty-seven. "I never sent thank-you notes. I always thought, well, grandmothers, they understand."

When he got the thank-you notes, Ross thought his grandmom was "pretty funny." But then he realized: "Oh-oh, I guess I'd better send her a thank-you." The upshot? "I'm completely reformed," he vowed. "I promise to send her thank-you notes from now on."

When grandson Tye Gribb, twenty, received the thank-you notes ("Not a very subtle hint," he said), he assumed he had been singled out for the grandmotherly reprimand. He was relieved to learn his cousins and siblings had been similarly reminded.

Still, it took him six weeks to finally write his thank-you. By that time, it was more of an apology note. "I apologized for being so late, then I apologized because I hadn't sent thank-you notes before, then I apologized because she had to send me the stamp."

Tye also swore he's a changed man. "I'm entering the age of responsibility," he predicted.

Among the grandkids, the whole affair created good-natured finger pointing. In her own defense, Allison Wheeler, twenty-three, said that in years past she had thanked her grandmom, unlike her brother, Ross, "who is horrible with thank-you notes, just terrible. He doesn't thank anybody."

Then there was Amy Gribb, twenty-three, whom I tracked down in Idaho. She already had used several of the thank-you notes from the box. Her grandmother's efforts "have made me think of sending thank-you cards to people I might never have thanked before," she said. "Gram had a great idea."

Indeed, Amy said her grandmother had taught her a lesson. And what could be a greater tribute than this? "When I use up this box of thank-you notes," she said, "I plan to buy another one."

Coincidentally, after learning about Wilma's technique, I heard from several other grandparents with similar complaints about unappreciative, ill-mannered grandchildren. Wrote one:

I send cash gifts to my two grandchildren in California for all their birthdays and holidays. They never send me a thank-you. If I call and ask if they received my gift, they'll say thanks. Otherwise, my cancelled check is my only indication that the gift arrived.

My granddaughter will soon turn 18, and I'm considering sending her a check and "forgetting" to sign it. This would force her to get in touch with me, if only to garner my signature. Is this a good idea?

I responded that it might work, sure, but it's a roundabout way to teach a lesson. A better idea, I wrote, is "the Wilma Wheaton method." It's been field-tested, it's a proven success, and if by chance it doesn't work, it saves you money: You don't have to send gifts to any ungrateful grandkids who don't send a thank-you.

Not all grandparents find such a receptive audience for their advice. The letter that follows is typical:

Dear Zazz: I just received a letter from my daughter-in-law informing me that if I wish to continue our relationship, now in its 14th year, I must keep my opinions about rearing children to myself.

For five years, I've silently watched my son and daughter-in-law give in to all of my grandson's whims and desires. The boy misbehaves, and they do nothing. His rebellious streak is hindering him in kindergarten.

Finally, I purchased a book on rearing children called "Dare to Discipline" and gave it to my son. He refused to take it and denied he and his wife need help. Shortly thereafter, his wife wrote me the letter. Was I out of bounds?

Could this woman be an overbearing mother-in-law? Or are her son and daughter-in-law too thin-skinned? Trying to walk the middle line, I told the grandmother:

If your son and his wife were less insecure, they'd be more receptive to your suggestions. But given the circumstances, heed their warning and keep your mouth closed.

The shame of this is that your grandson might have benefited from your input. Still, it is often best if a grandparent stays out of the child-rearing arena.

Children must be raised by their parents. You had your

turn. Now it's time to watch, hope, and have a little faith that those in the next generation will find their way.

Love your grandson and be supportive to your son and his wife. Perhaps one day they will feel secure enough to come to you for advice.

Among the saddest letters I receive are those from grandparents who lose contact with their grandchildren. Usually divorce is responsible. A man and woman divorce, she gets custody of the children, and the kids' paternal grandparents never see them again. Sadder still are stories such as this one:

Dear Zazz: My daughter died three years ago leaving children ages 9, 12 and 15.

At first, my ex-son-in-law needed me to help with the children. I gladly obliged. We got along well. But since he remarried, he hasn't allowed the children to have anything to do with me.

They send back Christmas and birthday presents and say they don't want anything from me because they have no intention of buying presents for me.

I don't want anything and I don't want to be part of my ex-son-in-law's life. I'm glad he has remarried.

However, I would like to be in contact with my grandchildren and buy them presents. What can I do?

My response:

As they build a new life together, your ex-son-in-law and his wife seem to be building walls to separate him from his old life. This is unfair and unkind.

If he won't listen to your reasoning, perhaps your grandchildren will. They're old enough to understand their mother's death and to appreciate your love for them. Without talking against their father, confide in them. Tell them how you care for them and want to be part of their lives, even in a limited way. They could be the bridge to help their father and his new wife understand how isolated you feel.

If all your efforts at reasoning with your son-in-law fail, a lawyer could help you determine what legal rights—for visitation or other involvement—you might have.

For National Grandparents Day, the second Sunday in September, I asked grandparents to share their thoughts about grandparenting. Scores responded. They offered their memories, gave advice, and wrote of love stories defined by a sixty- or seventy-year age difference.

Their letters detailed how so many grandparents are loaded with smarts, wit, good advice, and a capacity to be extraordinarily loving. Whether they were writing about their youth, modern times, or the art of grandparenting, they had a lot to say. A sampling:

• Fran Nunnally of Richmond, Virginia, wrote about accepting grandmotherhood.

> Our own grandparents are only dimly remembered as shadowy figures from another age. They are reminders of the succession of life, the march of generations—our mortality.
>
> Stepping into their shoes is awesome. But soon the doubts and the gloom are forgotten, dispelled by tiny hands and smiles.
>
> What advice do I have for today's grandchildren? One word: Read. Get to love good books. They'll be a comfort to you all of your life. When the glamour and noise of the boom box and the videos fade, your old familiar books will be there to comfort and sustain you.

• Janice Pauley of Ontario, California, wrote of how grandparents can serve as a link to the past. "I make my home a wonderful, magic environment for my grandchildren—the place where memories of their parents are stored. Offering them the treasures of old pictures and memorabilia, I bring the long-ago world to life again."

• "Good grandparents praise their grandchildren," wrote a grandmother from Texas. "Whenever I talk to my grandchildren, my favorite phrase is 'Your grandma is so proud of you!'"

• "Last week I left a message on my daughter's answering machine," wrote Muriel Fisher of Chicago. "My daughter told me that when my seven-year-old grandson heard it, he kissed the machine.

"My advice to grandparents? Just love them and they'll return more love than your heart can hold."

• I also heard from Marian McQuade, the West Virginia grandmother of twenty-nine who led the effort to create National Grandparents Day in 1978. "Everyone is a grandchild, no matter what your age is," she said. "Even if your grandparents are dead, you can continue being a grandchild by adopting grandparents in a nursing home."

Though I hadn't asked for comments from grandchildren and great-grandchildren, I heard from dozens of them. My favorite came from New Yorker Dan Whitten, thirty-one, who told about his great-grandmother's knowing humor:

> One Thanksgiving, Great-Grandma Lena stood up to give a toast. She said, "It's wonderful to have the whole family here. May we all be together to celebrate Thanksgiving in another 50 years!"
>
> Well, someone had to say to her, "Grandma, we might not all make it 50 years." She responded, "That's okay, I'll make new friends!"
>
> She didn't live long after that, but her remark was one of the fondest memories of my childhood.

Many grandparents gave advice and asked that their names be withheld:

• "If you think of life as a movie, then grandparents produced the cast of characters. Grandparents, in their wisdom, can often predict how the story will end, but we try not to interfere. Sometimes, we have to remind kids that we also enjoy going out for ice cream or pizza, or riding in a fast car with loud music. We're just a phone call away, but for some of us, the phone seldom rings."

• "I'm 80 and I give my family advice only upon request. I see all, hear all, and say as little as possible because I figure they might know more than I do."

• "There's a new breed—the modern grandmother. In her search for eternal youth, she flees to the Sunbelt to golf in the winter, and is removed from her grandchildren's birthdays, school plays, and their everyday joys and troubles.

"Is she any less loved than the traditional doting grandmothers? I don't think so. She may even be cherished for her zest and youthful appearance. Does it matter that her grandchildren need her now? Will they be available when she needs them? It's an interesting phenomenon—only time will tell."

• One grandmother, who also asked not to be named, told me this tale:

There was an Oriental family consisting of a grandfather, father, mother and young son. One day the father said he was taking the grandfather up to the mountains. His son asked to come along.

On their journey, the young son asked his father why they were taking the grandfather away. His father replied that the grandfather was old, and that he was going to leave him in the mountains to die.

The young son thought for a moment and then said, "Thank you for telling me. Now I know what to do with you when you get old."

The father stopped, looked at the boy and at his father, and then all three turned around and went home.

FREE ADVICE DAY

A Chicago shopping mall held Free Advice Day, and shopkeepers set up booths outside their stores.

Employees from the photo developer gave advice on how to shoot winning pictures. (Too many "Giant Thumb" portraits in your photo album? These folks had, excuse the pun, some handy tips.)

Clerks from the video rental store played Siskel and Ebert by suggesting worthwhile movies. (Their favorite flicks? Anything they had in stock.)

The shoe-repair shop had a table, too, manned by repairmen who called themselves "shoe doctors." "You need new heels," they advised. Or, "With new soles, your shoes will be good as new."

The shopkeepers had many helpful suggestions, though, in some cases, their free advice would end up costing you in the end.

There was, however, one booth in this Free Advice arena that wasn't part of the mall crowd. That was where I was stationed, along with my partner, Diane.

The mall had asked us to dispense advice for personal problems. We liked the idea. Why sit behind a desk answering letters when you can learn so much more by talking face-to-face?

Still, I felt a bit awkward—like Charlie Brown's friend, Lucy, with her five-cent pop-psychology stand.

Many people joked around. "You don't want to hear my problems," one woman said, "unless you've got a week."

"I don't have any troubles," a man told me. "I'm the luckiest guy alive."

And yet so many people, old and young, brought very personal troubles to our table. They walked right up and told their stories, not caring that other shoppers were listening in.

A lot of the problems were typical of what I read each day in the mail. The woman whose boyfriend got someone else pregnant. The man raising a son on his own. The girl who loves two boys, but not her boyfriend.

Some people needed more than advice. "I need a job as a janitor," one woman told me. "Please get me a job."

A Vietnam vet brought documents from the Veterans Administration. His problem seemed too complicated to explain in one sitting. "Take it all with you," he said. I didn't want to take his originals. Could he bring me photocopies? He disappeared into the crowd and never returned.

We posed for pictures, joked around, and gave away free newspapers. But then one shopper approached our table and told a powerful story that stuck with me. For days afterward, I regretted that I had answered this woman too quickly.

The woman said she was fifty-five and had just taken her mother to a hospital emergency room. A nurse asked for the sick woman's age. "Eighty-three," her daughter replied.

After the nurse had gone, the mother whispered to her daughter, "I wish you hadn't given her my age."

This was not an issue of vanity. It was, in the mother's head, a matter of self-preservation. "If the doctors think I'm too old," she told her daughter, "I know they're just going to let me die."

When the daughter had finished telling me this story, I suggested that she reassure her mother: This was a preposterous notion! Doctors don't discriminate by age.

But after I thought about it, maybe that wasn't enough of an answer. Maybe reassurances must come from society as a whole. Maybe our attitudes toward our elders, sick or healthy, made this eighty-three-year-old woman's anxiousness and paranoia almost inevitable.

On reflection, I decided to share this story in the column. Perhaps it would give readers something to think about.

The shoe doctors prescribe new heels to make old shoes young. The remedies for old people aren't always so easy. This was something I learned on Free Advice Day.

Coping with Adversity

"I HAVE A handicapped child," the caller said softly. "She is sad and unhappy. She's so lonely.

"Newspaper articles and TV shows tell us that parents of the handicapped are happy: Their children bring them joy. But I don't feel joy. I cry for my child every day. How do these people cope? How can they be joyful?"

This sort of call is not rare on our phone-in line. And the pain in the woman's voice was as gripping as any letter I've received. I had no easy answer for her.

But a few days later, I happened to get a letter from a woman named Tracy Kramer. "Yours is a column about people," she wrote, "so I'd like to tell you about a special person: Tommy Ansonia, my 19-year-old cousin."

Paralyzed from the chest down, Tommy is one of the country's oldest survivors with severe spina bifida, Tracy wrote. "This year, he completed high school—a monumental achievement. Tommy will never live a normal life, and he might not live much longer, but he is so happy and content: He teaches us to appreciate life.

"Friends and relatives from across the country will be gathering next week for a party to celebrate his graduation. Zazz, you're invited."

Before I finished Tracy's letter, the idea hit me: Perhaps this family could help answer the questions posed by the advice-line caller. The following Sunday, notebook in hand, I headed to Burbank, a Chicago suburb, for the party.

The sixty-five guests were eating dinner when I arrived. Many women wore flowers. I sat down with Tom's mother, Jean.

"When Tom was born, the doctors walked out of the room and said there was nothing they could do," she told me. "They gave him days to live, then weeks, then a year. Each day was a gift."

Tom's eyes are crossed and he has a learning disability. He has just one working kidney and wears a diaper. "But he isn't considered handicapped in our house," Jean said. "We tell him to do whatever he can and do it fast. He doesn't get sympathy and he doesn't want it.

"He's funny. I'll say, 'If you don't hurry, I'll kick you in the rear.' He'll say, 'That's OK, I won't feel it.' "

When kids ask Tommy why he looks funny, he doesn't flinch: He answers them. "He feels that'll make them more understanding with the next kid in a wheelchair," Jean told me. "He doesn't agree with parents who tell children, 'If you stare at that kid in a wheelchair, I'll smack you!' Tommy says, 'Let 'em stare. If they have questions, let 'em ask.' "

Tom's parents were both twenty-one when he was born. "Doctors said to put Tommy in a home," Jean said. "They told us not to have more children because we wouldn't have time to love them. But we had two more kids. Tom didn't strain our family life. He brought us closer."

Tom's parents didn't ask for a handicapped child, but they accepted his arrival in their lives. "I loved my wife so much, and she loved me and he was our son," said Tom's father, John. "That's all."

John and Jean said they view themselves as regular people, not superparents. But because their manner is so reassuring, doctors have often asked them to talk to parents of handicapped newborns. "Life is what you make of it," Jean said. "If you dwell on the bad, it hurts you and your child. Our life isn't easy, but whose is?"

Tom wheeled himself over and we shook hands. I asked if he ever gets depressed. "Maybe one day a month," he answered.

He reminded me that he's not a perfect kid. He has a temper. He talks back. "My mother will say, 'Walk over there and pick that up.' I say, 'I'll pick it up, but I'm not walking over there.' "

Tom was a devilish child. "I'd make my younger brother climb up on the counter and get me cookies." His mother never suspected him. He was in bed, paralyzed.

A rabid Chicago Cubs fan, Tom said he realizes that he may never live out his dream of being a sportscaster. And he said he knew, too, that his mother also needed care. She'd recently been told she had cancer. "Tom tells his mother, every morning, that he loves her," his Aunt Kathy told me. "He pours out so much love."

Later in the night, I spent fifteen minutes or so talking to Tom's grandmother. She made just the sort of comment that the distraught caller to my advice line referred to: "Tommy has been one of the joys in my life," she said. "He gives me a lot to live for."

Tom was just as upbeat. "I can't change how I was born," he said. "I just figure I'll go on with a smile."

The woman who called the advice line might have a child even more severely handicapped than Tom is. But perhaps, in the testimony of the Ansonia clan, she found some comfort.

Often, I've found that the best place to take a reader's problem is to someone who already has the problem—and has learned to cope with it. It's not just a matter of empathy. A person who has already suffered through something and survived it is more likely to say, "Hey, quit feeling sorry for yourself. Get on with your life."

A man's letter arrived unsigned, with no return address:

> **Dear Zazz:** Three years ago, I had several major operations. Part of my small intestines were removed. I lost all of my large intestines. My rectum.
>
> At 27, I must face living the rest of my life with a permanent ileostomy. The remainder of my small intestines are diverted through a hole in my abdomen. I wear a plastic bag attached to my stomach to collect waste.
>
> As a result, I've developed a poor self-image. I haven't had a date in three years.

He really hadn't changed. Except for the bag, he is who he was.

But, he said, the bag tormented him, angered him, and made him feel like less of a person.

He said he'd contacted a United Ostomy Association chapter. But most members were fifty or older. Things seemed easier for them. Most had spouses who loved them before and loved them still—to hell with the bag! Because of their age, they wouldn't have to wear the bag for forty or fifty years, as he would. As a young single, he couldn't relate.

"How can I get a better self-image?" he asked. "I want to start dating again but I can't." He signed his letter "Losing Out on Life."

If only he'd included his name and address, I would have gotten him on the phone with Marvin Bush. Bush had the operation in 1984, when he was twenty-seven. He could relate.

I called Bush and read him the letter. "After my surgery, I couldn't believe what I saw at my waist," Bush told me. "My eyeballs almost bugged out. I felt like a freak."

It didn't matter that he had a good job, that his wife loved him, or that his father, George Bush, was Vice President at the time. It would be up to him to overcome his resentment and depression.

"You can become a victim to the piece of plastic hanging from your waist," he said, "or you can gradually restore your self-confidence."

Acceptance is the key to recovery, he said. "Mine was emergency surgery. My alternative was to be dead. Given that, it isn't so hard to accept the operation. It saved my life."

I also contacted Rolf Benirschke, the former San Diego Chargers kicker who went on to host TV's *Wheel of Fortune.* He had an ileostomy in 1979. He said he was unmarried with plenty of dates. "At first, I asked buddies, 'How can I go out with women?' They said, 'Just jump in. Do it!'

"Sure, there are embarrassing moments. But people take their cues from you. If you're comfortable, they are. People can be unbelievably understanding."

In many ways, Bush said, his life is now easier and richer. Before the operation, discomfort was constant. He feared going to parties. What if he couldn't make it to the bathroom in time? "I appreciate simpler things now," he said. "I spend more time with my wife and daughter."

Bush knew the man writing to me was hurting: "But he has all the tools he had before. There's no prescription for confidence. Mine was rebuilt, little by little, with the support of family and friends—and a sense of humor."

The United Ostomy Association advises ostomates not to focus on how people will react. "I've dated many men," one ostomate said, "and I've found they're more interested in their own appendage than they are in mine."

"Don't lead your life with the pouch as your focus," Benirschke said. "Don't wear it on your sleeve. Take on life. Think how close you came to losing it."

After my column ran, dozens of ostomates wrote and phoned to offer encouragement to Losing Out on Life. One woman even saw me walking down the street in Chicago and stopped me. We talked for a while.

"I was nervous the first time I was going to make love after my ostomy surgery," she told me. "I told my boyfriend my story, and he paused for a moment, then responded, 'Well I never said you were a perfect asshole.'"

Other comments from ostomates:

- "Since my ileostomy, I've gotten married, fathered three children, gone scuba diving, traveled around the world and even jumped out of a plane (with a parachute). I'd rather have an ostomy than false teeth. To me, it's less trouble to take care of."
- "I'm 23, a wife and mother, and I've worn a urostomy bag for 19 years. I've witnessed the streamlining of the appliance. With fashion's looser styles, no one knows you wear one unless you tell them.

"When I was a teen, the ostomy pouch was not on my forehead. It didn't interfere with flirting or necking. When it came time for sex with a man, I told him as matter-of-factly as I could. Let's face it, Zazz, if you're a turn-on to someone in every other respect, he won't even notice the plastic."
- "People always notice my husband's smile and personality first and no one needs to know about his 'secret plumbing system.'"
- "I'm a 33-year-old black female who had an ileostomy in 1981. Before surgery, I was sick every day. I wished I had a bathroom in my kitchen, because if I ate even the smallest amount, I needed it.

"I felt devastated, too, after the surgery. But now I have my health, a husband who loves all of me, and a beautiful little boy. The Lord spared me—not to feel sorry for myself, but to show others that my life is just beginning.

"I'd like to tell 'Losing Out' that God doesn't give anyone more than he or she can handle. I'll be praying for him, myself and other ostomates."

UGLY TAUNTS

The most horrifying letter in the novel *Miss Lonelyhearts* comes from a girl who has no nose. What can Miss Lonelyhearts tell her? How can the advice columnist understand her shame and loneliness? Even though almost all people have felt ugly at some point in their lives, how can a man who has a nose truly understand the misery of someone without one?

I, too, receive letters from people with physical deformities—but not all of them are sad souls in need of pity. Many write to boost the morale of others. Every time I print a letter from someone who describes himself or herself as ugly, I get a small stack of supportive letters. After I printed the following letter from "Hurting," empathetic mail was especially heavy. Hurting wrote:

Dear Zazz: I'm a 42-year-old woman with three younger sisters, all married and beautiful.

My problem is that I am very ugly. All my life, people have told me how pretty my sisters were and how I was the ugly duckling.

As a child, children would often taunt me for being ugly. That continues until this day. I can't go to a shopping mall without younger people making fun of my ugliness. Once, children threw snowballs at me. I'm afraid to walk past a crowd of young people because they might call me ugly, or even attack me. I feel like a freak.

I get no support from my parents or sisters. I have no friends and am estranged from my relatives because of my looks.

I can't afford plastic surgery, so that's not a solution.

You don't know how ashamed I feel. I'm embarrassed and so lonely. Please help.

—Hurting

I responded:

Dear Hurting: Looks are just part of a person's total being. Many people who are not attractive are much beloved.

Yes, some young people can be cruel. But others have a lot to give. You shouldn't be afraid of all young people because of bad experiences you've had with some of them.

Perhaps you have a tendency to blame your looks for all of your personal problems so you don't have to deal with them. But the world is rich with people who will befriend and love you regardless of what you look like.

Make a forced effort to make others happy. Try to forget about your problems for a while. Perhaps at first you might not understand how this could solve your troubles. But this kind of effort can end up coming back to you.

I think my answer was sympathetic, yet it came from a direction she might not have expected. The empathetic responses came from other readers. One man wrote:

Dear Zazz: At seven, I was hit by a car, had my face crushed, and was pronounced clinically dead at the scene. By some miracle, I lived and now I am 44.

I was teased mercilessly in school for being ugly. Potential employers asked about my appearance. Even my ex-wife blamed me for poor reconstructive surgery.

For years I was hurting, too. But then I learned that no one's opinion of me is as important as my opinion of myself.

I'm now a minister. Hardly anyone criticizes my appearance anymore because I accept myself. I smile a lot. And I help others.

I may have a physical deformity, but it's easier to accept than a deformed character in a beautiful body. God values us for what we are in our hearts.

I can say, too, that our physical attributes seem to improve when our self-esteem does.
—V.E.B.

Though most letter writers offered Hurting encouragement and advice, some were more cynical and bitter. A woman wrote:

Dear Zazz: If you read the newspaper (other than your own column) you'd know that studies show people attribute positive characteristics to attractive people and negative ones to unattractive people.

This problem is compounded by the media. Why is it that young, slim, attractive white people are used to represent average Americans in TV commercials? When have we seen a handicapped person pitching shampoo? It isn't that the handicapped don't wash their hair.

Unattractive people, especially women, are treated like second-class citizens. I speak with authority, because I have a facial disfigurement made worse by bad corrective surgery. I know what it's like to enter a room and have people turn away.
—Without Hope

I replied: "What you say is true and sad, but if we can't change society overnight, we have to adapt." I offered this woman the letters that follow. I thought these letter writers had the right idea.

Dear Zazz: I have a nice complexion, nice eyes and a good figure, but due to a glandular problem, I must wear a hairpiece. Everyone notices. Their silence speaks volumes.

Yet I have compensated well because I recognize my positive traits and resist self-pity. Everyone is deficient in some way: Noses are big, tummies stick out, people are short or fat.

Hurting should build on her good points. Once, I saw a woman with an extremely disfigured face. She wore makeup, had nicely combed hair, and held her head up. I admired her immensely.
—Been There

A man wrote:

Dear Zazz: Hurting should recognize that people are not ugly, just different. I'm 32 and have been "fat and ugly" all my life. I weighed 240 in eighth grade. But I've always been noticed and remembered (one good thing about being different).

Hurting should get out in the world. There's so much to do and see. She might start with her local church. She shouldn't worry about what people might say. Nobody's perfect. And if other people are insensitive, just smile and wish them a nice day.

I want Hurting to know that she's not the only ugly person out there. I bet I'm uglier.
—F.W.

THE SECOND-GUESSERS

Once a week, fifteen second-guessers gather in a circle and rethink my advice.

They begin each session by reading my column out loud. They handle all the typical letters: lovers who can't live with each other, employees who can't stand their bosses, kids who can't get onto the cheerleading squad. It's rare that a question stumps the panel.

After giving their own answers, they read and rate my advice. Sometimes I get thumbs up, sometimes thumbs down.

Well, when I heard about these second-guessers, I decided to visit Chicago's North River Mental Health Center, where the group meets. They welcomed me with smiles and some blunt critiques. No one was afraid to tell me when they thought my advice bombed. And I felt relieved when they agreed with my answers.

Everyone in the group is a client in the city-funded day treatment program. Most are schizophrenic or manic-depressive. And counselors believe that giving advice is excellent therapy for them.

They look forward to their weekly "problem-solving" meeting. "It helps us realize that we're not alone," said Jim, a schizophrenic. "Everyone has problems."

They joke. They argue. They compliment each other's good advice and roll their eyes at not-so-good advice.

On the day I visited, they discussed a letter from a woman who threatened to kill her ex-boyfriend. When he left her, she attacked him with a knife.

The group discussed the power of love, the pain of rejection, and the reasons the letter writer needed therapy. And then, softly, Tony, a former barber, spoke up. "My ex-wife once went after my son with a knife," he said, describing how fine the line can be between love and hate. "My son was born retarded," he said, "and my wife took good care of him day after day until finally she couldn't handle it anymore."

On that horrible day, Tony grabbed the knife from his wife. His son wasn't hurt, but the boy later died of cancer. "The knife," Tony said, almost to himself. "It's always on my mind."

Tony is manic-depressive and a recovering alcoholic. He's intelligent and handsome, so it was hard to picture him as he was until a few years earlier—drunkenly wandering the streets and sleeping on benches.

Other people in the problem-solving group have also felt comfortable enough to reveal something about themselves.

Bobby once read aloud an advice column about an exhibitionist. "This reminds me of my problem," he said. He then told of his arrests for indecent exposure, and how chemical imbalances in the brain are thought to cause exhibitionism. "It was a major breakthrough for him," program coordinator Joyce Zick told me. "And everyone was very nonjudgmental, loving, and supportive."

The group told me they enjoy the lighter questions. Remember this Daily Double question: "When my husband and I pick up his mother for Sunday dinner, should 'the little woman' sit in the front of the car with her son, or in the back?"

"Put the mother in the trunk," joked Tony. Bobby suggested: "Put both ladies in the backseat and let them fight it out."

The schizophrenics take medication daily to control delusions and hallucinations. The problem solving "helps test their reality base," said Zick. "If someone comes up with a bizarre answer, the group says, 'I don't think you can do that.' "

The center's goal is to keep clients functioning in the community. "The mentally ill are people, too," said Jim. In fact, by playing advice columnists once a week, they often feel more normal than the so-called normal folks.

ASHAMED AND BEWILDERED

Almost every day on our phone-in line, soft and uncertain voices whisper that their world has collapsed around them.

"I'm pregnant and I want to die," says Bewildered, age fourteen.

"My boyfriend is forcing me to have an abortion," says Confused, age sixteen.

"I can't tell my parents," says Ashamed, age seventeen. "I hope I have a miscarriage."

The most disturbing part of my job is listening to their stories on the office answering machine. An astonishing number of the callers are young, naive, and pregnant. The sadness and confusion in their voices define their pain in a way no letter could.

Many whisper—apparently so their parents can't hear. During one girl's confession, a woman's voice in the background asked: "Who are you talking to?" The girl hung up frantically.

Many of the girls are inarticulate. Some cry. Almost all end their calls by pleading, "What should I do?"

No words from me can easily fix their predicament. But I do try to give a few basic messages in the column. I advise them to tell their parents. Parents tend to be much more supportive than kids expect, often rallying behind daughters to find solutions as a family.

The girls also need to see a doctor for proper prenatal care. Too many girls try to hide pregnancies or starve themselves so they don't show.

Though some pro-lifers rail against Planned Parenthood, I recommend the organization to girls in search of counseling, a shoulder to cry on, or information about options—from abortion to adoption.

"Planned Parenthood has seen every problem," I tell pregnant teens, "and can deal with yours." Indeed, the executive director of Planned Parenthood in Chicago told me of a twelve-year-old who came in alone. She wasn't pregnant. What did she want? "I'm having trouble taking care of the baby I already have," she said.

Such horror stories reflect a desperate need for sex education. And just as unsettling are all the hot-line calls we receive from confused teens who aren't pregnant—yet: "I'm a 12-year-old with a 16-year-old boyfriend. We love each other, but he wants me to have sex and I'm not ready. What should I do?" "My boyfriend makes me feel guilty because I won't go to a motel with him. He's 18. I'm 15." "Is it OK to have sex if you're a girl who has not yet had a period? I've heard it's safe because I can't get pregnant."

My message for these teens: Don't think you must have sex to be loved or to be mature. And don't succumb to peer pressure. (If you don't, you won't be alone: About 45 percent of teens are still virgins at high school graduation.) If you're going to have sex, adults telling you to "just say no" won't necessarily stop you. But for God's sake, be responsible. Your decision to have sex should be an informed one. Learn about sexually transmitted diseases. Use birth control. And recognize that it's natural to have sexual urges; you don't have to act upon them.

Of course, I know the limited impact of such advice. As long as the hot line is in operation, frightened teens will continue to call announcing their pregnancies. And I'll listen to their stories—sharing their regrets and wishing for some magical way to get through to them.

Abortion may be the most emotionally charged issue I deal with in the column. Whenever I hint that I am pro-choice, I inevitably receive letters from pro-lifers. Many make heartfelt right-to-life arguments, which I'm happy to print in the column. Others send hateful letters with photos of dead fetuses attached.

Readers send me field reports of hostilities between pro-life and pro-choice forces. One woman wrote: "How can I respond to a neighbor who continually gets me on the phone and calls me a 'baby killer'? I've had an abortion and make no secret that I'm pro-choice."

This pro-life extremist, obviously, was so committed to her cause that she behaved irrationally. But I've gotten many eloquent letters from right-to-lifers. One woman wrote:

Dear Zazz: My husband and I have tried to have a baby for seven years, but I'm infertile. To all you pregnant girls out there; I can't pretend to understand the details of your situation. But I am aware of your choices. And selfishly, I have a recommendation.

Your first and foremost alternative to unwanted pregnancy is adoption. Your decision to give your baby to a childless couple will bless persons tenfold.

To childless couples, you're not an outcast of society, you're a godsend—prayed for and praised. Pregnancy is only nine months of your life. You can finish school. And you'll have the peace of mind that your pregnancy was not a mistake, but a blessing for me and my husband.

I was shocked by one reader's response to this letter: "Listen, lady, God does everything for a reason. You should know that if you can't have children, there's a reason. I don't believe in children having children, so it's not a teen's job to conceive for people who can't.

"Lady, you're selfish! Don't think someone else should have a child for you. Think of someone else for once and quit feeling sorry for yourself. If you're lonely, buy a dog." She signed herself "Adamant."

The infertile woman certainly wasn't advocating that teens get pregnant so infertile couples can adopt children. Rather, she was offering her personal story to distraught pregnant girls who might welcome input about adoption. I found her letter courageous, and Adamant's letter unnecessarily harsh.

Many readers responded. One infertile woman made this point:

Under the right biological circumstances, any couple can have intercourse—and a child. But to be approved by an adoption agency, a couple must submit to incredibly close scrutiny, psychological testing, and discussions of their most private secrets. Their employers, family and friends must be interviewed to determine if the couple is capable of parenting. I know of no such screening for couples who can conceive on their own (even unmarried teens).

Maybe there is a reason some couples can't conceive. Maybe God knows that only some couples will be able to withstand the adoption process.

Before Adamant assumes she's better in the Lord's eyes because she can conceive and we can't, she should think again. Her child might take only five minutes to conceive. Ours is taking six years—and counting. Adamant owes a lot of people an apology.

THE GIFT OF LIFE

In October 1983, Stephen Armstrong shot himself in the head and saved several lives.

He was twenty-six, single, a former car salesman in suburban Chicago. "He was loved, and he was loving," his mother, Shirley, recalls. Yet he was unhappy and depressed and then he shot himself.

"The doctors explained the extent of the gunshot wound," Shirley later told me. "He was brain-dead with no chance of survival."

As Stephen's family grieved in the hospital waiting room, a doctor asked a very difficult question: Would the family consider donating Stephen's organs?

"I had other things on my mind. I had just lost my son," Shirley said. "But there was no pressure. The doctor was very comforting."

Overnight, the Armstrongs decided to make the donation. "Stephen's organs weren't doing him any good," said Shirley.

The next day, a transplant coordinator explained where Stephen's heart, liver, and kidneys were needed, how his corneas could give sight to two blind people. And after the woman brought out forms to sign, she said, "If you'll excuse me, I need to make a phone call. There's a family whose child is dying, and when they hear about your decision, they'll be crying with happiness."

At Stephen's funeral, a relative gave Shirley an article from the *Sun-Times.* It was about how a dying man in St. Louis had received several organs from an unnamed young Chicagoan who had just died. The news eased the Armstrongs' pain: Out of Stephen's death had come the gift of life.

Even before I became an advice columnist, I'd been a supporter of organ donations. For years, the back of my driver's license has carried my permission to "harvest" my organs after my death. My job allows me to bring this message to a larger audience, and so I devoted a column to the story of Stephen Armstrong.

Usually when young, healthy people like Stephen die, they are buried with their organs intact. Out of twenty thousand people who die each year nationwide and meet the criteria for donation, fewer than 15 percent become donors. This low percentage has little to do with survivors' reluctance.

I spoke with Mindy Malecki, a former transplant coordinator. She had organized a seminar to teach health care professionals how to ask for organ donations. "Most bereaved people, if approached appropriately, will agree to donate their loved ones' organs," she said.

Nurses and doctors are often too nervous or uncomfortable to broach the subject of organ donation with a bereaved family—so they don't. "They have to understand that for a family, being asked is often a consolation, not an imposition," Malecki said.

There are wrong ways to ask, however. Nurses shouldn't pressure survivors with such statements as: "If we don't get your son's organs, people will die." The best approach is to be gentle and compassionate. Time may be of the essence, but survivors can't feel they're being rushed into a decision.

At the seminar, Malecki taught nurses and doctors that their role is to relay information, not to persuade. They should approach a family in a private place, not at the patient's bedside. And to demystify organ procurement, Malecki taught them to tell families that most religions approve of organ donations, that there's no disfigurement, and that there can still be an open-casket funeral.

Shirley Armstrong appeared at the seminar, too. Her message: "It may hurt you to ask a bereaved family, it may hurt the family, but if you don't do it, it will hurt more. People will die."

My support of organ donations has not gone unnoticed by readers. Some, near death, have begged me to publicize their need for a healthy kidney, liver, or heart. One registered letter began: "Please, Zazz, I desperately need a kidney or I'll die. Can you ask your readers to think of me if something happens to someone they love?"

These letters are painful, but I won't write a column pleading for one individual, while ignoring those who are higher up on the waiting list. Some in the media have been doing such tear-jerking "human interest stories" for years. I think it is irresponsible and unfair interference. I've decided I won't play God.

Still, I use the column to help the cause. Another speaker at Mindy Malecki's seminar was Judy Kolodzey. Until five years ago, she was nearly blind. She told the story of her cornea transplant. She was on the operating table, sedated but conscious as the doctors worked, and suddenly, miraculously, she could see the lights on the ceiling. "Overnight, I had vision," she told me. "The next morning, the doctor stood across the room, held up his fingers, and I could count. One, two, three. . . .

"I know it's very hard to go to a family that has just lost a loved one. But if nurses and doctors see me, and the difference in my life, that might help them ask the question in the future."

Telling Judy's story in the column, I hoped, would be a reminder to readers that someday, they, too, could give the gift of health, of sight, of life.

Jerks

THE U.S. CENSUS Bureau has never taken an accurate count of the nation's jerk population. But judging from my mail, it is a healthy, thriving, and thoroughly obnoxious subsection of our society. Jerkiness crosses racial, cultural, economic, and gender lines—as well as most lines of good taste. Jerks come in all ages and sizes. (The worst ones come in extra-large: the bully size.)

Jerks work in our offices, shop in our supermarkets, and ride on our highways—usually on our bumpers. They seem to have special passes at movie theaters: Wherever we sit, they get to sit right behind us. They live in our cities and on our farms. Sometimes—don't you just hate it?—they even live right in our own homes!

Every day, I get letters from people complaining about the jerks in their lives. I find these letters to be among the toughest to answer. Jerks are rarely reasonable. They are often malicious. And if you respond to them by turning the other cheek, or by being honorable, fair, and pleasant, some jerks figure you're just an easy mark: They then devise new ways to take advantage of you.

Psychologists say that to many jerks, you are the jerk. They are so jerky that they see themselves as the victims in conflicts they create. That can make finding solutions even more complicated.

I've found that each jerk-confrontation must be considered individually. A few well-constructed sentences can go a long way in helping you vent your frustration. Outbursts of anger can send a message to a jerk: Don't mess with me, buddy! And, in some cases, even revenge is appropriate—if you feel better, the jerk feels worse, and you're not arrested. Often, however, for safety's sake, it's best to simply walk away from a jerk: If you've got high self-esteem, you won't feel like a wimp.

An advice column serves as a forum for people to bitch about jerks. So even if I can't come up with the perfect way to deal with every variety of jerk, at least I can give the victims an outlet to express themselves.

Some of the letters in this chapter will sound familiar. We all know jerks like these jerks. Other letters describe jerks whose stunts are more cruel than even the most cynical among us could imagine. Jerks fall into many categories.

THE UTTERLY SELFISH

A woman moved out of her New York City apartment and sent a change-of-address form to the post office. Most of her mail soon began arriving at her new home. However, some letters were still trickling in to her old address. She wrote:

> Recently I learned from former neighbors that the man occupying my old apartment has been writing "Deceased" on any mail addressed to me. He leaves the letters by the lobby mailboxes.
>
> He knows I'm alive. He just doesn't want to be bothered with my mail, and figures that if the Postal Service thinks I'm dead, carriers will quit putting my mail in his mailbox.
>
> I'm really steamed. What a selfish man! Is he breaking any laws? Should I confront him?

I replied:

> Wouldn't it be nice if the new tenant in your old apartment would never again receive important letters. Also, his citizenship would be revoked, locusts would descend on his apartment, and his skin would break out in boils.
>
> However, postal authorities tell me there aren't laws designed to nab jerks like him. The Postal Service recommends that you contact the manager of the branch officer that delivers mail to your old address. Explain what this man is up to, and make sure your forwarding address is on file.
>
> As for the man now living in your old apartment, resist the urge to sign him up for reams of junk mail. Just send him a short letter explaining: "I've informed the post office that I'm still alive. If you feel compelled to write on any mail of mine, 'Not At This Address' will be sufficient." Sign it, "Stay Healthy," followed by your name.

AUTOJERKS

There are many jerks on the highways, and they have many ways to annoy us. Consider the guy who rides your bumper, flashing his high beams. He refuses to let you into his lane when your lane is ending. Or he drives so obnoxiously, you feel like rolling down your window and cursing at him.

Well, don't.

Instead, when you meet him at a red light, roll down your window and politely say, "Excuse me, there seems to be something leaking from under your car. You'd better pull over and check it out."

He will. You'll get miles up the road, away from him. You'll also get a large measure of satisfaction.

Be careful, though. After I gave this advice in my column, a man wrote to say he was an autojerk and if anyone pulled that stunt on him, he'd "meet the clown at the next traffic light and make him apologize." He didn't get any more specific.

PREFERENTIAL-TREATMENT DEMANDERS

A waitress wrote that her restaurant has a policy of giving discounts to uniformed police officers—as a courtesy and as a crime deterrent. One day, five off-duty officers, all women, came into the restaurant in their street clothes and demanded the discount. The waitress asked her manager. He reiterated the policy: They must be in uniform. The women were belligerent. "I showed them no disrespect and gave them fine service," the waitress wrote. "And when I went to clean their table after they left, I found one penny in front of each of their plates." The waitress taped the five pennies to the letter she sent to me. She asked that I track down the officers and return their money: She didn't want it.

COME-ON ARTISTS

"Whenever I run into Ben, he tells me how far his bedroom is from where we're standing," a woman wrote. "He always winks and has this mischievous smile on his face. I think he's just creepy. How might I respond?"

I told her if she's not interested in making the excursion to his bedroom, she should keep her distance: "Say, 'Sorry, Ben, I have no plans to go in that direction.' If he gets even more obnoxious and overbearing, add: 'I'm glad you always keep track of the mileage to your bedroom. As for myself, I like to keep track of the distance between myself and the nearest jerk. Right now, I estimate I'm about two feet away.' "

BULLIES

Most of us meet our first brutes when we're children. In fact, many young people write me in desperation: How do they deal with the school bully? And bullies can be male or female.

"I'm certain that a girl at school stole my gym shoes," wrote a junior high school girl. "I don't have solid proof, but the shoes this girl wears look exactly like the ones taken from my locker.

"Now my mother says I can't get new shoes until I get the old ones back. I'm afraid to confront this girl. She's rough and mean, and I don't think she'll give me back the shoes anyway. How do I explain this to my mother?"

She signed herself "Shoeless."

When her problem came across my desk, I couldn't believe how similar it was to an experience I had in my youth. I wrote back to the girl and told her the story that follows:

I was a sophomore in high school when my sneakers were stolen from my gym locker. An eyewitness told me that "Glenn," the school's all-conference football player and all-around tough guy, had stolen them. I got up my courage and approached big Glenn, mumbling that I had lost my sneakers. "If you see them, Glenn, could you let me know?" I asked. "The sneakers have my name written on them."

Glenn scowled at me, said he hadn't seen my sneakers and didn't expect to. He then encouraged me to get lost. I sized up his feet: Though he was big, his feet were my size.

A month or so passed. One morning I came to school and learned that Glenn was walking around with sneakers that had ZASLOW written on the side of them in big letters. I would have to confront big Glenn or I'd be forever branded a wimp.

So I did. I said something like, "Ummm, I think those are my sneakers, Glenn." I'll never forget his response. He said, "No they're not."

I argued the matter a little longer. He acted as if the fact that

ZASLOW was written on his sneakers was a mere coincidence. And so I had to make a decision. Should I try to beat up the school tough guy? Or would it be smarter to kiss my sneakers good-bye and safely get on with my life?

Call me a wimp, but I opted for the latter. And so I told Shoeless: "If confronting the girl who stole your sneakers yields no results and turning her in to school authorities would somehow endanger you, you might want to kiss your gym shoes goodbye, too.

"Tell your mother it might not be safe for you to get into a battle over your shoes. If she can remember the tougher times from her youth, she'll understand and buy you new shoes."

Many readers disagreed with my advice. They wrote of the benefits of standing up to young bullies. One man wrote:

> I was a quiet child and toughs took advantage of me. Like you, Zazz, I was scared when I saw this young thug wearing my shoes—with my name on them. But I was more afraid of my father's reaction if I came home without my shoes. So I confronted the jerk.
>
> A fight started and, out of fear and anger, I beat the you-know-what out of the thief. Not only did I get my shoes back, but the thug ended his reign of terror at the school. I believe that if Shoeless is sure who stole her shoes, she should take whatever action is necessary to get them back— not only to prevent further problems, but also as a matter of principle. It's not always wise to be a wimp.

A woman wrote:

> Your answer to Shoeless brought back painful memories. When I was 11, I was beat up daily by an overgrown 14-year-old girl. She would pull my long hair, punch me, and she once gave me a black eye. I was terribly afraid of her.
>
> But one day she shoved me in front of a speeding car, and I got so angry that I pushed her down the stairs at school and threatened to beat the daylights out of her. She believed me. I had quit being a mouse, but I never became a bully.

When bullies grow up, they continue to pick the weak and the meek as targets.

A sixty-seven-year-old woman with arthritis wrote me to say

she lives alone on social security: "A bully lives next door to me. He's unfriendly, even mean to me. The other day he shoveled his driveway and dumped all the snow on the sidewalk in front of my house. What can I do?"

I replied:

If life were fair, it would snow only on certain houses— your neighbor's, for instance.

You could try talking to him or voicing your complaint in a well-worded note. But if he's such a jerk, reasoning with him could be impossible. In that case, you'll have to wait and catch him in the act of dumping his snow on your sidewalk. Get a loud siren. Every time he dumps a shovelful of snow on your property, blast the siren. He'll certainly be taken aback—and afraid of what you might do next.

Let's hope his day will come. Maybe in the spring.

Many readers had advice for this woman. One man sent money for her to hire kids to shovel her sidewalk. Another made this offer: "The next time that bully pulls something smart, let me know and I'll come over and beat his brains out—or give him a new set."

I found the suggestions involving guns, bows and arrows, and "man-eating snow-blowers" to be a bit strong. But I was impressed that so many readers showed their support. Their message: Bullies beware!

EVANGELJERKS

Several readers have written asking how to deal with the overbearing "missionaries" who solicit donations at airports. If you've ever been in an airport, you've probably been accosted.

Here's the scenario and my advice:

You're hurrying to catch your plane and you're stopped by a smiling guy in a wig and an outfit from another planet. He carries paperback Bibles, speaks in an odd, singsong voice, and wants you to convert to his religion before you get to gate B-7.

He also wants as much money as you can give him and talks vaguely of children in orphanages. You tell him that you support only charities you've heard of, and don't give money to strangers in airports. The evangeljerk just keeps smiling and talking, using words like peace, love, and orphanage.

That's when you should say: "You know, I've often thought about converting to your religion, but then I meet a jerk like you, and I realize how wrong it would be!"

SPOUSES WITH EXCUSES

A woman called our hot line and angrily announced: "I caught my husband with another woman. He admits he had been seeing her, but says he shouldn't be considered a cheater because there wasn't sexual intercourse. Am I crazy, or old-fashioned? Or do I have a right to feel betrayed?"

I replied: "I'd hate to play poker with your husband. I'd catch him with cards up his sleeve, and he would deny he was cheating because his hands weren't in my pocket.

"If your husband wants a reconciliation, insist that he confess, ask forgiveness, promise to be a good boy—and broaden his definition of cheating."

Another woman wrote: "My husband didn't come home the other night until 3 A.M. I trust him: He was just out with the boys, having fun. But I had expected him home by midnight, and I was worried sick.

"When he got in, I asked, 'Why didn't you call?' He answered: 'I couldn't find a phone.' I'm sure every bar he went to had a phone. Boy, was I steaming! Any advice?"

My response: "Tell you husband that AT&T counts 1,861,542 pay phones in the United States—and next time he's going to be three hours late, he'd better find one of them and call you.

"Let him know that on a scale of one to 10, you rate his excuse as a zero. Don't let him get away with it again."

DASTARDLY PEOPLE WHO'D STEAL YOUR LIVELIHOOD

A waitress at an upscale restaurant wrote about a coworker: "She's nice enough on the surface, but I'm almost positive she's making off with some of my tips. How do I prove it or confront her?"

The solution I suggested: "Have a friend eat dinner at one of your tables. At the end of the meal, your friend should call over your co-worker and say: 'I've got to leave now. Could you give this tip to my waitress?'

"He'll hand her $10 and take off. Then you'll come out of the kitchen. If your co-worker doesn't fork over the full tip, you'll have your evidence."

DASTARDLY PEOPLE WHO'D STEAL YOUR KID'S LIVELIHOOD

What sort of people would conjure up a plan to hijack a paper route from a hardworking twelve-year-old boy? You're right: Jerks!

The boy wrote to me to say that two customers on his route had called the newspaper to complain about his deliveries: "Both have sons my age who told me they wish they had my job. I think the customers hope to get me fired so their sons can apply for my route. What can I do?"

I advised him to tell his supervisors about his suspicions. That could protect him.

As for your two rotten customers, resist the urge to get even. Make sure their newspapers land on their porches, not in the bushes. Keep their papers dry. And don't toss tomorrow's edition through their windows.

This might be a helpful experience for you. When your days as a paper boy are over, you'll certainly meet more people who'd step on you to get ahead. The earlier you learn to be wary of such louses, the better.

CITIZENS YOU WISH YOU COULD ARREST

One question I'm frequently asked: What should a person say to a blatant litterbug in a public place? Even when litterers are strangers, there's an urge to admonish them, and tell them to pick up after themselves.

A similar question: What, if anything, might one say to folks who feel it's not necessary to pick up after their dogs?

My responses are related: "If you see someone littering, you might say, 'Excuse me, I think you dropped something.' They may glare at you or ignore you, but they may be sufficiently embarrassed and feel obliged to pick up their litter.

"As for the dog walkers, you can always say, 'Excuse me, I think your dog dropped something.' The dog owner won't be as apt to pick it up, but again, you'll have made your point."

JERKY AND PROUD OF IT

I wrote a column about the annoying green-grass enthusiasts who turn on their sprinkler systems and end up watering the sidewalk. I said it's rude to passersby. A few days later, I got a letter from a woman who signed herself "Concrete Waterer." She wrote:

> I water my concrete to keep people off my property. I don't own a dog and I'm sick of cleaning up after other people's pets.
>
> I've erected "keep off the grass" signs and purchased every product imaginable. Nothing seems to keep animals and their masters away—except watering the sidewalk.
>
> Now, people and their pets detour into the street and bypass my lawn. For the first time in six years, I haven't had to clean up after neighborhood dogs.

I replied:

> I assume you're unconcerned about water shortages. You don't seem worried about chasing pedestrians (senior citizens, kids) into the street, possibly into the way of oncoming cars. And I don't know whether you realize that the sidewalk isn't your property.
>
> Yes, people who allow their dogs to abuse other people's lawns are rude and selfish. There are no easy solutions to this problem. But watering concrete as a deterrent? For how many hours? Wasting how many gallons of water? I'm sorry, but I think your technique is equally rude and selfish.

BIGOTS

A white teenage girl wrote to say that her parents disapproved of her Puerto Rican boyfriend, and often made racist remarks about "useless Ricans." I suggested:

If you have a VCR, go to your local video store and rent "Guess Who's Coming to Dinner." The movie eloquently examines parents' concerns and misgivings when a daughter brings home a fiance of another skin color.

The parents in the movie learn to be accepting. That's a big step, and in the case of your parents, such a transformation probably won't come overnight. Your relationship is obviously a shock for them and their rude comments are their way of dealing with it. Perhaps watching the movie with you will help them control their bigoted attitudes.

My answer resulted in several racist letters, including this one:

Dear Zazz: If a man teaches his children to be proud that they're white, he is no more of a bigot than the blacks who say "Black is Beautiful." They have Black History Month and the Miss Black America pageant. What do whites have?

Only whites are put down for being proud of their race. You suggested that people watch "Guess Who's Coming to Dinner." The movie could have been titled "Guess WHAT'S Coming to Dinner."

I wouldn't cross a black Labrador retriever with a white poodle, or a Negro, Rican, or gay with my white kids.
—White and Proud of It

I replied:

Dear White: You can certainly be proud of your own identity, but you must maintain your respect for people who are different. I found the tone of your letter and your choice of words to be absolutely racist. I suspect you know this, since you conveniently didn't sign your name.

I'm not especially proud to have you as a member of my human race.

By the way, mixed-breed dogs are in great demand and are often healthier.

THE JERKS YOU RAISED FROM INFANCY

"Speechless Mom" wrote to say that she went to her son the doctor for a physical: "He did a good job. I was very proud of him. But now he has sent me a bill. Should I pay it?"

I told her that if her son was too thick to realize all the motherly things she'd done for him over the years, she should pay the bill, let the matter drop, and find herself another physician.

Many readers had better ideas. Wrote one: "That doctor's mother should send him a bill for the nine months she carried him, for all the times she wiped his nose, for all the food she fed him, for all the clothes she bought for him, and for all the money she spent to send him to school to be a doctor."

Another reader advised this mother: "Write on the bill 'Do you mean it? signed, Mom' and mail it back to him in an envelope marked personal. If he responds in the affirmitive, just don't pay him. He wouldn't dare give you trouble about it. He'd be too concerned about the potential newspaper headline: 'Dr. So-and-So Sues Mother For Services.' "

JERKS WHO INFLUENCE THE NEXT GENERATION OF JERKS

A woman named Sherle Adams called me to tell of an experience she had in a twenty-four-hour photocopying store in Schaumburg, Illinois.

Sherle, a communication analyst, was a customer in the store at about 1:30 A.M., when a woman in her thirties came bouncing into the place. "She had this bubbly voice," Sherle said. "She was just ecstatic. She talked about how thrilled she was to find a photocopying store open in the middle of the night."

The woman happily told the store clerk that her son, a junior high school student, had swiped the answers to an upcoming test from his teacher's desk. "This woman said she had to make a lot of photocopies of the answer sheet so her son could sell them to his friends the next day," Sherle recalled. "In her heart, she thought she was being a wonderful mother by helping out her kid. You could hear the happiness in her voice."

There were a few other customers in the store. All looked on in disbelief. Sherle wished she'd followed the woman into the street. "I'd have told her that she ought to stop and think what she's doing to her son. She's lost sight of a mother's role. She's teaching him that it's all right to steal and to cheat, and if he can make money doing it, all the better.

"There's a ripple effect, too. She's copying the answer sheet for her son, who sells it to the children of other mothers. It's wicked."

We can only speculate about how many children in Schaumburg forked over a few bucks for a copy of the stolen answer sheet. Maybe the sale was so public that the teacher got wind of it and punished the boy. The shame is that the mother, most likely, would lament only that he was caught.

Sherle hoped that some good might come from relating the story in my column. Perhaps some parents would see a bit of themselves in this woman—and rethink the way they're raising their kids.

"I wish Leo Durocher had never said, 'Nice guys finish last,'" Sherle told me. "That line is quoted again and again. It's become a sad philosophy for our society."

Swimming Upstream

A DECADE AGO, on the night of his senior prom, Joe admitted to his date that he had never slept with a woman. "She wanted to have sex in no uncertain terms," he recalls. "I had to tell her no."

Still, Joe discovered his sexuality that night. He and three buddies dropped off their dates and finished the night together. In Joe's words: "I guess we all 'came out' on prom night."

It was the first time that Joe and his friends acknowledged to each other that they were homosexual.

Joe, twenty-seven and a banker, told his story at a dinner party in his Chicago home. He had prepared a great Italian meal for his friends, Todd and Dan. I was there, too. Making house calls, I find myself observing and writing about a host of life-styles. Joe's invitation had just the right tone:

"As an advice columnist, you undoubtedly receive letters from straights complaining about gays, gays who want to be straight, straights who think they're gay, gays who wish they looked like Judy Garland, etc., etc.

"If you come for dinner, my friends and I can give you some insights. We're all professionals whose careers would be destroyed if we revealed our sexuality."

So there we were, having a serious discussion and some laughs, too. All three men talked of how they struggled against their homosexuality. Todd, thirty-one, said he remained celibate from ages seventeen to twenty-one. "I thought, 'This will pass,' and when it didn't, I thought, 'I'll make it pass.' Eventually, I had to accept myself."

All were suicidal at times in their youth. At eighteen, Joe overdosed on Scotch and Librium: He spent three months in a coma. "If I could, I'd be straight," he told me. "I'm not the sort of person who elects to swim upstream."

Though his friends said they're now comfortable with their

sexuality—"When I realized what I was, I decided to like what I was," said Dan—they, too, said their lives would be easier if they were straight. All feel alienated from some family members. And they wish they could be more public about their personal lives. "It's natural to want to walk arm in arm with someone you care about," said Dan, whose family may be the most accepting; he has slept with a lover at his parents' house.

The men talked of gay-bashing. Joe said a police officer had recently roughed him up for playing his car radio too loudly. "I was near a gay bar," Joe said. "He knew what I was and where I was going. He kept saying, 'You people.' I was terrified. If I was a straight guy with a loud radio, he'd have told me to turn it down. Period."

I asked a slew of personal questions. As a reporter, I'm always curious, but was I out of line? "Straight people usually don't ask any questions," said Todd. "They don't want to know." If more straights were more interested, he said, they'd gain a better understanding.

A growing acceptance of gays in the last decade has been offset by paranoia and animosity fueled by AIDS. Dan said he wishes more straights would join the fight that for gays is an everyday battle. "We all know people who have died of AIDS," he said. "AIDS is an important factor in our being. I've been to Vietnam. I've seen death. Now, again, I see it all around me. All of us need help dealing with friends who have AIDS."

Joe said he tested negative for the AIDS virus. He told of a friend who tested positive: "Every time he gets a cold, he thinks he's going to die." Should everyone be tested? The men weren't sure. "Psychologically," said Dan, "testing positive can destroy you." The men said they practice safe sex—and pray to be spared.

Their advice for straights? Try to understand that homosexuality is genetic in nature. Indeed, Todd believes he was gay the moment he was conceived. Joe added: "People might think their hairdresser or waiter is gay, but they never realize that their doctor, lawyer, or priest might also be. All we ask for is mutual respect."

On the stereo, Judy Garland was singing about "the man who got away"—a song "all of us can relate to," said Joe. He talked of fatherhood: "I envision paying a woman to carry my baby." And, as the night drew to a close, he told me about his own father, whom he hadn't talked to in five years. "When I was growing up," he said, "my parents kept saying, 'Marry an Italian girl.' Well, now they'll be lucky if they get an Italian."

GAY STRUGGLES

Being gay in America today brings with it a host of legal, moral, medical, family, and discrimination issues. I get an unending stream of mail from homosexuals because there are so many potential dilemmas in their lives.

One gay man wrote to tell me about Bob, his live-in lover of five years:

> We had a wonderful, loving relationship. When Bob died, I was beside myself with grief.
>
> After the funeral, Bob's brother and mother came to our house and took things they said were his. Some items were gifts I gave him. Others were items we bought together that had sentimental value. I was not in the right frame of mind to argue. I let them take whatever they wanted.
>
> Now, six months later, Bob's mom wants to pick up 'the rest of Bob's things.' Most of what she's talking about belonged to both of us. What can I do?

Sadly, such stories are becoming common as more gays live together openly and as more people die of AIDS. But the fact is that umarried couples, whether homosexual or not, have no rights to inherit from "roommates" who leave no will. Only legally married couples have the benefit of joint-property laws.

I told the surviving roommate that if reasoning with Bob's family was fruitless, he should get a lawyer: "You'll need receipts for items you alone purchased. Bob's next-of-kin will be entitled to half of the property you bought together, but receipts will at least allow you to retain your half."

A lawyer I contacted to help me answer this question said he had recently represented a lesbian whose lover died. Disagreements between the dead woman's family and her lover went beyond property claims. "They even fought over her ashes," the lawyer told me. "As absurd as it sounds, we ended up splitting the ashes."

Most letters I receive from homosexuals center on their alienation from their families, and their struggles to come out of, or remain in, the closet. A thirty-year-old man wrote that his immediate family knows he is gay and is respectful. However, his eighty-eight-year-old grandmother has been trying to get him married for ten years. Over his objections, and not realizing his sexual prefer-ence, this grandma plays matchmaker by giving his phone number to eligible women. "I know she means well," the man wrote, "but enough is enough."

I advised him to consider telling her straight: He's not. "You might be surprised to find her very accepting," I wrote. "Many people who live eight or nine decades have seen so much in their lives that they're not easily shocked or offended."

Among the saddest letters I receive are the ones from people who have long repressed their homosexual urges. Denial may be the most painful way to deal with being gay.

A sixty-year-old Catholic man wrote to say that as a teen, he had homosexual relations with men. Later, he joined the Army and was discharged for being a homosexual. In his letter to me, he explained:

> A doctor in the service was very understanding. He told me if I found a homosexual partner, I might live a happy, fulfilled life.
>
> Well, I didn't take his advice. Instead, I listened to a priest who told me to repent and go straight. I spent decades pretending to be a heterosexual. I never got married, but I also never returned to homosexuality.
>
> Now I'm retired, regretful and very lonely. My only solace is knowing that I won't die of AIDS, unless I get it through a blood transfusion.
>
> I am writing this letter as a warning to young people with the same problem. If they know in their hearts that they are gay, they shouldn't pretend to be anything else.

He signed himself "Alone."

I told him that his life isn't over and it's not too late for him. If he got involved in the gay community, he might get the support and companionship he'd missed all his life.

After I printed Alone's letter, I heard from several ministries that seek to "help people come out of their homosexuality." Their contention is that homosexuality is a result of emotional and psychological needs not met in childhood. "Though it is not the worst sin, it is not acceptable to God," one minister wrote.

I also heard from Dignity, a Catholic support group for gays and lesbians. The group deals with the question: "Doesn't the Bible condemn sex between two people of the same sex by calling it an abomination?" Dignity's answer: "Yes, it does, but the Bible condemns a lot of things. It condemns to death stubborn children and a man who picks up sticks on the Sabbath. It calls camels and eagles abominable things. All of this indicates that the many prohibitions of the Old Testament cannot be rashly quoted or easily understood outside their particular historical and cultural contexts." Dignity's goal: "Those of us who find ourselves both homosexual and Christian—and happy to be both—want to work within the church to help it and to be helped by it."

Most readers who commented on Alone's letter focused on the issue of whether homosexuality is sinful. But one letter writer made this well-taken point:

> Alone blames his loneliness on the fact that he never pursued homosexuality. I doubt his priest recommended he spend his life feeling sorry for himself and never forming close friendships. Why does our society assume that sexual activity is always a key component of intimacy? Isn't it obvious that sex may or may not be part of a close relationship? Inside marriage as well as out of it, friendship is the real treasure, not sex.

I try to be accepting, respectful, and open-minded when dealing with homosexuality in the column. This invariably results in bitter hate letters from homophobic, irrational readers. But it also leads gays and lesbians to send letters thanking me for being understanding and supportive.

Still, I've been accused a few times of insensitivity toward gays, and some of these accusations have had merit. Especially when I began giving advice, I didn't always consider a question from every conceivable angle.

One instance where I had to rethink and recast my original answer came after this letter:

> **Dear Zazz:** I'm in a sticky situation. My job involves matching people together to share hotel rooms. If people are coming to a conference or convention and need roommates, I match them up.
>
> Now I've got this client who is a lesbian and wants me

to find her another lesbian. She's insistent, but I don't want to jeopardize my job. What should I tell her?
—Uncomfortable

I replied:

You're not running a sex partner service. It's a roommate service. Firmly tell this to your client. Besides, how would you know whether potential roommates are lesbians? You'd have to ask them—and that's certainly not part of your job, is it?

Nothing against this woman's sexual orientation, but she might not be the right customer for your service. She seems to be looking for action, rather than someone to share the hotel bill. Don't match this woman with anyone unless you're certain she'll behave herself and not embarrass or hit on her roommate.

Dozens of lesbians were offended by my answer. A sampling:

• "Suggesting that this woman not be matched with a roommate unless she behaves herself is indicative of the myths and homophobia lesbians must fight every day.

"I've requested lesbian roommates in hotels and during college. I don't want to share a room with a person who may condemn me for what I am. I don't want to deal with hate, fear and ignorance.

"Your advice doesn't allow for the very logical possibility that the lesbian client is already monogamously involved. Heterosexuals haven't cornered the market on fidelity. Your advice supports the myth that if you put a lesbian in a room with another woman, she will try to seduce her."

• "To understand why a lesbian might want to room with a lesbian, it could be helpful for you and your readers to pretend you're not straight for one day. Live life as a secret. Don't talk with anyone about your boyfriend, girlfriend, hopes for marriage, or who gave you the flowers, etc.

"Uncomfortable should have told the client that her request would be cheerfully accommodated if another lesbian made a similar request."

• "Maybe the lesbian wanted a roommate who wouldn't spend all her time asking if she'd seen the hunk by the pool, or other inane, insensitive questions. Or maybe she wanted a roommate who wouldn't bring a man to the room. I challenge you, Zazz, to prove you're not a jerk and answer my letter."

I answered all the letters, which led several gay magazines to write about the stir and the many "apologies" I issued. I told all the letter writers that I'd discussed the issue with friends and colleagues, both heterosexual and gay. I said I was too quick to assume the lesbian client was using the roommate service as a dating service. Maybe that was her intention, but there was no evidence to unequivocally confirm this.

I certainly didn't mean to imply that all lesbians are promiscuous or preoccupied with sex. But I can see why so many gays were sensitized to the issue. Heterosexual ignorance and intolerance are rampant.

So many gays send me letters detailing mean-spirited behavior by straights. One man wrote to say that when he was younger, he had posed nude for gay magazines: "Now a co-worker has discovered an old magazine with me in it. He is blackmailing me for money."

There are innumerable ways straights set out to hurt gays. Consider this letter:

> **Dear Zazz:** I am a lesbian, but I don't flaunt it at work.
> For 14 months, a female co-worker was coming on to me. I knew she was heterosexual, so I was confused by her advances. I tried ignoring her, but she was persistent.
> Then I broke down and wrote her a note telling her I had feelings for her. I was shocked when she took my note to the personnel department. She said I was sick and disgusting.
> Why would she tease me and then stab me in the back? Do some straight people have that much hatred for gays?
> —Shocked

My response:

> Maybe you mistook friendliness for advances, and you assumed she had feelings for you because you had feelings for her. If that was the case, perhaps she was shocked by your note. Still, her response was harsh and hurtful.
> If your co-worker's advances were indeed as unmistak-

able as you perceived them to be, she sounds like a sick, cruel woman. Then again, she may have been attracted to you and found it safe to flirt. When you responded with a note, however, maybe she got scared that she'd acted on her homosexual feelings. Turning you in might have been a panic reaction.

Whatever the case, you'd be smart to stay far away from this co-worker.

Gay readers again lent me their input. Wrote one: "Many lesbians could tell a similar story of harassment by a straight woman testing her power of flirtation. Invariably, the straight woman runs to the authorities when she's successful. It's not only that such women hate lesbians; they also hate being confronted by the lesbian within themselves."

My column allows me to see the depths of homophobia. For instance, whenever I write about a gay topic, I invariably receive an unsigned hate letter from a certain reader whose envelopes bear a Maryland postmark. His profane rantings and sick illustrations are just about the scariest mail I receive. I hear from him several times a month. Even when I write about AIDS patients who are children, this reader scrawls "pervert-lover" or "sodomite-defender" across my columns and mails them back to me. If he gets a copy of this book, I assume I'll hear from him yet again.

Gay issues, especially AIDS, generate mail from profoundly paranoid and uninformed readers. I've gotten letters from people asking if they can get AIDS from masturbation, shaking hands, or riding on elevators with gay coworkers. I thought it ludicrous when a supermarket checkout clerk asked if she might get AIDS from gay customers' dollar bills. Then I learned of a *Los Angeles Times* poll indicating that 10 percent of Americans believe AIDS can be contracted by handling money.

A woman wrote me to say she was worried about her sixty-five-year-old friend, who was sexually active with several partners: "She believes that, at her age, she cannot contract AIDS. No one has been able to convince her that old age doesn't make you immune to the disease."

Misinformation about AIDS results in different responses from different people. A mother wrote to tell me about her son and daughter, both in their twenties, who believe AIDS is a disease almost everyone will have in the future. "They say there are all sorts of ways to get AIDS, even through insect bites, and that the government has covered up these facts so there isn't a panic," the mother wrote. "As a result, my children believe it doesn't matter whether they are sexually careful or not. They are behaving in bold ways—as if there's no tomorrow. I'm wondering if other young people today are adapting this fatalistic 'devil may care' attitude."

I passed out photocopies of this woman's letter at some of Chicago's famous Rush Street singles bars. I was impressed with the sensible outlooks of many young bar-hoppers I spoke to. Most said this woman's children were in the minority. They spoke of being more cautious than ever, of once-promiscuous friends who are now abstaining. Many said they were horrified that this woman's children could be so ignorant and unconcerned about how their actions might hurt, or kill, their partners.

"I know people who do background checks," one woman said. A bar doorman told me: "A lot of people think there will be a cure, and until then, they'll take precautions. Of course, if a girl is outrageously hot, then some guys will take a risk." Added the doorman at a bar down the street: "Some people are fatalistic about AIDS. They say half the world will have AIDS in ten years, so why not go out with a bang? But most people are cautious about sex to the point where they're saying, 'I don't need it that bad.' "

In an effort to keep customers coming in, and to keep them alive, Rush Street barkeepers told me they installed condom machines in both the women's and the men's rooms.

Some readers write with their "solutions" to the AIDS epidemic. One man pointed out that "the best way to avoid catching AIDS and to tackle the teen pregnancy problem is abstinence. But abstinence is not a practical answer unless something can be done to enable an individual to better control his or her natural sex drive." This man's answer: masturbation. "Not once," he wrote, "have I seen anyone suggest a program to encourage masturbation as an effective way of attaining abstinence. Instead of dispensing safe-sex information in the schools, why don't experts like the surgeon general promote masturbation?"

I replied that this was an interesting idea, but it wouldn't work. Once boys and girls discover one another (or boys discover boys, and girls find girls, in the case of homosexuality), they invariably prefer each other's company to being alone. Masturbation, I said, would be more of a stopgap than a cure-all.

Then there are the people who have misguided notions about

what to do with the growing number of AIDS patients. I try to refute their suggestions only after acknowledging their fears. One letter writer suggested that a school be opened for children with the AIDS virus: "People with AIDS who are still able to work could teach these kids. The kids and teachers could come from all over the country. That way, normal people in schools wouldn't be infected."

I responded that herding kids into a leper-colony-style school would be cruel and unnecessary. I quoted the federal Centers for Disease Control, which recommends that students with AIDS continue going to their schools because the risk to others appears "nonexistent." I added: "Yes, we must make sure that children with AIDS don't infect other kids. School policies must be studied. But any solution must be a humane one."

Several readers wrote to say they liked the concentration camp idea, and that I was "pro-homo" and "pro-pervert" for arguing against it. In their irrational rage, they'd lost sight of the real issue: children's health.

Readers regularly send me antigay literature and propaganda. One mailing from a group called Christian Family Renewal began: "Just when you thought your children were safe from homosexual advances, Congress introduces House Resolution #709—The Gay Bill of Rights." Murray Norris, the group's president, offered this message in his mass mailing: "Homosexuality is not going to go away until you take an official stand on the issue."

Norris's rantings were sent to me by a concerned woman who'd received it in the mail and was terrified by it. She wrote:

> Why do people who preach prejudice think they are more Christian than the poor souls who bear the brunt of that hatred? If homosexuals can't live in our neighborhoods, nor earn a living in our workplace, what is to become of them? You may not be able to answer my question, Zazz. But you can speak out for compassion and understanding. You offer a moderate voice to thousands of readers. I hope some are listening.

I responded that the mailing was, indeed, frightening: "Substitute 'Jew' for the word 'homosexual' in this letter and it could have beem written a half-century ago by the hate-mongers in Nazi Germany." The Gay Bill of Rights was designed to provide equal rights for homosexuals in such areas as housing and employment. But

Norris suggested that the resolution sought to permit homosexuals the legal right to sodomize our children. It was a total distortion of the resolution, and I said so in the column. The hate mail in response was predictable.

In such a homophobic society, it is no wonder that the stigma of homosexuality can follow a person beyond the grave. Among the saddest letters I receive are the ones from the friends and family of people who died of AIDS. One survivor wrote:

> What rankles me most is the knowledge that from now on, Jim's name will become synonymous with the comment, "He died of AIDS."
>
> That label wipes out an entire lifetime of achievement. Already, his friends have been branded with guilt by association. AIDS robbed our society of yet another fine individual. But everyone will remember Jim only as an AIDS victim, not as the intelligent caring, smiling person who was always helpful and loving to others.
>
> And Jim's lover? He must deal not only with Jim's untimely death, but also with the people who tell him that he most certainly has AIDS, too.

I told this woman:

> It is up to you and others who loved Jim to keep his memory alive. Remind anyone who will listen that he was a wonderful, caring man. And don't be resentful when people talk of how he died of AIDS. By identifying AIDS victims by their personalities and accomplishments, maybe you'll help others to be less fearful and ignorant of the disease. By building understanding, you can make life easier for those now suffering from AIDS.

Consumer Alerts

A GOOD ADVICE-COLUMNIST must be a consumer advocate of sorts. Some people view my office as a quasi-governmental protection agency. The questions they send in have nothing to do with the usual subjects: cheating lovers, lazy spouses, broken dreams, etc.

Instead of cheating lovers, they write about cheating grocers: "He never really deducts for all my coupons. He just pretends to."

Instead of lazy spouses, they complain about lazy ballet teachers: "My daughter says her ballet teacher tells the whole class, 'Alright, dance in place,' and then goes outside to smoke a cigarette."

Instead of broken dreams, I hear about broken pipes: ". . . and until the landlord fixes them, I'm going to keep on holding back the rent."

Naturally, I can't deal with all these consumer woes in the column. If someone's blender breaks and the company won't honor the warranty, I might be able to give advice on how to deal with the stress and emotional heartache. But the problem itself is more suitable for the *Sun-Times*'s "Action Time" columnist.

The consumer issues I do choose to handle are the unconventional ones. Perhaps the most intriguing product-complaint story I ever received came from a woman I'll call Brenda.

"I'm a lawyer," she wrote, "and after dating another lawyer for five months, I felt close enough to him to make love. Because I'm conservative and worried about AIDS, it was my first sexual encounter in a year.

"Well, the condom broke, I got pregnant, and my boyfriend now says the 'new rules' of society dictate that pregnancy is solely a woman's responsibility. He wants nothing more to do with me."

Brenda felt alone, helpless. She had to let off steam. So even though she knew she had no legal recourse, she called Schmid Laboratories, maker of Ramses prophylactics, to complain about the torn condom. She told me:

Basically, they gave me a form speech over the phone. They talked about "the chain of liability." They said there are so many factors that might have caused that condom to tear. Maybe it somehow got damaged during delivery, or on the store shelf. Or maybe my boyfriend was an idiot when he put the thing on.

The person I talked to was very nice, but she was giving a memorized speech. She said she'd see about getting me a reimbursement. I asked if that meant Schmid would support the child for the next 18 years. She kind of laughed and said, "Well, you know, that's not what we mean."

A few weeks later, Brenda got a cordial letter from Phyliss Barber, Schmid's manager of regulatory affairs. Barber's letter apologized for "whatever inconvenience you have experienced."

Soon after, the refund arrived: a check for $1.75.

Though still anxious about her pregnancy, Brenda couldn't stop laughing. How was she expected to raise a child on $1.75?

"They also sent me this cute little envelope so I could send back any unused samples for them to examine. And they specifically said 'unused,' as if I'd be stupid enough to send them the used condom."

Brenda never cashed the check. "I keep it for the sake of humor," she said. "I show it to friends."

Well, I couldn't resist calling Barber. It seemed to me that $1.75 refund checks are kind of silly. Wouldn't Schmid be wiser to simply point out to complaining customers that condoms aren't 100 percent foolproof? After all, it's written right on the package.

Barber had an explanation. Schmid is regulated by the Food and Drug Administration. There is a section in the FDA's "1976 Medical Device Amendment" that calls for manufacturers to "replace, refund or repair a device" if it proves defective. "We definitely cannot repair our devices," Barber said. "So we refund or replace."

Schmid receives only a handful of complaints each month and is committed to "rigid quality control," Barber said. "People may call and say they don't like how it fits. We keep records on all complaints. We like to see if there's a trend."

The $1.75 wasn't intended to satisfy Brenda's need for money to raise a child. But the refund was issued to remind Brenda that she is a valued customer, Barber said, adding: "My job is to use good business sense to keep us within regulations."

Shortly after receiving the refund, Brenda had a miscarriage, which she said was more emotionally painful than the unwanted pregnancy.

The good news was that Brenda left her selfish, inconsiderate boyfriend. He also must have come from a bad batch. (If he bought the condom, he's the sort of jerk who would have said the $1.75 belonged to him.) She was smart to be through with him.

UNDERCOVER POET

To protect readers from getting hoodwinked and ripped off, I keep my eyes open for suspicious activities and scams. Sometimes, I even go under cover. (But don't worry, Mom, I pick safe issues. Poetry, for instance.)

Investigative reporters think they have better things to do than cover the poetry industry. Not me. And besides, the poetry beat is wide open. One day I grabbed it—and took off on an undercover investigation that lasted six months.

I'd noticed that the "New American Poetry Contest" had been advertised heavily in mass publications such as *Parade* and the *National Enquirer*. In the ads, editor and publisher John Campbell explained: "I want to find exciting new poets! Even if you have written only one poem in your life, be sure to enter."

Now I'm no poetry editor, but if I were searching for the next Robert Frost, the *National Enquirer* wouldn't be the first place I'd sink my ad dollars. I'd be afraid I'd get too many poems about diets of the stars, fights on the *Roseanne* set, or Madonna's love spats.

I suspected what Campbell was up to, with his $1,000 grand prize and his promise to print winning poems in a deluxe *World Poetry Anthology*. He was looking for the easily flattered.

So I entered his contest under cover. "In your photo, you look wise and poetic," I gushed in my application. Because I thought Campbell was more interested in customers than good poets, I wanted to enter a poem with little potential. I wrote the poem below in four minutes. The title: "Questions?"

> You say you love me, but then again,
> I've got questions if it's true,
> Like where? And how? And what? And when?
> And the biggest question: Who?
> Who have you been out with, babe?

Who have you been kissing?
Better speak up, and fast, my babe,
Or it's me who you'll be missing!

Three months later, a "poetrygram" arrived with good news. "Questions?" had won an honorable mention! In his letter, Campbell encouraged me to frame and display my award "with pride."

I pictured would-be poets across America opening their poetrygrams and framing their awards. Very suspicious.

Well, a month later, on January 15, 1988, I received another poetrygram. This time, Mrs. Eddie-Lou Cole, poetry editor, was writing to wish me "a most happy and poetical New Year." In a form letter, she called my winning entry "a sensitive, wonderful poem, and one I feel deserves to be read and enjoyed by poets worldwide." She said she was working on a book of poetry "by some of our world's greatest poets, and the exciting news is: *I'd like permission to publish your poem in the book!*"

She reminded me: "Even Robert Frost was 'unknown'—until he became published!" My poem, she promised, would be printed "on the finest of rich acid-free papers." The "luxurious hardbound and gold-embossed" book will "preserve for posterity some literary gems which might otherwise be lost to oblivion. Truly a milestone in publishing history, it may be displayed with pride for generations to come."

She gave her age (seventy-nine), then concluded: "I love you as a poet" and "I believe in you."

Nice letter, huh? Well, she also sent an order form for the $69.95 book. The good news: I could buy the book for $39.95 (two for $59.90) as an "honorarium" discount. For $10 more, I could dedicate my poem to a loved one; for $45, they'd print my photo; for another $45, an "award-winning" artist would illustrate "Questions?" (How? With question marks???)

So there you have it. For one book with "the works": $139.95. And you can bet that there were plenty of would-be poets across America who would pay to see their poems in print.

Well, when I wrote a column outlining my investigation, I also offered advice to readers with a literary bent: "Write poems, show them to your friends, read them aloud to your children, try to get them in legitimate anthologies—but if you're a real poet, don't blow it! Save your money."

I never would have guessed how many readers of my column

had actually entered the contest—and even put up cash for the book.

Some wrote just to say thanks. "My husband thought something seemed fishy," wrote one woman, "but I guess I was so happy that Mrs. Cole loved my poem, I was willing to pay to be flattered. Now I'm just embarrassed. After your column, I deposited my poetry-grams and my certificate in the trash."

"I entered the same contest you did," wrote another reader. "Like you, I received a reply indicating that I am oozing with un-tapped talent. They didn't want to lose me! With my award came the pitch for the $39.95 book. I could also enter more poems, at $5 each. There must be a lot of gullible people in the world."

I also heard from poets who earn money writing for legitimate anthologies. "Those ridiculous poetry scams are the bane to the reputation of modern poetry," wrote one poet. Another explained: "Poetry is thought to be such a minor art—poets don't expect to earn money—that it never occurs to people that poets easily can be scammed. I'm a poet myself, with the ruthless bull detector that Hemingway said all writers must develop, so I usually can smell these 'contests' miles away."

Several readers wrote to encourage me to continue my investiga-tion. "You soon will receive an invitation to attend a poets' conven-tion in Las Vegas, where you will meet many famous poets (other honorable-mention winners, no doubt)," wrote one contest winner who now knows better. "Of course, you will pay your own way and book your hotel through the poetry organization."

He was right. Soon enough, I was invited to the convention. Judging by the brochure photos, most of the previous year's twenty-five hundred winners were older, smiling women in long, flowing dresses. (Mrs. Eddie-Lou Cole, at seventy-nine, looked like one of the younger participants.) The poet laureate wore a giant crown, and those in her court wore Olympiclike ribbons. Also, Milton Berle was pictured, with no explanation. The scene looked like a surreal beauty pageant.

I didn't attend the convention, so some important questions remain. Was Milton Berle an honorable mention winner, too? How much do those poetry crowns cost? And why were there so few men at the convention?

Well, I'm still on the poetry beat, still looking for answers. The investigation continues.

A PHONE CALL AWAY

In preparation for a consumer-oriented column I wrote in December 1988, I journeyed through my house, collecting all sorts of food products, medicine, shampoo, and cleaning supplies. I then sat down with twenty-four cans, jars, bottles, and boxes, and was ready to write.

Boy, I could have written a phone book.

Maybe you've noticed: These days, if you have a question, a comment, or need advice about a product, you can get instant attention. Hundreds of products offer toll-free numbers right on the package. You call, and a friendly "agent" is at your service.

I phoned twenty-four hot lines. My questions were often unconventional, but every agent treated me cordially, if a touch quizzically. Highlights:

• The box of Pepto-Bismol tablets warned: "A darkened coating on the tongue may occur from Pepto-Bismol's beneficial medication."

Though the condition was termed "harmless and temporary," I phoned 1-800-543-7270 and asked: What if you have a big date and a big dark tongue? How long is "temporary" and how dark is "dark"?

"It can become almost blackened," the agent said. "It comes from the active ingredient mixing with the hydrogen sulfide in the bacteria in your mouth. It goes away after you stop using the product. Don't worry."

I asked if she gets a lot of calls about this. "Oh yes," she said, almost wearily.

• One ingredient in Nabisco's Oreo cookies is whey. So what's whey?

I dialed 1-800-932-7800 and an agent told me: "It's derived from milk and is used in Oreos as a protein."

"Is there double the whey in Double-Stuf Oreos?" I wondered.

"I'm not sure," he admitted. "Interesting question."

• The Green Giant green beans can warned: "Green Giant recommends use by December 1990."

So what happens in 1991? I called 1-800-328-4466. "The beans don't self-destruct," the agent reassured me. "They might be discolored. You wouldn't want to eat them. But look, you still have two years. Don't worry."

• My jar of Ragu Gardenstyle spaghetti sauce, however, was cause for worry. I knew I'd bought it a while back, and the label boasted "no preservatives." Uh-oh.

I called Ragu, 1-800-243-5804. The agent had me read her the "batch number" from the jar. "Wow," she said, "that jar's four years old! Its shelf life was only two or three years. I wouldn't use it."

For sentimental reasons—the jar accompanied me through three changes of address—I still couldn't bring myself to throw it out.

• The agent for Band-Aid, 1-800-352-4777, was more reassuring. My old Band-Aid box had a seven-year shelf life before the bandages would be less effective at "absorbing wound fluids."

In an age when most packages are cardboard or plastic, I asked why Band-Aid boxes are still made of sturdy metal: "People love them," the agent said. "They put buttons in them."

• Sweet 'n Low packages carry this blunt message: "This product contains saccharin which has been determined to cause cancer in laboratory animals."

When I called 1-800-231-1123, the agent said federal regulations require the statement, "but don't worry."

"The lab animals spent their lifetimes drinking the equivalent of the saccharin in one hundred cans of soda," she said. "If you're using Sweet 'n Low occasionally, I wouldn't worry."

(The song "Don't Worry, Be Happy" was at the top of the music charts at the time. It seemed as if it was the theme song for these hot lines.)

• My Schick razor package asked: "Shaving questions? Call 1-800-SHAVERS."

My question: How do I avoid cutting my Adam's apple? "You need a fatter neck," the female agent joked. For some reason, I'd have preferred to talk to a male agent on this one.

• Maxwell House coffee's packaging announced that it sponsored the 1988 United States Olympic team. That surprised me. I'd read that caffeine was banned at the Olympics.

The Maxwell House agent (1-800-431-1004) didn't know, but he was a quick thinker. "We produce several brands of decaffeinated coffee," she said. "Maybe that explains it."

• When I called Pillsbury Best chocolate chip cookies (1-800-328-4466), I asked if that hyperbolic product name hurt sales for Pillsbury's regular cookies. "We call all our cookies 'best,' " the agent said. "We don't have best and average, only best."

• The perky agent for Dole pineapple chunks (1-800-232-8800) promised to send me a stack of pineapple recipes.

I asked her what question she is asked most frequently. "Our recipes call for using a Number Two can, and people don't know what that means," she said. "Every day they call and ask."

So what's a Number 2 can? "Twenty ounces," she said.

Why don't the recipes call it a twenty-ounce can? "Good question," she replied.

• The box for SuperSoft ClingFree claimed: "ClingFree is: Thicker! Better! Does More!"

When I called 1-800-242-1718, I didn't mention that the phrase "ClingFree is does more" is incoherent. But I did ask why thicker is better. The agent gave a dissertation on static-control testing.

So how many people call these hot lines? Well, to find out, I called Procter and Gamble Company, which offers toll-free lines for all of its one-hundred-plus brands. The company receives eight hundred thousand calls a year.

Two thirds of the calls are "information-seeking" and a third are complaints, said spokeswoman Linda Ulrey. "It's an expensive operation, but it gives us a good pipeline to consumers. If people can't get quick answers, they might decide never to use the product again."

Agents are given four to six weeks of training to learn about the products they'll be describing and defending. They're also taught to show respect for all callers, no matter how stupid their questions may be.

Ulrey declined to talk about the strangest or most humorous calls P&G receives. "We don't like to talk about that," she said. "We don't want consumers to feel their questions aren't being taken seriously."

Working Stiffs

IN ONE WAY, at least, little has changed since I left *The Wall Street Journal.* I still cover business and the working world. Except, these days, I usually don't get asked about stock option strategies.

Instead, a factory worker asks me if he should report stoned coworkers. A woman wonders if a sequined dress is appropriate for the Christmas party in her plant's lunchroom. A clerk happens upon her boss's pay stub and regrets spreading his big-number salary around the office. A man asks if it's gauche to request a doggie bag at a business lunch—especially if he isn't paying.

People often write to me after they get fired, but usually there's not much I can do. One woman called in sick to her job so she could attend *The Oprah Winfrey Show,* which is shown live in Chicago. The jig was up when her boss spotted her in the TV audience with a healthy smile on her face.

Office-romance questions come in droves—and in many varieties. I've even gotten complaints that companies encourage office flings. Consider the letter from "Stuck at Home." Her husband's company bars spouses from its "working weekends" in Florida, yet always sponsors an employee dance contest on the beach. The left-at-home spouses are left with visions of cute single secretaries doing the rumba by moonlight with their married bosses.

Once, an entire law office wrote for advice:

> Our problem? Sexual tension in the workplace. We don't have any. Each of us is fairly attractive, intelligent, open-minded, liberal, fun-loving, and happily married. We've read in your column and elsewhere about sexual adventures among co-workers, and are wondering why we're not lusting after one another.
>
> Being in the business, we also try to identify with "L.A. Law" on TV. However, our practice does not include

rendezvousing in the file room, dallying on the office couch, or interviewing clients who offer tips on the latest techniques.

They were obviously kidding—weren't they? In any case, I told them: "Your letter proves there can be good humor in a legal office—and that's scads more fun and much less risky than sexual tension. Long after 'L.A. Law' is canceled, your marriages will be in prime time."

Work-related problems run from the mundane to the gravely serious. Readers want to know how to deal with coworkers who steal their staplers, hit them up for loans, have powerful body odor (a frequent question), or are sleeping their way to the top. They ask how to respond to sexual harassment: One man in his early twenties said he was fighting off a female boss in her fifties. They write about dishonest bosses (a woman suspected her manager of embezzling five hundred thousand dollars), and the evils of nepotism. (One reader told of the supervisor who hired her two children. The kids were coming to work late, falsifying time sheets, getting reimbursed for exaggerated expenses, and earning more than employees with decades on the job. "If life were fair," I told the letter writer, "your supervisor's children would come to work only as photos in her wallet." As it was, there was little she could do.)

A woman wrote of discovering that a new business associate was a man she'd dated nine years earlier. "I slept with him back then, got pregnant, and had an abortion," she explained. "I didn't give him the details, and we soon lost contact. Now we've been thrown together in a business situation and it's awkward between us."

Offices are the perfect environment for busybodies to thrive. The person who wrote the letter that follows signed herself "Concerned." Maybe so. But she was concerned about something that was none of her business.

Dear Zazz: A co-worker has become romantically involved with another person in the office. He's quite taken with her. She's pretty and sweet and seems to like him a lot.

The thing is, I know she was sexually abused as a child. Since these unfortunate people often have hidden emotional problems and are poor marriage material, do you think I should discreetly mention this to my co-worker before he becomes involved with her?

—Concerned

I replied:

Dear Concerned: No way! Let the romance blossom without your interference. As they get to know each other, chances are she'll confide in him about her past. And if she doesn't, that's her decision. It would be unfair of you to meddle.

She may be dealing very well with emotional scars from her childhood—through counseling or on her own. In fact, she could be terrific marriage material.

Your concern is to be appreciated. But they could be the couple of the year. You may even end up dancing at their wedding. And if you do, dance with your mouth shut.

Every occupation comes with its own problems, some of which didn't seem to be problems until recently. A teacher wrote that he thinks it's important to hug his students: "Often, that's the best way to comfort children in the wake of a death, their parents' divorce, etc.

"Society and my principal remind me to be careful. These days, a teacher who hugs a student is looked at suspiciously. Yet I feel a teacher needs to show compassion as well as impart knowledge."

I advised this teacher to be discreet:

The awful realities of child abuse make parents nervous and scared. So all of us, not just teachers, have to be careful in our dealings with children. Try to avoid situations where your actions might be questioned. Sometimes a kind word or a caring pat on the back can work as well as a hug. Still, trust your judgment. If you feel a distraught child could use a hug, don't hold back.

Many workers use my column to educate the public about their jobs—and to give pointed advice. There are aspects to these people's jobs that we never consider—nor do we realize how annoying we can be when we're dealing with them.

A truck driver complained that motorists assume he can stop his truck in a heartbeat:

> Well, it's not so easy to bring a 70,000-pound truck to a halt. With all those little cars darting in and out around is, it's a wonder there aren't more accidents.
>
> Sometimes, I get so upset by selfish people in cars that I have to pull over to the side of the road. When I'm agitated, it's harder to drive, and I don't want to hurt anybody!
>
> Yes, I know some truckers are jerks. But I just wish car drivers would give a little more consideration to the rest of us on the road. If not for us "jerks," motorists wouldn't have their cars (we truck the cars to the dealerships), their clothes, their food, their anything.

A woman who sells lottery tickets for a living outlined her pet peeves:

> I'm on my feet eight hours a day, with long lines of people yelling at me to hurry up. Some people don't like standing in line, so they crowd around the counter. Then the yelling increases.
>
> A lot of people mumble or speak broken English, so I can't understand what numbers they want. If I ask them to repeat themselves, they glare at me like I'm the one who doesn't understand English.
>
> Also, when the machine is almost out of tickets, it prints pink tickets. There's nothing wrong with these tickets; they're legal. I get in trouble if I don't sell them. But so many people refuse to take them. It makes my job that much harder.

(In a just world, a customer would win a few million bucks on a pink ticket, and return to her store to share his winnings. I told her this, but she knew better: The odds would be astronomical.)

People often write me to defend their loved ones. The wife of a heating repairman wrote to say she's tired of the abuse her husband takes from the public, the state's attorney's office, and the media:

> When people say heating repairman, it's often in conjuction with the words 'scam' and 'ripoff artist.' My husband does good work at a fair price. He often has to leave our

house at 2 A.M. in below-zero weather to fix someone's heater. He has worked Sundays, holidays, and even Christmas. Then, sometimes, people say he charges too much and won't pay him anything.

Please, Zazz, tell your readers that when their furnaces break down in the dead of winter, it is my husband who is out there freezing all night to make you warm and comfortable.

I got just one letter supporting the repairman's wife. It was from a woman in Texas, who told this story:

A homeowner sent for a repairman to fix the furnace. The repairman arrived, took a hammer from his tool kit, and proceeded to tap the furnace in a number of places.

"It's okay now," he said. "That'll be twenty-five dollars."

"That's highway robbery!" shrieked the homeowner. "I want an itemized bill."

"All right," the repairman said, and wrote out a bill:

"For tapping the furnace . . . five dollars.

"For knowing where to tap . . . twenty dollars."

MUTINY IN THE SKY

One day, above the clouds between Chicago and Miami, I met a man who takes abuse for a living. "And through it all, I have to smile," he said, and grimaced.

He offered me a soft drink, peanuts, and a piece of his mind. He knew I was an advice columnist. I knew he was a flight attendant. We had reason to talk.

"Tom" stood in the aisle by my seat for a half hour. "I've got advice for flight attendants everywhere," he said, "Take notes. I've got a lot to say."

Figuring he'd give me good grist for a column, I got out my notebook.

The woman on my right, who had been reading a mystery novel, closed it up to listen. She had no choice. Tom leaned over her as he spoke to me.

"Why are people so rude to flight attendants?" he asked. "They treat us like dirt. They forget that the reason we're on board is for their safety. They think we're here just to listen to their complaints and to dish out food. People think we're just space waiters!"

Passengers kept squeezing by him on the way to the bathroom. "It's not our fault that the plane is late or that the bread is two days old or that you can't carry on everything you own. I don't make the rules."

Nor does he make the seats. "If your knees are in your nose, I'm sorry. But it's not my fault. People vent their frustrations out on flight attendants."

Tom said he'd been an attendant for nine years. He was based in Florida. He liked the freedom of his job, the many days off, the benefits, the free trips. But he said he hated the way some people treat him. And on one overseas flight from somewhere to somewhere else (he asked me not to give specifics), he fought back. He said he has felt better ever since, and he recommended that other flight attendants follow his lead when they've had it with rude passengers.

Tom's fateful flight was troubled from the start. Due to mechanical foul-ups, it boarded six hours late. So by the time the 380 passengers got into their seats, they were predictably irritable.

As he does on most flights that are terribly late, Tom announced that the first round of mixed drinks would be free. Such decisions are his to make. Sometimes his superiors at the airline complain. "Tough," he told me. "I'm the one who has to deal with passengers. If they don't want me giving out free liquor—it only costs them thirty-seven cents a bottle—then let *them* work a plane that's six hours late."

On this particular flight, even the free drinks couldn't calm the angry mob. "They started grabbing at flight attendants, pulling our sleeves," Tom recalled.

The plane got airborne and a new problem was discovered. A computer error—mixed with an odd method of assigning seats in Europe—had smokers in every other row, rather than in the rear. "It was horrible," Tom said. "People were furious. One guy started hitting me with his valise. That's when I went crazy."

Tom fought off the passenger with the valise and made his way through the mutinous mob to the front of the plane. He took the microphone and made a decision that he was certain would end his career as a flight attendant. The public address system crackled and Tom boomed: "WHO THE HELL DO YOU PEOPLE THINK YOU ARE? Do not pick on your flight attendants! Go to your seats and we'll straighten things out!"

There was silence. The other flight attendants looked shocked. The passengers fell back in their seats. Everyone knew that what

Tom had said was not the airline's patented public address patter. But what happened next surprised Tom. The passengers erupted into applause. Suddenly, they had a new respect for flight attendants. "Suddenly, they understood," he said.

Row by row, Tom regrouped the smokers, far from the non-smokers. He got the dinner service under way. And he got word out: Passengers with complaints should write to the airline. He even gave people the customer service address—a practice he has continued.

"I want people to know that flight attendants try to be congenial and pleasant," he said. "But if we're pushed too far, we'll fight back."

Well, I wrote a column about Tom, and then things really started flying. Food servers wrote angry letters taking exception to Tom's reference to "space waiters." Wrote one: "True, waiters and waitresses aren't responsible for people's safety (except in choking incidents), but that doesn't make them lower forms of life than flight attendants."

Frequent flyers responded to Tom's breast-beating with sharp comments and horror stories of their own:

• "Tom asked unhappy passengers: 'Just who the hell do you people think you are?' My answer: We're the people who supply your paycheck, pal!"
• "After a delay of several hours, we boarded our plane and were told we could have a free cocktail for our trouble. (That would have been a little strong for my young daughter.) Even though we hadn't eaten since breakfast and it was now 6:15 P.M., all we were given was a bag of potato chips. We were hungry so we asked for an extra bag or two. The space waitress acted like we were stepping way out of bounds with our request.

"Tom seems to think free drinks are the proper solution to delays. That shows you the mentality of the airlines."
• "On a flight to Tokyo, I was in the window seat and next to me were two very polite Japanese women who spoke no English. I motioned to them when I wanted to go to the restroom and they remained standing until I returned. That made me reluctant to leave my seat again.

"So when it got cold, I used the call button to request a blanket. An hour later, an attendant arrived and seemed angry I had disturbed her.

"Flight attendants wonder why we're rude. They're on board for

our safety and comfort. Unfortunately, they think we're just there to be in their way."
- "Female flight attendants are helpful, courteous, friendly and congenial—if you are a male passenger. The few male attendants appear to be gay, so they also pay more attention to men. I've waited too long for a soft drink while a 'man-crazy' flight attendant grins at a male in Row 7."
- "My daughter got airsick on a crowded flight and threw up all over both of us. I asked the attendant for a towel and was told that because the dinner service was under way, she couldn't help us.

"I told her I had nothing to use to clean us up and that other passengers would surely not want to eat their dinners smelling or seeing the mess. She took a towel off her cart, threw it at me, and said, 'This is all I have. It'll have to do.'

"I wasn't asking her to take care of the mess. I only wanted something to use to clean it up. I no longer fly on that airline."
- "Tom sounds like he's been in the ozone too long. If I had been on the flight where he yelled, 'Who the hell do you think you are?' I would have yelled back: 'One of the asses who spent hundreds of dollars to be treated like this!' Free drinks? Big deal."

Naturally, flight attendants wrote to defend Tom—and themselves.

Wrote one: "Most people are pretty easygoing. However, some don't realize that delays, missed connections, lost luggage, special meals that weren't boarded, and domestic quarrels before 'leaving on a jet plane' are not a flight attendant's fault."

Another flight attendant, a woman, took issue with the flirting charge:

> One of your readers seems to think that we're only interested in the men on board and the best way to pursue them. Well, on most flights, we don't have time to chase anyone. Not that it really matters, because a number of male passengers find the time to pursue us—through the plane, the airport, the airport parking lot, and in some instances, to the hotel on layovers.
>
> I don't just attend to male passengers. I can't begin to count the number of times I've listened to stories about grandchildren from elderly passengers, talked to families

about their vacations, and tried to comfort people on their way to funerals.

I offered space in the column to all comers. A dialogue, I always figure, helps leads to understanding. The friendly skies needn't just be an advertising line.

SECRETARIES SOUND OFF

Secretaries Week 1988 was nearing its end, and a lot of awful bosses had assumed they'd done their duty. Maybe they brought flowers. Or took "the girl" to lunch.
Whoop-dee-doo.
If they really wanted to please their secretaries, they could have followed some of the suggestions offered in my column during Secretaries Week in April 1988.
A month earlier, I'd asked secretaries to give advice:

> You've all been watching your bosses for a long time, observing the mistakes they make and the ways they could improve (as managers and as human beings). Well, get out your stationery! Write me a letter giving advice to your bosses. The most insightful, creative and helpful entries will be eligible for the grand prize: A party for up to eight friends or members of your secretarial pool—a Secretarial Pool Party, if you will.

Some secretaries lauded their employers. But scores of others had sharp advice for bozo bosses. A sampling:

• **Quit being a slave driver.** "Anytime my typewriter was off for a minute, my boss shouted, 'Whatcha doin', Edythe?' So one day, I responded, 'I'm throwing up. Would you like to hold my head?' That was my finale in that job."
Another secretary told how her boss changes the time on her desk clock so she'll work an extra ten minutes. "I'm smarter now," she wrote. "I bring a watch. When he says, 'Leaving early?' I respond, 'Nice try!' "
• **Don't be so cheap.** A boss took his four secretaries to lunch for Secretaries Week. They were appreciative until he told them to deduct ninety minutes from their time sheet for the long lunch.

- **Use a real phone.** "Don't yell, 'Speak up, damn it! I can't hear you,' when you're talking to me on that horrible car phone."
- **Quit asking me to lie for you.** "I'm tired of your wife asking me, 'Did he really have a meeting last night?' "
- **Organize your own vacation.** "It takes me half a day to find the cheapest rate for your family's plane fares. But on your six-figure salary, I know how important that is."
- **Quit blaming your secretary.** I heard many complaints about bosses who miss deadlines or fail to return calls and say it's their secretary's fault.
- **Clean up.** Some bosses have decade-old paperwork in their "in" basket and ancient lunches in their desks. "Clean up your act, or I'll set your office on fire," one secretary advised.
- **Learn the difference between machines and humans.** "You treat me like any other piece of office equipment. Just as I don't say 'Good morning' to my typewriter, you don't say 'Good morning' to me."
- **Learn the words "Excuse me."** "When I'm on the phone, he sits in his office and yells, 'Hey Ruth!' " one secretary wrote. "If I don't respond, he comes out and just starts talking."

Among the hundreds of comments offered by other secretaries:

- "If you're going to make the moves on me, do it now or quit teasing me forever."
- "Quit eating all the food on my desk while I'm in the bathroom."
- "Blow your nose in your own office. For some reason, you only blow your nose directly over my desk."
- "I'd appreciate a pat on the back, not on the butt."
- "My boss, a lawyer, can go into great detail on the proper way to put a stamp on a letter, and yet he'll give me a three-page will and say, 'See if you can figure this out.' "
- "I've heard enough about your hemorrhoids."
- "I don't mind that you chew tobacco. Just don't leave your 'spit cup' on my desk."
- "Get a job you know something about and quit this one."
- "Please refrain from grousing when the personnel office sends you reminders about Secretaries Week. I don't mind that you don't observe it. Just don't complain to me about it."

The winning entrant, understandably, wanted to remain anonymous. Her funny memorandum concluded: "The only advice that makes any sense is for my boss to spend just one day doing my job."

QUITTING WITH STYLE

Millions of American workers have the same daydream. It usually develops after years of being overworked, underpaid, and mistreated by the boss. It's the what-if? dream.

"What if I quit right now, with fourteen pizzas in the oven?" muses the pizzamaker.

"What if I run away and leave the boss to do the dishes?" dreams the dishwasher.

Well, to celebrate my first Labor Day writing the column, I saluted those people who actually made their what-if? dreams come true.

There's something daring and romantic about quitting a job in the middle of whatever you're doing, and waltzing out the door, never to return. I call it "quitting with style."

Sure, most bosses deserve two weeks' notice. And I didn't intend my column to encourage irresponsibility. But, I figured, a lot of readers are always itching to assert themselves to tyrannical bosses. They deserved a few good ideas.

I told of the Eastern Airlines pilot who got frustrated waiting in a long line of jets to take off. He taxied his plane, loaded with passengers, back to the terminal and disembarked forever.

There was the Louisiana judge who quit in the middle of a defendant's testimony; the Michigan bus driver who stormed off a crowded bus; the auto upholsterer in Ohio who won $1.9 million in the lottery and hired a band to play "Take This Job and Shove It" for his boss.

More than sixty thousand Americans quit their jobs every day, according to the U.S. Bureau of Labor Statistics, and those who desert their posts with style have some great stories to tell. I heard from scores of them.

A Dictaphone operator from Indiana wrote to say that his boss relentlessly took advantage of him. One day, our hero left a message on his Dictaphone: "Knock, knock. Who's there? Dictaphone. Dictaphone Who? Dictaphone and your crummy job up your ass, because I quit!"

Many who quit with style told me they did so for ethical reasons. A Wisconsin bakery worker said she objected to the sale of day-old sweet rolls as fresh. Finally, her boss told her that if she didn't like the way he operated, "you can get the [expletive] out!" So she did, calmly walking past a mob of customers.

Sandra was a receptionist in a windowless Chicago office when she worked for "a beast" who verbally abused every employee.

This boss wanted Sandra to monitor his company's parking lot for cars belonging to customers from a dog-grooming shop next door. Then he'd call a tow truck to haul their cars away.

"Our office had no windows, so he expected me to see through a brick wall," Sandra said. "Well, one day he asked, 'Whose goddamned Cadillac is on our lot?' I still hadn't developed X-ray vision, and I was very busy with the phones. I totally lost my cool."

She considered vaulting over her desk and choking him, but instead, walked out forever, leaving him to handle her wildly blinking phoneboard.

Several waitresses and secretaries said their most satisfying career moves were out the door. Gina, a Woolworth's waitress, told me of how her boss once offered a ten-cent raise, "as a big favor." Gina saw it as a big insult, and her customers egged her on to quit. "It made my day to see the manager running from table to table, trying to fill my shoes."

I was also told about a young research chemist who had spent three years separating a certain substance into its components. It was excrutiatingly tedious work, done for starvation wages.

The young man was a Ph.D. candidate, and his egomaniacal adviser demanded top billing when the important research was published. Having done all the work, the Ph.D. candidate balked.

The adviser wouldn't yield, so the young chemist took the two flasks of separated compounds and poured them together. The phrase "all that work down the drain" was never more appropriate.

Quitting with style, of course, demands proper execution to avoid embarrassment. Mary once worked in a restaurant and brought along her two children in the summers. While she worked, the kids played with their toys in the storeroom.

"One day, I stormed off my job, went out the door, and slammed it behind me," Mary wrote. "But within seconds, I sheepishly walked back in. I was so angry, I'd forgotten my children. I collected them and their toys, and once again, slammed the door behind me."

Okay, so her first exit was a false alarm. Still, I saluted her style in the column. She could have just left her kids there forever.

My favorite "quitting with style" story came from a woman in Texas:

> **Dear Zazz:** I once worked as a live-in housekeeper for a couple with two small boys. The father worked, the mother didn't, but she was out all day, every day.
>
> I cared for the boys, cleaned the nine-room house, managed the household accounts and did the shopping, cooking and laundry—all for $300 a month. When my paycheck bounced three times in three months, I decided to quit with style.
>
> After breakfast, when "Mom & Dad" left the house, I dressed the boys and took them downtown by taxi. We stopped by an employment office, and I was hired for another live-in position with a lovely family. I then rented a van and took the boys home.
>
> After giving them lunch, I put the kids in for a nap. I packed my things in the van and straightened the house at the same time. Oh, I also made dinner.
>
> When "Mom & Dad" came home, I met them at the door and said, "The boys have eaten, they're watching TV, they're bathed and ready for bed. Your dinner is in the oven and here are your keys. Goodbye! Good luck! Congratulations! You're now PARENTS!"
>
> I walked out, and drove off to my new job and home.
> —Saved in San Antonio

Now that's style!

Writing Off the News

IN THE *SUN-TIMES* building, the bustling news-room is on the fourth floor. My office is an escalator ride away—on the third floor.

I rarely need to venture into the newsroom. Shelley, my assistant, picks up the day's mail in the paper's mailroom, sorts it, and piles it all on my desk. I have a computer in my office on which I write the column and draft responses to readers' letters. I press a few buttons and my columns go directly to the newspaper syndicate in New York. I could go months without ever visiting the *Sun-Times* newsroom.

And yet, I find myself drawn to the bustling fourth floor. Newsrooms, it's been said, are where the earliest drafts of history are written.

From the time I was a kid, I've identified myself as a reporter. That's what I wanted to be. Then that's what I was. My detour into advice giving didn't really change how I view myself. I'm still a guy who itches to be covering compelling stories.

So I'm always looking for ways to write columns "off the news." Others in the media have chuckled when they've seen me at a press conference or the scene of a crime, scribbling away in my notebook. "You'd try to find an advice angle at a fire," a smirking TV news cameraman once said to me.

Well, maybe. But the challenge would be to offer advice more significant than "Don't play with matches." If I can't lend some new perspective to a news story, I generally back off.

Sometimes, though, an event in the news seems absolutely suited for the sort of reader-participation column I'm trying to write. I guess what I really consider myself is a hybrid of sorts: an advice reporter.

THE CHILDREN OF WINNETKA

On any other Friday night, the bicycle racks at Hubbard Woods Elementary School would be empty.

But on the unforgettable evening of May 24, 1988, more than fifty abandoned bikes stood side by side in the racks, an eerie reminder of the school's day of terror.

Even if you arrived late to the scene, as I did, you needed no explanation. You could imagine panicked mothers and fathers speeding to the school, praying to find their children safe. You thought of how tightly they must have hugged their kids, and how they drove them home with their car doors locked.

A bizarre, mentally ill woman named Laurie Dann had opened fire inside this school in the wealthy Chicago suburb of Winnetka. She killed an eight-year-old boy and wounded five other children. When school let out, she was still at large. In the wake of that horror, no parents could permit a child to ride home by bike on the streets of Winnetka.

And so here it was, after 9:00 P.M., and one by one, boys and girls were returning for their bikes. Every ten minutes or so, another car drove up. A child would get out, walk tentatively to the bike rack, and wheel his or her bike back to the car. Then a parent quickly loaded the bike into the trunk.

Almost every kid would sneak a backward glance into the small park across the street. There, the TV networks, cable TV crews, and a host of local stations had set up a maze of wires and cameras connected to satellite trucks. The TV lights directed at the school cast a powerful, unnatural glow on the bike racks. Like a hundred cars with their high beams on, the TV lights ignited the bikes' safety reflectors. Safety, of course, was on everyone's mind.

What brought these kids back for their bikes? Perhaps they sought a feeling of security. Without the bikes stored in their garages, they, too, remained victims of the tragedy. Getting back the bikes might have been an attempt to feel whole again.

In the days that followed, counselors tended to these children of Winnetka, trying to heal their psychological hurts and soften their nightmares. But the tragedy also had a profound impact on a lot of other people. Many more children died in a school bus crash in Kentucky the week before, but the calculated rampage directed at Winnetka's children seemed far more chilling. There were implications on many fronts.

A psychologist told me that in countless therapy sessions across Chicago that week, patients felt compelled to discuss the tragedy. They asked about Dann—and wondered about themselves. All of us have some degree of rage inside of us. How does one turn into the monster that Dann became?

Another frightening aspect was that Dann, by occupation, was a baby-sitter. Police knew she had a history of strange behavior and violent acts, yet she purchased guns without being questioned. None of the parents who employed her knew of her record. So her outbursts fueled the fears of parents everywhere: Whom could they trust to care for their children?

In Winnetka, counselors and officials offered whatever reassurances they could. As Winnetka school superintendent Donald Monroe explained, it was a task not unlike promising someone struck by lightning that it never strikes the same spot twice.

And what of those outside this small community? Millions in the Chicago area and beyond watched the grizzly event unfold on live TV, culminating in Dann's suicide, just after sunset, in a barricaded house not far from the school. These people had questions, fears—even psychological scars.

After writing about the night I spent in Winnetka, I told readers my column could be a forum of sorts. If they had a question or comment related to the tragedy, they could write, or call my hot line. Whether they wanted to voice their concerns about child care, refute or reassert the right to bear arms, or share their prayers for the kids who remained hospitalized, my column would be an outlet.

The office hot line began ringing the morning the column appeared, and hardly stopped for several days.

A woman called and told of witnessing a murder when she was nine years old. For years, she was afraid to go outside. She couldn't sleep unless the door was bolted. Her advice for the parents of Winnetka: "Listen to your children. Respect their fears."

Another woman called: "My son is mentally disturbed. When he cut my throat, it was a cry for help. He's getting help now, but it's too late for Laurie Dann." Some people must be forced into psychiatric care and prevented from buying guns, she said. "Our society must redefine civil rights."

A man from Winnetka called to say his neighbors shouldn't dwell on Dann's rampage: "The more you make of it, the more kids think they should make of it. Parents here go overboard on everything—cars, academic achievement. They shouldn't go overboard on this."

Readers gave advice, shared their own experiences, and intelligently looked at the tragedy from a variety of angles. A sampling:

• "Maybe the National Rifle Association could hold seminars for children in Winnetka to explain why Dann was carrying all those guns."

• "I was a friend of Laurie Dann. She was well-adjusted for most of her life. What happened, I think, was partly due to a bad divorce. There was a lot of money involved, and a lot of activity by divorce lawyers. The divorce left Laurie feeling displaced."

• "What are we to make of all the media attention? When an innocent black child is gunned down by gang crossfire, it's not big news and counselors aren't dispatched to help traumatized witnesses. If we cry for the children of Winnetka, we must also cry for the dead children of Chicago's South Side."

• "Perhaps Dann's parents were wealthy enough to influence authorities and protect her from getting arrested. In a poor neighborhood, a Laurie Dann would have been taken away long ago."

• "TV sitcoms are full of jokes about 'shrinks' and 'funny farms.' How can a person who needs mental health care see it as anything but degradation?"

• "Society doesn't understand that the brain, like other parts of the body, can get sick."

• "I've been a baby-sitter and now have kids of my own. As long as we pay people less to care for our children than to clean our homes, this sort of problem won't go away. Good pay will attract good baby-sitters. Parents have money for VCRs and vacations. Child care should be a priority."

• "I'm a stand-up comic, and the Friday of the tragedy, I was on stage. My heart wasn't in it. I had survivor's guilt. Between sets, I'd run to watch the TV news at the bar. All I wanted was to be home, holding my kids."

• "Laurie Dann's parents told friends that her bizarre behavior was 'under control.' I was a teacher for 40 years, and whenever a child displayed aberrant behavior, parents were defensive. They made excuses, thinking the problem reflected on them. One such troubled student is now an adult. Last year, he was convicted of murder. Perhaps Dann's parents gave excuses. Help should have started when she was a girl."

• "The tragedy made me feel guilty, as if, somehow, I could have done something: not necessarily in Winnetka, but maybe I could have joined the voices calling for better day care or gun control. I've never even written my congressman."

• "My sister is mentally ill. If she didn't get help, who knows what she might have done? What's frightening is that there are thousands of Laurie Danns out there, undiagnosed and untreated."

THE LOST LOVEBIRDS

Scott Swanson and Carolyn MacLean were such a romantic couple. As students at Wheaton College, they were always making goo-goo eyes at each other. They were inseparable.

It seemed to be quite a tragedy, then, when the two good-looking, well-to-do students disappeared off the face of the earth. Their parents and their friends were sure the two lovebirds had met foul play. Indeed, the evidence looked grim.

The couple had spent that fateful day, April 2, 1988, at Carolyn's grandmother's house in Michigan. They then set off, hand in hand, to drive to Wheaton, Illinois, where they had classes the next day at their small Christian college. They were all smiles: Scott, who was attending Wheaton on an ROTC scholarship, seemed thrilled that he was about to be commissioned as an officer. Carolyn seemed thrilled that Scott was holding her hand.

But that evening, their red BMW was found abandoned in a downtown Chicago alley. The keys were in it. The motor was still running.

Had they been killed? Kidnapped? The media got wind of the story, and kept an anxious public well informed.

What was it like to be tortured with worry and heartache? Through their tears, the couple's parents gave the details.

How did their friends and classmates show their concern? The students held prayer vigils and toured the countryside tacking up MISSING posters.

And were law-enforcement agencies doing all they could to solve the mystery? You bet! The Chicago police, the FBI, and the state police in three states put an army of agents and detectives on the case. Dogs sniffed their way through Michigan forests in search of fresh, shallow graves. Helicopters buzzed the highways, looking for clues. The police announced that an inmate who had recently escaped from prison was a prime suspect.

Well, four tense months passed. The search continued. So did the prayers, the tears, the media coverage. And then in late July, America got the good news: The lovebirds were alive, well, safe, secretly married, and still good-looking in their new home in San Diego. They'd faked their whole abduction, it turned out, and run away together to spend the rest of their lives in each other's arms.

While hiding out in California—with fake names, dyed hair, and wildly fictional identities—they were well aware of the frantic search for them back in the Midwest. In fact, they would frequently go to the library to read accounts of the investigation—and interviews with their heartbroken parents—in the Chicago papers. What sort of perverted pleasure could they have gotten from this?

When the story broke, I felt compelled to address the lovebirds issue in my column.

"Call in the tracking dogs!" I wrote. "You can land the search helicopters! And when this prayer is over, call off the vigil! The kids are OK! But excuse me for not saying, 'Whew!' I'm angry, and I didn't even tack up one poster!"

True, kids run away from home every day. But a lot of them have the decency to call their parents from a pay phone or send a letter in an unmarked envelope saying, "We're safe. Please don't worry."

The lovebirds' loved ones had a right to feel awfully ornery. I half expected the couple's parents to announce: "It's a good thing the kids are alive, because now we're going to kill them!"

But instead, Carolyn's dad said, "I don't think they ran from us. They ran to something else. They were interested in perfect love."

Perfect love, huh?

Well, yes, exactly. The couple went on TV to explain that they wanted to wrap themselves in each other—to build what they termed "a perfect love." They quoted the Bible a lot, too.

So I posed this idea to readers:

"Maybe those of us in love who didn't run away, triggering a nationwide search, have a few thoughts on ways to make love perfect. Maybe we can advise the no-longer-missing lovebirds on love and matrimony, so they don't have to vanish again."

I invited comments, by phone or by letter, and promised to pass them on to Scott and Carolyn: "Maybe you have advice for the couple's family and friends. How can they respond to these two selfish and irresponsible kidders? How might they teach Scott, 23, and Carolyn, 22, that they're adults now?"

Most of the hundreds of readers who responded were livid about the lovebirds. Several called for them to be publicly spanked. One woman asked that they be sentenced to scrub police station floors for one hundred years. Readers offered the couple suggestions, observations—even invitations.

Joanne Sequist invited Scott and Carolyn to a Parents of Murdered Children meeting. She said the couple might benefit from stories people there tell.

In 1983, Joanne's nineteen-year-old daughter disappeared from her suburban Chicago home. "It's difficult to explain a parent's pain," she told me, "when they're dragging a nearby river for your child. My family trudged through forests in 90-degree heat, hoping to uncover some sign of her. On sleepless nights, I'd stare out the window hoping to see her walk up the driveway.

"Then, after an agonizing five months, she was found strangled, dead."

Joanne suggested that Scott and Carolyn contact her to volunteer for "I Search," a group that helps parents search for missing children.

Here's a sampling of other comments that readers asked me to pass on to Scott and Carolyn:

- "As a taxpayer I financed your adventure. So if anyone offers you a movie or book deal, I want my share."
- "You're spoiled, cruel, heartless, arrogant brats—and I'm being charitable!"
- "When I think of the many times I prayed for you two, it makes me want to vomit."
- "I think everyone in Chicago should be allowed to slap each of you across the face."
- "You blew your chance to be an officer through ROTC, Scott. You should be made a private. Then God have mercy on your soul, because no drill sergeant will. I'm a retired sergeant; if I led your section, I'd bust your buns."
- "Quit quoting the Bible! Remember the Bible tells us to honor our parents and not bear false witness."
- "I lost my only child to cancer. You two ought to visit a children's cancer ward and observe parents' love for kids they may soon lose."
- "They should auction off your BMW and give the proceeds to charity."
- "Maybe you should be forced to do TV commercials reminding

people to 'Phone First!' Had you phoned someone, so much heart-ache could have been avoided."
• "Please vanish again, this time from the media. By writing about you, Zazz fell for your deplorable scheme."
• "Perfect love? No, I wish you two perfect justice: May you have children who grow up to pull the same stunt on you."

A minority of readers were more charitable. Some felt sorry for the couple. One woman wrote:

> The kids are mentally ill and need help. How do I know? Grandiosity is the tip of the iceberg: In San Diego, they said, people were attracted to them because they were 'so much in love.' Another sign is their hostility toward their parents: How could they enjoy giving them such pain?
>
> Many people think psychotherapists love patients into sanity. Not so. If Scott and Carolyn are to be punished, let an expert do it! You've never really been miserable until you've been punished by your therapist.

A few readers came to the couple's defense. "Let's not be judgmental," a man wrote. "They acted in the name of love. Parents are hurt by children in many ways, but must be forgiving. No crime was committed. Yes, time and money were expended, but the escapade made for a great mystery in the media. How fortunate that this episode ended happily!"
A few readers said the public's "bloodlust" was more disgraceful than anything the couple did. A man wrote: "We got the happy ending—they're alive—so let's celebrate. Does society's mass anger mask disappointment that we didn't get the unhappy ending?" Wrote another: "Would we be happier if they were found dead? Then the taxpayer's bill would include the costs of a coroner, a manhunt for the murderer, and his trial and life imprisonment. Should we now erect public stocks and come by to spit at them? Since they're alive, should we beat them to death?"
Yes, this reader's foul-play scenario might have been more costly, but the couple's impact on society went beyond dollars expended. Indeed, one of the most chilling letters I received was from a woman who told this story:

> Ten years ago, my friend and her fiance vanished from a gas station where the fiance was an attendant. The cash regis-

ter was found cleaned out and police suspected the couple of stealing the money and eloping. Police never really listened to our claims of foul play until the couple's badly beaten bodies turned up.

When police caught the murderers, they learned that my friends were alive for some time after the abduction. Logic dictates that they couldn't have been saved, but I still wonder: What if the police hadn't suspected my friends of running away? Would they have acted more quickly?

I'm afraid that Scott and Carolyn's legacy might now be this: The next time a young couple disappears, police may be even more inclined to label them runaways.

THE BELT LOOPS OF GEORGE BUSH

During the 1988 presidential campaign, hundreds of newspaper columnists wrote thousands of columns and many millions of words on the subject of how to get elected. Even after it became inevitable that George Bush would win, every pundit in America felt an obligation to give the man advice. He'd ensure victory in the election, they said, only if he followed their game plans, heeded their warnings, and convinced his wife to dye her hair.

Pundits can be pompous.

Though I'm in the advice business, I had no idea how to win the presidency. So I held off giving Bush or Michael Dukakis advice.

And yet, whenever I saw Bush on TV, I recalled the day in April 1980 when he and I had met. And I realized that maybe there was good advice to be found in that memory. I couldn't resist. I had to write an advice column on the subject.

In 1980, I was a senior creative-writing major at Carnegie-Mellon University in Pittsburgh. As editor of the school paper, I hosted the Pennsylvania Collegiate Press Association conference. Attended by thirty-one student editors, it was pretty small-time.

That week, Bush and Ronald Reagan were battling each other in Pennsylvania's primary. Remember, those two were adversaries before they teamed up in the 1980 general election.

A friend of mine was a Bush volunteer. He suggested that the candidate address the student journalists. Bush staffers loved the idea, especially because my friend promised a crowd of five hundred student editors.

I was thrilled to have such a big-time keynote speaker. But what if Bush found out that there were only thirty-one of us? I felt compelled to run around campus, trying to drum up a crowd of impostor student editors. I also had to give a campus tour—emphasizing emergency exits—to Bush's no-nonsense secret service men.

A few columnists arrived a day early to capture the "mood" of these five hundred young journalists. (There were only a handful of moods to capture, but we offered a host of strange observations about America. We rambled; the columnists nodded.)

On the morning of the speech, there were twice as many press corps members as there were student journalists. But luckily, word of mouth had brought out hundreds of "impostors"—art majors, engineering students, my frat brothers. Assuming they were surrounded by student editors, the reporters prepared stories on Bush's encounter with "five hundred of tomorrow's media leaders."

Bush arrived on schedule. He was tall, friendly, polite. As he and I spoke backstage, he kept repeating my name. (He never missed. It was "Jeff" every time, which made me wonder about his preelection *Nightline* performance: He kept calling Ted Koppel "Dan," as in Rather.)

I led Bush onstage, introduced him to the crowd, and took a seat behind him. He was impressive. There were a few hecklers, and he had sharp comebacks that drew cheers.

He was roughest on his opponent—describing Reagan's fiscal plans as "voodoo economics."

It was quite hot and Bush took off his suit coat. From my seat behind him, I immediately noticed that he had missed a back belt loop—maybe even two. As a result, his belt scrunched up his shirt. He looked disheveled, but endearing: It proved he's only human. After the speech, I considered pointing out the belt loop, then figured: "That's what aides are for."

I never saw Bush after that day, but this story isn't over.

In February 1982, after Bush was already Vice President, folks in the media recalled that he once had labeled Reagan a practitioner of "voodoo economics." Bush insisted he never uttered the phrase: "I challenge anyone to find it."

NBC News immediately dug up the videotape of his CMU speech, which also showed me behind him, staring at the back of his pants. That speech became the most infamous of his failed 1980 campaign.

But Bush, of course, came back again. And now that he's President, what advice might I give him?

Perhaps, this: Don't sweat the small stuff, Mr. Bush. You can miss the belt loops, just get people's names right. And, of course, remember that anything you say can and will be held against you. The videotape will catch you every time.

The only other advice I have is for Mrs. Bush: She needn't color her hair. In fact, if I were a dedicated columnist, I'd sample the mood among, say, student journalists, and determine that young America is ready for a natural woman—a First Lady with white hair.

But I won't bother with such a survey. One thing I learned from the 1980 campaign is that the mood among student journalists is suspect.

PREVENTION: THE ONLY CURE

Our greatest health threat is not AIDS, cancer, or drug abuse. No, according to 220 future physicians, the world's greatest health threat is the danger posed by nuclear arms.

A few days before the 1988 fall election, these 220 students from Philadelphia's six medical schools sent an open letter to the next President. It was as powerful and heartfelt as any statement issued during the campaign:

> Because we accept the professional responsibility to treat disease and diminish pain, we are working to prevent the massive and unprecedented death and suffering that would result from a nuclear conflict.
>
> It is well established that there can be no adequate medical response to nuclear detonation. The hopeless reality is that antibiotics to treat rampant infection would be scarce, morphine to treat agonizing pain would be unobtainable, and hospitals to bed the injured would be rubble.
>
> Physicians would be few in number and helpless in providing health care. We know that where treatment of disease is ineffective, prevention remains the only cure.

Neither candidate responded to the letter. But I thought it worthy of coverage in my column.

The students had each pitched in $5 or so to help buy a $1,700 ad in the *Philadelphia Inquirer.* My parents live in Philly, and my father was moved by the letter. He passed it on to me, and I called the phone number in the ad.

The election was long over by that time, and Lucy Miller of the Physicians for Social Responsibility told me the response had been underwhelming. Just five people had called. And besides me, the only other media interest was from Tass, the Soviet news agency.

The letter had been drafted by Roger Spingarn, a fourth-year med student at Philadelphia's Hahnemann University. He went door-to-door asking students to get involved. About sixteen hundred were approached.

Some told him it was inappropriate for med students to make a political statement. Several feared that signing the letter might prevent them from landing the residency of their choice. And of the 220 who did sign it, 3 asked to be anonymous. "They're med students on military scholarships," explained Spingarn. "They feared retribution."

Spingarn didn't want to come off as some radical. He said he fears for the world and deeply feels more of us need to take a stand. To me, parts of the letter he drafted read like poetry:

> We call on you, the next president, to demonstrate unparalleled leadership. See that we use our extraordinary minds and not flex our short-tempered muscles. You have a great opportunity to lead a nation, to lead the world. Please call for an immediate halt to the nuclear arms race, initially through a mutually verifiable moratorium on testing.

I ended my column by saluting the med students for their concern, and wishing Bush the courage to follow their suggestion.

The reader response to this column was slight. I got fewer than a dozen letters. But these letter writers said they and their families were moved by the med students' efforts, pleased that I had devoted a column to the subject, and motivated to take action themselves.

These are the letters that matter most to me.

It's Not Just a Column, It's an Adventure

IN MY JOB, I'm expected to know everything about everything. It's as if I've taken out an ad in the yellow pages under "Expert." The calls—from the media, big business, small social clubs, you name it—arrive in a steady stream.

I've been asked to judge every conceivable contest: ice cream eating, rib sauce recipes, Halloween costumes, teenage stand-up comedians, student essays, ceramic vase making. Playwrights have sent me their plays to critique, poets their poems, get-rich-quick schemers their schemes.

Almost every day, the phone rings, and I'm expected to give sage advice off the top of my head.

Morning radio DJs routinely give me unannounced wake-up calls demanding instant wisdom. I'm not always sure where my dreams end and the 7:00 A.M. radio bits begin. (The subject is often the same: sex.) When I didn't answer my phone one morning—I was out of town—a Chicago radio DJ sent a reporter to do a live interview with the doorman of my building. The question for the doorman: "What do you think his advice would be if he were here?" I thought that was reaching a bit, but it gave the doorman a chance to share his thoughts with thousands of listeners.

TV stations also want my expert opinion in areas where I'm no expert. A Chicago sportscaster asked me to play Monday morning quarterback after the Bears lost a game 49 to 7. Short of "Don't pout" and "Try to do better next time," what could I say? Well, I advised Mike Ditka, the Bears' hot-tempered coach, to go easy on the boys. I also suggested that the players' wives not cut back on their love and affection because of the embarrassing loss. I declined to give any advice on playing football, however. I knew Coach Ditka wouldn't want to hear a peep from a nonexpert like me. The night before, he'd thrown a wad of gum at a fan who'd offered unsolicited advice.

Print publications have my number, too. A *Life* magazine editor called. Because of a momentary rebirth of the miniskirt, they were doing a fashion spread on legs. "Why are legs so important to men?" she asked.

"Well, ummm . . ." Off the top of my head, I had no answer.

"We're under a tight deadline," the editor told me.

It's tough to be witty on demand, especially when I have to write five columns of my own each week. But that's the challenge of this job. It's part of the thrill. So I asked if I could call *Life* back. I stared at the walls for a while, trying to think of a line that was quotable, on-target, but not sexist. Finally, I came up with something. In surprisingly big print, *Life* ran it as follows:

> We asked advice-to-the-lovelorn columnist Jeffrey Zaslow if he could please shed some light on this whole legs business. "A lot of women talk with their legs," he observed, "and a lot of men listen with their eyes." Then he added, possibly as an afterthought, "The shorter the skirt, the longer the conversation."

Shall we discuss it?

Star magazine was doing a takeout on Eddie Murphy's love life. "The sexy superstar is terrified of money-grabbing gold diggers," the magazine reported, "so he has condemned himself to a wild bachelor life." The magazine asked me to advise Eddie. My advice ran in a sidebar under the headline, MAN-TO-MAN ADVICE TO HELP SUPERSTAR FIND MISS RIGHT. I played it straight. I said that since everyone laughs at Eddie's jokes, he should look for a woman willing to tell him when he's not being funny. Also, a gold digger would ask him about his cars, his houses, his boats. Someone who really cared would say, "Tell me about yourself."

Glamour magazine called to ask: "At the end of a business lunch is it proper for a woman to put on lipstick right at the table? Would she be taken less seriously by associates, both male and female?"

The answer I came up with: "A businesswoman is still a woman. While she shouldn't attempt a full makeover at a business lunch, there's nothing wrong with applying a few strokes of lipstick. She should just do it quickly, quietly, and accurately, avoiding the cheeks and chin. And obviously, she needn't feel obliged to offer her lipstick to others at the table."

I added: "As a man, I hate it when women are so afraid to have lipstick wear off that they rarely use a napkin and only allow their teeth and tongue to touch their forks. I'd much prefer a business-woman who eats like a human being and then puts on more lipstick at the end of the meal."

Woman's Day asked a variety of holiday questions. Among them: Is it appropriate to send a Christmas card to a friend who recently had a death in the family?

My response:

> If your normal Christmas card is an illustration of Santa on a surfboard with bikini-clad helpers, then, no, it's not an appropriate card to send to someone in mourning. But do send a simple, staid card letting your friend know she's in your thoughts. It can act as a sympathy card, a friendship card, and a subtle reminder that life needs to go on. A new year is approaching.

This job calls for a lot of personal appearances and speeches. I enjoy getting out and meeting people, and love giving speeches, but I sometimes wonder what I've gotten myself into. Am I a writer? A personality? A what?

Why did I agree to dress up as the "Celebrity Santa Claus" for a zoo society cocktail party? There I was, a skinny, pathetic-looking Santa, roaming a crowd of well-dressed, well-heeled zoo patrons. Zoo officials had neglected to figure out a way to inform people that it was I in the costume. And since there were no kids at this party, no one was too interested in making my acquaintance. The crowd would part as I approached. Few people even smiled at me. I gave up on the ho-ho-hos early in the evening, and by the end of the night, was glad no one knew this strange Santa was me. Feeling awkward and embarrassed (and worried about my credibility), I hid out for long stretches in the petting zoo.

I believe it's important to appear at charity events and on telethons. But these have led to strange experiences, too. On the Jerry Lewis telethon, organizers wanted me to answer phones behind an ALL THAT ZAZZ sign. However, they forgot to make such a sign. So they sat me at a desk with four other people, behind a CELEBRITY LOOK-ALIKES sign. My coworkers on the phone bank: "Marilyn Monroe," "John Wayne," "Michael Jackson," and "Barbra Streisand." Viewers easily guessed who those people were. But who was the fifth person, that strange curly-haired blond guy at the end?

"Burt Reynolds," I replied to coworkers who kidded me about it the next day.

Sometimes, I feel awkward at personal appearances—as if I'm being overly celebrated. The Delaware County Symphony outside Philadelphia invited me to narrate its *Nutcracker Suite.* I did my reading, backed by the sixty-five-piece orchestra, and at the end, took a bow with the conductor. He and I went offstage, and came back for another set of bows that made me feel self-conscious. The conductor was a man worth applauding: He'd studied his craft for years, and had worked hard preparing this orchestra for its performance. At the same time, I was being applauded . . . for what? I was a guy who knew how to read. Bravo!

I've appeared in several high-society fashion shows, where people have asked my advice on clothing and accessories. (Remember: I had to buy two suits when I got this job.) Then there was the time I hosted an arts council Valentine's Day dance, where women had to pay a buck to dance with me. (As a dancer, I raised just six dollars for the arts council.)

I've learned to diplomatically turn down some of these appearance requests. But event organizers have subtle ways of making me feel guilty. I don't usually charge charities for speeches. But there are a lot of nonprofit quasi-charities out there. "We can pay you an honorarium," one woman's club officer told me. "If you need it, we can pay you." Naturally, I politely declined the honorarium.

At speeches, different audiences want different advice from me. When I addressed a group of investment-conscious physicians, several of them asked me for insider trading tips from my *Wall Street Journal* days—to heck with the lovelorn advice. Speeches have also led to morning-after phone calls. An insurance man heard me speak and then called to give me advice: "You need a good life insurance policy, and I may be able to help."

People often come up to me after my speeches to give honest appraisals of my column, my diction, my posture. I gave a speech to a Chicago women's group whose average member was about seventy-eight years old. They were a receptive audience, and they especially liked my more risqué anecdotes. Anyway, that morning, I'd appeared on *CBS This Morning,* and during that interview, my head was strangely cocked to the side. I wasn't even aware of my cocked head, but it sure looked odd. Well, a woman at that speech came up to me to say she'd seen me that morning on the show: "I said to my husband, 'What a shame. That boy has some sort of spinal disease.' It hurt to look at you. My husband will be glad to know you're healthier than you looked on TV."

The fact is, I'm not always comfortable on TV. That's understandable, considering some of the TV shows I've been involved in. Perhaps the most disconcerting one was a TV pilot called *American Heartline.* I wasn't told many details before I was flown out to Hollywood to be a panelist.

The premise of the show was this: Three people with problems were interviewed one at a time by the show's host and three panelists, as a studio audience looked on. Then the panel got to vote on who told the saddest, most compelling story. That person got a cash prize. Viewers could call a toll-free number to make donations to the losers.

In the pilot, the first contestant said her husband had four months to live and she wanted to take him on a cruise before he died. She was in tears and was shaking as she said she couldn't afford the cruise.

Contestant number two was an extremely overweight Vietnam veteran who needed money for a weight-reduction program. Number three was a woman who gave her son up for adoption sixteen years earlier, and subsequently learned that her son was deaf. She desperately wanted to find him and tell him that she didn't give him up because of his handicap. She needed money to hire a detective to track down the boy. She told us she was a teacher of the deaf: Guilt feelings drove her into the profession. When I asked her what she might say to her son if she got to meet him, she responded in sign language.

I felt uncomfortable through the whole process. This was kind of a pathetic *Queen for a Day.* Was I playing God? Were we unfairly using these people to make good TV? (Or bad TV?) Was the show helping people or embarrassing them at their time of trouble?

During a commercial break, the panelists had to pick a winner. We all agreed that the poor woman with the dying husband was the most deserving. This was obvious to anyone who heard her sad story. But the show's producers said they preferred some drama in the selection process. They asked me to change my vote to the woman with the deaf son. For the sake of show biz, I agreed. But when I cast my vote, mumbling in the studio audience—highlighted by hisses—let me know they weren't pleased with my lack of good judgment.

Meanwhile, another panelist, the bishop of Los Angeles, offered to give his exercise bike to the fat Vietnam vet. The audience applauded. The whole experience was surreal. On the red-eye flight back to Chicago, I questioned what I really was doing in this advice job: Was I helping people or exploiting them? That TV pilot never made it to the air, but such unresolved feelings have continued through several other TV appearances and pilots.

On the one hand, these TV shows are very exciting. On the other, I wonder where I'm lending my name, my face, my reputation.

Despite all of these diversions that come my way, I try never to lose sight of my foremost responsibility: the column itself. I was hired to write five 600-word advice columns a week, fifty-two weeks a year. And truthfully, getting back to my computer terminal to write them can be both a relief and an obsession.

There is a rhythm to my job, and I'm caught up in it. Readers' lives are part of my life. I think about their questions before I fall asleep. Answers and turns of phrase hit me as I doze off.

In the morning, invariably, I reconsider. I roll out of bed, and usually, I'm tapping away at my minicomputer even before my first cup of coffee. I can't resist hitting on my still-groggy wife for feedback. My refrain: "Well, how about this for an answer?" Her response: "Uh-huh."

I guess I love this job.

Sometimes, I envision myself writing the column as an old man—an eighty-two-year-old boasting that I have the wisdom of an eighty-three-year-old. On other days, when the woes of the world are wearing me down, I wonder just how long a hitch I'm in for.

It's natural for people to ask me whether I'll last in the column as long as my predecessor did—thirty-one years. "That depends," I tell them.

"On what?" they ask.

"I don't know," I say, because an honest answer man admits when he hasn't a clue.

But I do know this: It's a rare job in journalism that offers such entree into readers' lives. Every day, I have a chance to help people, to make a difference. I don't always succeed, but I am captivated by the challenge of trying.

After I'd been in the job for about fourteen months, a reader called to ask that I write a column detailing what I'd learned in my rookie year.

As I listened to her request, I thought, "Well, my answer could fill a book." And in a sense, I've responded to her in these nineteen chapters.

Still, I think there is a way to sum up the most important thing that this job has taught me.

I've learned that everyone has a story to tell, and a good advice-columnist is nothing if not a good listener.

The real thrill, for me, comes from the people I meet and write about along the way. That's what intrigued me so when I took the job. I suspected then and know it now: "All That Zazz" isn't exactly my column. It's everyone else's.

And that's what makes it such a great adventure.